HALLE BERRY

Also by Frank Sanello

Reel v. Real: How Hollywood Turns Fact into Fiction

Spielberg: The Man, The Movies, The Mythology

Jimmy Stewart: A Wonderful Life

Eddie Murphy: The Life and Times of a Comic
on the Edge

Stallone: A Rocky Life

Julia Roberts: Pretty Superstar

The Opium Wars: The Addiction of One Empire
and the Corruption of Another

The Knights Templar: God's Warriors,
The Devil's Bankers

Upcoming

Faith and Finance in the Renaissance: The Rise
and Ruin of the Fugger Empire

To Kill a King: An Encyclopedia of Royal Murders and
Assassinations From Ancient Egypt to the Present

Soap: A History of How the World Cleaned Up Its Act

HALLE BERRY
A Stormy Life

Frank Sanello

First published in Great Britain in 2003
by Virgin Books Ltd
Thames Wharf Studios
Rainville Road
London
W6 9HA

A catalogue record for this book is available from the British
Library.

ISBN 1 85227 092 6

Typeset by TW Typesetting, Plymouth, Devon
Printed and bound in Great Britain by CPD Wales

For Nigel Cairns

CONTENTS

ACKNOWLEDGEMENTS   ix
1. AN ENDING AND THE BEGINNING   1
2. LIVING HELL   23
3. THE BIG SCREEN AND THE BIG TIME   29
4. WHITE ROOTS   47
5. INTEGRATING BEDROCK   67
6. LOSING ISAIAH, REGAINING RESPECT   75
7. BLACK QUEEN TAKES WHITE KING   83
8. INJUSTICE   87
9. DEMOTED TO PRINCESS   113
10. FRIENDS AND MENTORS   117
11. INTRODUCING . . . ERIC BENÉT   125
12. THE ACCIDENTAL MOTORIST   143
13. ACTING UP A STORM   149
14. GRATUITOUS PRUDERY   155
15. SCREEN GODDESSES AND MONSTERS   163
16. HALLE'S COMET   177
17. STAND BY YOUR MAN   197
18. BILLION-DOLLAR BABE   205
19. WEATHERING ANOTHER STORM   215
EPILOGUE: THRIVE ANOTHER DAY   221
FILMOGRAPHY   229
TELEVISION   245
PICTURE CREDITS   251
ABOUT THE AUTHOR   253
INDEX   255

ACKNOWLEDGEMENTS

Daniel Abraham, Kris Andersson, Edith Barcay, Professor Joseph Boone, Dr Daniel Bowers, Ellen Bersch, André Brooks, Charles Casillo, Carrie Cohen, Louis Chunovic, Dr Gary Cohan, Hector Dejean, Ghalib Dhalla, Michael Dorr, Anita Edson, Mike Emmerich, Maribel Escalera-Ulloa, Stephanie Goldfarb, Cyrus Godfrey, Lawrence C Goldstein, Mary and Art Goodale, Dr Stephen Graham, André Guimond, Scott Hill, Dr Scott Hitt, Chris Hix, Frederick Hjelm, Brad Kane, Steven Kay, Chuck Kim, Gary Kirkland, Lin and John Knorr, Pamela Lansden, Robert Lent, Dr Bertrand Levesque, Michael Levine, Will Litchfield, Christina Madej, Charlie Medrano, Paul Manchester, David Marlow, Kevin Moreton, Jim Murphy, Tom Packard, Ross Plotkin, Dr Dale Prokupek, Lee Ray, Linda and Phil Reinle, Dr William Resnick, Ray Richmond, Doris Romeo, Marjorie Rothstein, Sarkis, Catherine Seipp, Rob Senger, Bryan Smith, Monica Trascendes, Peter Trimble, Christopher Villa, Dean Wong, Jeff Yarbrough, Joan Zlogar and the exceedingly patient staff at the Academy of Motion Picture Arts and Sciences' Margaret Herrick Library in Beverly Hills, California.

I especially want to thank my agent, Dorie Simmonds, and my editor, Kirstie Addis, for making this project happen, and my long-time mentor, James Robert Parish, for his invaluable guidance and research assistance.

1. AN ENDING AND THE BEGINNING

In early 2003, two of the most prominent black women in America lost their fathers within days of each another. The death of one man made the network news and was reported in newspapers around the world. The other man's passing was noted in a single tabloid of dubious reliability and in a brief obituary in his hometown newspaper that contained unsavoury allegations about the deceased not normally associated with death notices – based perhaps on the old belief that it's not kind to disparage the dead.

The pop star Whitney Houston's father, John Houston, 82, died on 2 February 2003, after a long battle with diabetes and heart disease. One of the reasons his death received so much press attention – other than his daughter's fame – was that in September 2002 John Houston had filed suit against Whitney demanding $100 million for allegedly helping get marijuana possession charges against her dropped and for negotiating a $100 million deal with her label, Arista Records.

John Houston – a one-time artists' manager who had guided the career of his ex-wife, Whitney's mother, the gospel singer Cissy Houston, who had been a member of Aretha Franklin's backup group the Sweet Inspirations – also alleged in his suit that attorneys representing his John Houston Entertainment LLC in Newark, New Jersey, had provided assistance to the 39-year-old pop diva in 2000 after security guards at an airport in Hawaii found half an ounce of marijuana in her handbag.

Over the course of two nights in December 2002, the syndicated American television news programme *Celebrity Justice* aired two interviews with the ailing Houston, who insisted that the multimillion-dollar lawsuit was a business matter rather than a personal attack on his daughter. 'I never thought about suing my daughter,' Houston said from his hospital bed. 'I never thought about it that way. I thought about suing the corporation that belongs to Whitney, and she happened to be right in the middle of it.'

At one point during the hour-long interview, John Houston turned to the television cameras and addressed his daughter directly: 'You get your act together, honey, and you pay me the money that you owe me. If you do that, you haven't got a lawsuit.'

Whitney had made peace with her father and was at his bedside in a Manhattan hospital when he died. By that time, his corporation had dropped the lawsuit against the singer and sometime movie star. Whitney's publicist also released a statement that said, 'The entire family is greatly saddened by the loss of someone they all loved so much . . . John and Whitney loved each other and always will.'

The tabloids claimed that the singer got her revenge by boycotting her father's funeral at the St James AME Church in Newark, New Jersey, but the more reputable *New York Daily News* reported that she did attend one wake at the Whigham Funeral Home in Newark and another wake – but not the funeral – at St James.

News cameras showed Whitney Houston braving a blizzard as she left the church. Her press representative, Nancy Seltzer, said, 'Whitney spent the majority of the day with her father yesterday [7 February 2003], privately, in the viewing room of the funeral home. She attended the wake ceremony later that night in the church.'

Rather than boycott the funeral, said Seltzer, her client chose not to attend in order to avoid the mob of paparazzi that had descended on the church. The publicist even claimed that the $100 million lawsuit had not caused a rift between father and daughter. 'Whitney saw him before he died, and they were never estranged,' Seltzer said. It may have helped that father and daughter were no longer litigants against each other when he died. Cissy Houston attended both wakes and the funeral, even though she had been separated from her husband since 1980 and divorced in 1993.

The Oscar-winning actress Halle Berry's father, Jerome Jessie Berry, 68, died just over a week earlier on 24 January 2003 at the Indian Hills Nursing Home in Cleveland, Ohio, where he had been battling Parkinson's disease for years.

It's difficult to determine how the actress felt about this moment of closure. Her publicist did not release a statement to the press after her father's death. Halle had so distanced herself from her father – an estrangement lasting more than two decades – that, when I phoned the publicist's office, an employee refused even to confirm or deny Jerome Berry's passing. Unlike Whitney Houston, Halle Berry was not at his bedside when her father died. According to the tabloid, the *Star*, she also did not attend the memorial service on 1 February 2003 at the Second Mount Olive Baptist Church in Cleveland. The *Star* ran a photograph of the actress and her husband emerging from the trendy Fred Seagal clothing store near Beverly Hills, California, allegedly on the day of her father's funeral with a headline that scolded, SHE GOES SHOPPING AS DAD SHE DESPISED IS LAID TO REST.

Why had Halle, who is normally accessible and gracious to the point of volubility with the press and fans, suddenly become so tight-lipped about a major event in anyone's life like the loss of a parent? What caused her to turn away?

Jerome Berry's obituary in the *Cleveland Plain Dealer* suggested an explanation when it reprinted a year-old quotation about her father attributed to the actress.

> He was an alcoholic and abusive. I don't think I really dealt with that pain until recently. Thank goodness we had our mom. She gave us a home. She gave us belief. And she gave me and my sister Heidi a sense of self-worth. It was an unbelievable struggle for a divorced white woman with two little black girls.

The Star quoted family members as saying it was Jerome's dying wish to see his famous daughter before he died – a wish that was not granted. Halle's half-sister, Renée Berry Graves, said in an interview with the tabloid before their father's death, 'Dad told me that he'd be the happiest man alive if Halle would just pick up the phone and call him.' Graves also said in the interview that the family had begged Halle to forgive her father and visit him so he could die in peace.

Halle appears never to have made the phone call or visited her father in the nursing home. He died, apparently unforgiven, by his famous daughter.

Death, it seems, failed to free Halle from a relationship that survived only in the form of recriminations and resentments. But, troubled as it was, the dynamic between father and daughter helped make Halle Berry the woman she is today and contributed, however painfully and negatively, to the indomitable drive that has made her the most successful and respected black actress of all time.

The aftereffects – perhaps better described as aftershock – of this dynamic continue to this day. This is how it began.

Halle Maria Berry was born on 14 August 1966 at Cleveland City Hospital, the place where the actress Dorothy Dandridge, whom Halle would later play in a TV movie, was born in 1922. The future star's first name came from her mother's favourite department store in Cleveland, Ohio, Halle Brothers, which has since been converted into an office building and whose exterior now serves as the fictional department store on the American TV series, *The Drew Carey Show*.

'My mother was shopping in Halle Brothers in Cleveland. She saw their bags and thought, "That's what I'm going to name my child,"' Halle says. One of the most beautiful actresses in the motion-picture industry today was named after a handbag.

The hospital where Halle was born is a sprawling, forbidding monolithic complex of buildings that to the superstitious might have seemed like an omen of ill things to come for the tiny biracial child. Her father, Jerome Berry, was an ex-GI, an orderly at the Veterans Administration Hospital in Cleveland and black. He later worked as a bus driver for the Bluebird travel lines. His wife, Halle's mother, Judith, (née Hawkins) was a psychiatric nurse at the same hospital – and white. They met at work.

Judith Berry was born in Liverpool in the UK and her parents emigrated to the US when she was six, growing up in the Cleveland suburb of Elyria. A photograph of her in her twenties wearing her RN's (Registered Nurse's) cap reveals that she was as beautiful as her daughter would famously turn out to be.

Halle was the couple's second child. Another daughter, Heidi, had been born four years earlier. (The tabloids claim the sisters are estranged, but no mainstream media have reported the rift.

The *Globe* claimed Halle said of her troubled relationship with her 38-year-old sister, a married mother of two who still lives in Ohio, 'We fought a lot. We fought for real, sometimes drawing blood. I don't know, but part of me feels that we never recovered from the fighting adolescent years. I moved away from home at such a young age that the relationship never quite repaired itself.')

To call the first four years of Halle's life Dickensian is to understate the nightmarish world she and her mother and sister inhabited. Before Judith Berry kicked her husband out of the house when Halle was four years old, Mrs Berry and Heidi endured horrific physical and emotional abuse. 'He was an alcoholic. He battered my mother,' Halle has said.

One of Halle's earliest memories is that of her father hurling the teacup-sized family dog, a Maltese terrier, against the wall, which made the unfortunate pet almost bite its tongue off. Although she was only four, the incident has remained seared in her memory and was still fresh in 2002, when she said, 'The blood and that image. When somebody mentions my father, that's the first thing I think about – that dog flying across the room. I remember saying, "God, let him leave!" so that my life could get back to normal.' (Interestingly, as an adult, she would end up owning four Maltese – perhaps as emotional replacements for the unfortunate terrier her father abused.)

Other early memories include slaps, punches and fights at the dinner table. When Jerome would begin beating Halle's mother, her sister Heidi would try to intervene and end up getting beaten herself. Halle herself was never touched, and to this day she feels unwarranted guilt at having escaped her father's physical abuse while the rest of the family suffered. Psychologists call this phenomenon 'survivor's syndrome', and it has plagued many concentration-camp inmates who escaped the gas chambers during the Holocaust.

There was a simple reason Jerome Berry never laid a hand on his younger daughter. Whenever he became drunk and belligerent, unlike her feisty sister, Halle would leave the room. She recalled, 'He never hit me. He beat on my sister, but never me. I felt a lot of guilt. When my sister saw him hitting my mother, she would jump in and get hit, but I would run and hide.'

Although Halle escaped physical abuse, her emotional scars may be just as thick as her battered sister's. The *Los Angeles Times* recently ran an article on adult survivors of childhood abuse that noted:

> It was long believed that a youngster would not be harmed by witnessing the abuse of another in his home. Now, researchers suspect that the resulting fear is psychologically as corrosive as direct abuse of the child. And while sexual abuse may still be the most shocking form of mistreatment, many clinicians are beginning to believe that emotional abuse . . . wreaks the greatest damage in the long term.

In 1976, when Halle was ten, Judith allowed her husband to rejoin the family. As an adult, Halle justified her mother's unusual decision by explaining, 'My mother said, "I'm going to give it a shot," because she wanted us to have him in our lives.'

But the old abusive patterns emerged and Judith kicked Jerome out of the house again after less than a year. Nineteen seventy-six was not a happy year for Halle – she would call it 'the worst year of my life' – mostly because of her father's presence. Between the ages of four, when he left, and ten, when he returned, Halle seems to have forgotten the abuse and replaced it with an idealistic fantasy of her departed father. The reality, when he returned, was 180 degrees away from her idealised recollection.

Halle said of Jerome's return in 1976, 'I had longed for my father a lot until that time. But he was not the image I had made my daddy out to be. If I had lived with him any longer that year, I know I would have turned out to be a very different kind of person.'

In a 1998 documentary about her daughter that ran on the Lifetime cable channel in the US, Judith Berry smiled as she described the man she married, even though he would eventually turn out to be something quite different from her initial estimation of him. 'He was very personable, very charming, good-looking, could sing, sounded just like Johnny Mathis – you couldn't tell the difference. He was really outgoing. That's kind of the way I remember him when I met him.' Still smiling, Judith Berry added that she didn't realise at the time that alcohol was a big problem for him until several years into the marriage. It's puzzling and an ironic variation on the old dictum, 'Physician, heal thyself', that Judith Berry, despite her training as a psychiatric nurse and counsellor, allowed her troubled husband to return in 1976 and wreak his havoc a second time. Judith Berry's acquiescence suggests she may be a codependent personality, someone who tolerates abuse from a loved one with the unlikely hope that somehow the abuse can be turned into love.

Codependency is often treated with a twelve-step programme along the lines of Alcoholics Anonymous; and, like alcoholism, codependency may have a genetic component. Judith may have passed on the 'victim' gene to her daughter, who has also tolerated abuse in her adult relationships with men.

The American CoDA website www.codependents.org offers a 22-item check list of patterns and characteristics to help possible codependent personalities determine whether they suffer from this syndrome. As this account of Halle's life and loves unfolds, readers may agree that nine of these 'markers' for codependency could apply to the star's behaviour. These include finding it hard to work out what she is feeling; changing or denying how she feels; putting her own interests to one side in favour of others' and not asking others to fulfil her own wants; finding it hard to identify what she feels; seeing herself as completely committed to others' welfare; heaping presents on others; and being afraid to express sentiments or points of view that diverge from those of others.

Halle believes that it was her father's alcoholism that destroyed her parents' marriage. 'My mother couldn't deal with it, and he left. He came back a few years later, but he wasn't any better. He was like a stranger to us, and then he just disappeared.'

Halle elaborated on the traumatic effects of her father's return. 'He spent a year with us. It was probably one of the hardest years of my life as an adolescent, dealing with him coming back into the family and trying now to be a disciplinarian, trying to be a father when for the first ten years of my life he really wasn't there.' Halle has said she was terrified of her father and greatly relieved when her mother kicked him out of the house.

Although Jerome left, Judith worried about the effect his brief return had had on her children, and she sent Halle to a psychologist. That initial encounter turned into a lifelong process of self-examination under the guidance of a professional. Her mother, Halle said, 'saw that my mental state was at risk, and she made sure I had an appropriate outlet for discussing my feelings. To learn at such an early age that there is a calm and effective way to process emotions was a lesson I've never forgotten.' Ongoing therapy, she has said, has not prevented her from making mistakes, but at least it allows her to examine her problems with objectivity and keeps her 'grounded'.

As an adult in her own romantic relationships, Halle seemed to repeat her mother's pattern with Jerome Berry: she would tolerate abuse from a spouse or lover for a while, then cut the transgressor out of her life like a malignant tumour.

Her father ruined her self-esteem, but, in a brilliant example of smashing lemons to make lemonade, Halle fed on her feelings of inferiority and became a compulsive overachiever. 'I realized I always had a feeling of not being enough and that came from my father leaving. It came from so many things that I never felt good enough. I really suffered low self-esteem for many years.' She began overcompensating for this early on, in school and later in beauty pageants, modelling and finally as the most successful black actress today.

Nineteen seventy-six was a pivotal year for Halle for another reason: it was the first time her racial identity became an issue. Until she was ten, the family had lived in a black neighbourhood in the inner city of Cleveland. After Jerome Berry had left his wife and children, Judith moved her daughters out of the city to the almost all-white Cleveland suburb of Oakwood Village to take advantage of its superior school system.

'First we lived in an all-black neighborhood, and my mom felt on the outs,' Halle says. Her mother's sense of alienation was furthered by the fact that all of her white relatives turned their backs on her and her mixed-race daughters, as did Judith's black in-laws. 'She was alone, and she made it happen and survived.'

Judith recalls her family's pariah status in urban and suburban Cleveland. 'We suffered a lot of prejudice in both neighbourhoods because I was white and my children were interracial. We got a lot of prejudice from the black community.' Prejudice followed them to the white suburbs, whose inhabitants considered Halle and her sister black, not biracial.

Halle says, 'She moved us to an all-white neighborhood to afford us a better education, where my sister and I were the odd ones.' She describes the transition as 'culture shock'. Photographs of their two-storey, brown-brick and white-clapboard, suburban home with lots of trees and bushes and a spacious lawn indicate that Halle and her sister had a solid middle-class upbringing, thanks to her mother's generous paycheque as a nurse practitioner (a nurse who has additional education to specialise in a specific area of medicine – psychiatry in Judith's case).

Children are often notoriously cruel, and Halle's new white suburban classmates were no exception. White kids, she says, made fun of her delicate facial features and nicknamed her 'Pug Nose' and 'Buttons'. When peers saw her with her mother, they would ask Halle if she were adopted. When she insisted that Judith was her biological mother, they called her a liar.

Children can also be creative in their cruelty. For an entire year during her childhood, Halle recalls receiving a box of Oreos in the mail on average once a week. At the time, she thought she had a secret admirer and didn't realise until years later the malicious symbolism of the Oreo cookie as it represented her racial composition: black on the outside, white on the inside. Other kids called her and Heidi 'zebras'.

Halle remembers another painful incident where her parentage was questioned and denied. In the third grade, a student had seen her mother and told Halle they couldn't be related by blood. The child repeatedly said, 'You're black and you're mother is white, so you're adopted.'

Halle was lucky her mother was a trained psychiatric professional who wanted her daughters to have a healthy sense of self and their racial identity. Technically, Halle was of course biracial, half white and half black. But the world tends to be an either/or place: you're either white or you're black, regardless of your parentage.

It has been inaccurately reported that Halle grew up confused about her racial identity. This myth gained special power in 1993, when she played the *Roots* author Alex Haley's mixed-race grandmother in the TV miniseries, *Queen*. But, from an early age, Judith made sure her daughter knew exactly who and what she was.

One of Halle's earliest memories is of Judith sitting her down in front of a mirror and saying, ' "Look at yourself. What do you see when you look at your skin?" I said, "Brown." She asked, "What colour do you see when you look at my skin?" I said, "White." She said, "That's right: you're black and I'm white; but that doesn't mean I'm not your mother, that I don't love you. You are a black little girl." ' Halle credits her mother with teaching her to identify herself as black because that's how everyone else would classify her based on her looks. Strangers wouldn't know she was biracial, Judith told her daughter, and they wouldn't care even if they knew.

Halle says, 'I'm discriminated against like a black woman, as if I were one hundred percent African-American, so that's what I feel I am.' She is content with her identity as a black woman, even though she once confided to a reporter that she has always wished she had her mother's 'beautiful blue eyes'. (In a photograph that contains a tight, cheek-to-cheek close-up of mother and daughter when Halle was a young adult, they have almost identical features, except that Halle's hair is curly and her lips are a bit fuller – and of course Halle is a few shades darker, but only a few. However, the most significant thing about the photograph is the almost palpable love for each other evident on their faces.)

Fortunately, as much as her father damaged her self-esteem during his brief time with the family, her mother indoctrinated her with a lifelong belief in her own worth, her invincibility and the power to accomplish anything she set out to do – life skills that would eventually carry Halle to the very top of her profession. Her mother gave her 'life, love, and everything. She always instilled in me that you are good, you are smart, you are beautiful, you are capable of doing whatever it is you want to do,' Halle has said.

Never during her fourteen-year acting career has the press ever brought up a subject that Halle addresses on her official website, www.hallewood.com. In a sublink at the site labelled 'Inner Beauty', she poses a question to herself: 'It seems like you don't identify with the white side of your heritage. Why is that?' Her answer is that she does indeed identify with her white heritage though, even while she was young, she didn't *feel* white. Throughout her life she has been aware that she is biracial but the other children at school tended to assume she was black and didn't believe her when she said her mother was white. So she eventually decided not to worry about what other people thought.

Actually, it took a nightmarish divorce and the public humiliation of being labelled a hit-and-run driver to liberate Halle finally from the burden of other people's opinion of her, she has admitted elsewhere.

On the same website, Halle recounts her mother's telling her that people wouldn't believe she had a white mother unless she wore a sign on her forehead. Even if they did believe her on that topic, though, many people think even an ounce of black blood in you means you are black.

At an early age, Halle says, she decided to let other people categorise her any way they cared to. Her sense of self and self-esteem would not be determined by the colour of her skin or which ethnic group she chose to be a part of. She went about her life, being herself, 'and let the issue of [her] race be the issue of those who had a problem with it.'

Although she attended the almost all-white Heskett Middle School in Bedford Heights, Ohio, there was one powerful black role model, her fifth-grade teacher, Yvonne Nichols Sims, who remains close with her former student to this day. 'She was the first person other than my mother to help me understand what being black was all about and what my struggle would be,' Halle says.

Sims's effect on her sounds almost mystical the way Halle describes it. 'An angel appeared. Here was a strong, powerful black woman who was very in control of who she was and very involved in black culture and black history. She came along and scooped me up and made me realize that I was OK being myself and loving myself and my blackness.'

According to a seventh-grade classmate, Hank Wojda, the struggle for Halle didn't begin until she attended Bedford High School in Bedford, Ohio. At Heskett Middle School, Wojda said,

'Halle was definitely the prettiest girl in school. Halle was very popular, and there was no hint of any racial prejudice in [middle school] – but at Bedford High it was harder for Halle. She suffered through a lot because she was biracial.'

In middle school, Halle was a class monitor, and Wojda remembers how she performed an act of kindness towards a total stranger – him. 'I was in trouble. I think it was for skipping school. Halle was the official office monitor sent to get me out of class to see the principal.' Wojda said he was very nervous about being reprimanded by the principal and was amazed that 'this sweet, petite girl' tried to calm him down. 'She was half my size, but her voice and demeanour impressed me.' The memory of her kindness is still fresh to him almost a quarter of a century later.

At Bedford High, Halle felt compelled to achieve, to excel and overcompensate because of her race. And, as she would later do in her film career, she found herself in the onerous position of being the trailblazer for people of colour. At least she had the help of Yvonne Sims, who transferred to Bedford High when Halle did and served as her guidance counsellor in both middle and high schools. 'I swear to this day she followed me through the whole school system,' Halle said.

Sims's initial impression of Halle was that of a 'quiet little girl', but, with the self-assurance the guidance counsellor instilled in her protégée, Halle blossomed at Bedford High, where she made the cheerleading squad, became editor of the school newspaper and a member of the honour society. She was also elected freshman class president and prom queen during her junior year. 'If there was an organization, I wanted to be the head of it. I wanted the best grades. I wanted to be the best at everything,' Halle recalls.

All along the way, she met resistance based on her race. 'I was told at first that I couldn't be a cheerleader because our school didn't have any black athletes and because there had never been a black cheerleader. They'd say, "You're really good but . . ." Halle proved the pessimists wrong and eventually became head of the cheerleading squad.

'I thought if I made the honour society they would know I was as smart as they were; if I ran the paper I'd control what's in the paper and make it diverse; if I'm a cheerleader, I'm going to be the captain.'

The reaction to her election as prom queen was an eye-opener and made her realise how tenuous her acceptance by the white student body was. She was accused of having rigged the election. In 1993, she said, 'I felt like I was accepted there until it came to being the prom queen.' In 2001, she was still obsessing about this long-ago injustice: 'I ran for prom queen and won, but they accused me of stuffing the ballot box. I won by such a landslide, they couldn't believe that little ole black me could beat all those white beauty queens.'

Yvonne Sims chuckles and says of her protégée's landslide victory, 'It would have taken an awful lot of illegal ballots to have been placed in that election box for it to come out the way it did.'

School officials suggested that she share the title with the runner-up, whom Halle described as a 'beautiful blonde'. But Halle rejected the offer. 'I said, I'm not sharing anything.'

Then the school suggested a coin toss to determine the winner. Halle picked 'heads' and won again. 'But that experience stuck with me. I could be president and head cheerleader, but they were white and I was black and I was different.' The incident made her realise her entire life would be a struggle and it took a long time for her to get over it. For years, she has said, she never felt 'equal'.

'When I realized I didn't blend in was the year that I won the junior prom queen [title]. The reality smacked me [in] the head, then I realized they accepted me, but not as the symbol of beauty.' This latter realisation would pursue, even haunt, her for the rest of her life and create two conflicting emotions. She never felt quite beautiful enough again and would reassure herself by winning one beauty pageant after another, then go on to the ultimate confirmation of one's attractiveness, fashion modelling.

Furious, even though she had won the coin toss, Halle at first fantasised about not turning up. Bedford would host a high school prom without a prom queen. Her mother urged her to attend and warned that people would say she was afraid if she didn't attend. Her absence would allow her enemies to have the last word.

And Halle herself felt a certain racial burden to attend the event after her initial decision to boycott it. 'But then I thought, "History will say the first black queen didn't even show up." So I said to myself, "Go, represent, and deal with your personal issues later," ' she says.

So she decided to savour her victory in person but on her own terms by arriving half an hour before the prom ended. When she at last made her entrance, the entire prom committee was standing outside the auditorium, frantic that the star of the show wouldn't be there.

Her date for the prom caused more problems. According to Halle, she went to the prom with the son of Bedford High's principal, a white man, who, Halle later said, 'wasn't too interested in anything interracial. The principal's disposition wasn't too good when he saw that.'

Voting-fraud allegations had the effect of reinforcing Halle's identity as black rather than biracial. On her website, she says that the experience had the outcome of making her feel more of a connection to the black community because, despite the fact that she herself was half white, she was experiencing exactly the same discrimination as her friends who were fully black. It was exactly what Judith had warned her about many years before – though her mother was white and Halle therefore had white blood in her, many people were ignorant of the distinction and it therefore didn't make any difference against racism.

But Halle also reveals on her website that she isn't bitter about being considered all-black and has turned what some might consider a burden into a blessing. She's an optimist who always sees the glass as not half full or half empty, rather as overflowing. She has realised that it actually puts her in a very good position to be considered completely or exclusively black. Because of that she can carry on with what she has been doing and, in the process, explore new areas for other black women in both television and film and make those who have in the past been educated with racist teachings to be more receptive. She notes that, if she can destroy the negative pictures that exist of black people and the negative stereotypes that the public associate with black people, then there will have been some profit from her life.

Some have felt Halle's past struggles were not as harsh as they have been portrayed.

Kelli Hichens, a white classmate at Bedford High, feels that Halle has overemphasised the discrimination she encountered as a teenager, but then again Hichens wasn't a black girl in a predominantly white school. Hichens has said, 'Halle was a very well-liked girl in school. She had friends who were both black and white, and I know many boys would have liked to have dated her regardless of color.'

Another classmate and a close friend at the time, Terrie Fitzwater, believes Halle hasn't exaggerated the racism she endured, and the ludicrousness of the ballot-box-stuffing charge proves it. 'You couldn't really do that [stuff the ballot box],' Fitzwater says. 'Because when you went up to vote they had your number and crossed it off after you voted.'

Halle doesn't want to portray herself as a martyr and realises children can be cruel for a variety of reasons, not just because of skin colour. 'It was just teasing. The fattest kid got teased, the kid with the biggest glasses got teased, the kid with the best grades got teased. My problem was no worse than theirs,' she said.

While Halle was discriminated against by many students, she found others who were happy to her accept her regardless of her colour. 'I got hit on pretty equally by both [black and white boys]. I didn't have a preference.' At least once a month, her mother would tell her, 'Bring home whoever you want as long as he's a good guy and treats you well.' That was a piece of advice Halle would disregard with disastrous results time and again in later life.

Besides the racial element in the prom-queen controversy, Halle felt it also reflected on her looks. 'I had worked hard to be accepted,' she recalled years later, 'but, when it came to being a standard of beauty for the school, they didn't want me. That taught me: no more dancing bear.'

Actually, insecurity about her looks compelled Halle to continue the 'dancing bear' act in a series of beauty pageants, where her participation helped quiet the internal voice that whispered, 'You're not pretty enough. You're not good enough.' And always, festering right under the surface, lay the suspicion that many of her socialisation problems in high school were due to the fact that 'you are not white'.

Even after she became an internationally known movie star, Halle felt the race card was still being dealt in her life. After the ballot-box-stuffing allegations, she realised, 'I could be president and head cheerleader, but they were white and I was black and I was different. I realized that I always have to keep fighting. It made me feel like I wasn't beautiful; that they don't see us as being beautiful.'

The prom-queen brouhaha made Halle feel so humiliated that the once gregarious student withdrew from school activities during her senior year and kept to herself. But somehow Halle managed to put a positive spin on this lonely period in her life as she turned the rejection into a challenge to prove her worth constantly. 'Now I had a chip on my shoulder, and now I couldn't wait to get out, get out into the world and show these SOBs that I'm going to be somebody and one day you're going to want to remember that you knew me because I'm going to go out and do something fabulous.' She admits that at the time she didn't exactly know how or what 'fabulous' thing she was going to accomplish. 'But I felt like, "I'm going to show them . . ." '

A battery of pageant judges begged to differ with Halle's insecurity about her looks, although, unlike the rest of her meticulously planned and calculated career, her path to the beauty-queen runway was a fluke she did not engineer or even seek. When she was seventeen, and without informing her, her then boyfriend sent her high school yearbook photograph to the Miss Teen Ohio beauty pageant. 'Three weeks later I get a letter saying you have been selected as a finalist. So I decided to go [as Miss Cuyahoga County], wore my prom dress and surprisingly I won Miss Teen Ohio.'

She then went on to compete in the 1985 Miss Teen All-American Pageant, which according to *Pageantry Magazine* has a reputation for discovering 'stars of tomorrow', and this woman who was unsure of her attractiveness not only won the Miss Ohio title, but went on to achieve the national title as well.

In 1986, she walked off with another Miss Ohio title, which allowed her to compete in the Miss USA pageant. 'When I was winning, I thought, "Hey, who paid these people off?" It really wasn't that important to me. I wanted nothing more than to go back to my high school and say, "Hey, guys, who stuffed *these* ballot boxes?" '

She came in second in the Miss USA contest, losing out to an *Ur*-WASP, a blonde, blue-eyed beauty from Texas, Christy Fichtner, whose win seemed to reinforce Halle's belief that white beauties had an easier time of it than black beauties. To add insult to disappointment, when she failed to win the Miss USA pageant, her high school boyfriend, the originator of her many trips down the runway, dumped her. It must have been some consolation to the 'loser' that Bob Hope invited her to join him for a three-week tour of seven countries as part of the first Bob Hope Miss USA/USO tour.

Winning first runner-up in the Miss USA pageant also qualified Halle to compete in the Miss World contest in 1987 in Hong Kong, according to a Lifetime documentary about Halle. She lost that one, too, but was placed a respectable third, and her fashion sense was already evident as she won the consolation prize of 'best dressed'.

Still, a nagging voice told her that beauty was only a door-opener. But when she opened the door she had to rely on more than a stunning physical presence. Halle has said, 'Beauty can be used as a tool to draw people in. But once you're in, you've got to be able do something. If you can't then you're just another pretty face.'

The universe of beauty contests can often seem like major displays of narcissism and exhibitionism, but Halle wasn't there just to show off and get her ego massaged. She was also in it for the money. In 1993, looking back on her past on the runway treadmill, she said her primary motivation was to win money for college tuition. 'We were very middle-class people. Not upper middle. Not lower middle. And I knew that my mother couldn't afford to flat-out send me or my sister to college. So my only hope was through scholarships and grants.' By 1993 there may also have been the feeling that her runaway résumé detracted from her efforts to be taken seriously as an actress.

Despite the reinforcement of winning so many beauty contests, her success did not automatically reinforce her desire to become some kind of professional beauty, be it model, actress or singer.

After high school, she enrolled in Cleveland's Cuyahoga Community College. During her brief tenure in college, Halle majored in journalism, but found the in-your-face requirements of being an investigative reporter made an uncomfortable fit with her personality. While in college, she has said, she did an internship at a TV station one summer – 'and they'd send me out on stories, but I couldn't ask people questions'. (Interestingly, the late George C Scott, an otherwise tough customer, also abandoned his journalism career when he found interrogating subjects excruciating, as have other stars, such as Brad Pitt and John Goodman (Roseanne's TV husband) – both of them college-journalism majors.)

Halle has said of having to ask tough questions, 'I felt it was too intrusive, so I decided journalism wasn't for me. I wanted to be a journalist, but I just couldn't do it.' For one of her first assignments, her teacher provided a list of questions to ask an inner-city family whose house had been burned down. 'I accompanied the lead journalist and had these questions, but I was just bawling. I so lost my composure that it upset the family. I didn't have the skin for the job.'

Halle by now had developed a hide toughened by surviving an abusive childhood, racism and allegations of voter fraud, so investigative journalism doesn't seem like such a tough job by comparison. *Pageantry* magazine has suggested a more cogent reason – public 'adulation' – why Halle forsook the reporter's notebook in favour of the pageant and fashion runways. 'Pageant success at age 17 and the audience adulation from the USO tour proved stronger than the promise of some day anchoring Cleveland's 6 o'clock news,' according to *Pageantry*.

Losing the Miss World pageant may have been a blessing in disguise. Instead of being sidetracked by the traditional year of shopping-mall appearances, ribbon cuttings and all the other numbing PR that pageant winners must endure, Halle used the twelve months she would have wasted playing Miss World to pursue even bigger and better career opportunities – first as a model and then as a sitcom star, ultimately finding movie superstardom. 'You're exploited if you want to be,' she said in 1993. 'Only good things came out of my pageant days.'

Over the years, Halle's opinion of her beauty-queen career has evolved and sometimes seems self-contradictory as her experience is refracted through her present state of mind and self-image.

In 2001, she had only praise for her time with the tiara. 'It was very shallow in many ways, because it perpetuated my physical self a lot more than I ever wanted to, but very significant in a way because I gained a lot of confidence in myself. That confidence has served me throughout my life.'

She even turned her personal victories into a triumph for her entire race. Pageant judges, she recalled, were 'taking too much heat' because none of the black contestants was among the finalists or semifinalists. 'They couldn't deny us any longer. So, did I win for real, or was I the black girl who won to make a statement?' Halle says she still doesn't know if she was a token, but at the time her victories made her feel accepted. 'As shallow or superficial as it may have been, in that moment I felt like I am as good as they are.' Halle still seems haunted by the false accusations of ballot-box stuffing at Bedford High.

But, only a year after she had lauded the self-confidence that winning pageants had given her, she appears to have changed her mind and badmouthed the phenomenon that made possible the rest of her record-breaking career. In 2002, she dismissed the entire pageant universe. 'I did it for three years. I hated it; it was the most boring work I ever did. There had to be a better way to make a buck!' she said with a derisive laugh. 'Not being able to have a say. Being a human coat hanger . . .'

But in 1995, she had felt just the opposite. 'Pageants teach you how to lose and not be devastated. It was great preparation for Hollywood.' Halle wasn't exaggerating the beneficial effects of pursuing a tiara. One of the Miss USA judges, Kay Mitchell, was an agent from Chicago, and she was so impressed by Halle's beauty and stage presence that she urged her to move to the big city, Chicago, and embark on a modelling career. Halle took the agent's advice.

'Kay made it [modelling] sound so glamorous: "Come to Chicago, you can live with me in my downtown apartment on the 54th floor. I'll get you started." ' The agent even volunteered to pay for her model's portfolio, saying, 'You're gonna be fabulous,' Halle recalled in 1998.

Another judge, pageant producer and agent, Syd Freedman, was also struck by Halle's loveliness, and he turned out to be a terrific prognosticator of future greatness. Freedman was impressed with Halle's effervescence and said, 'I think she had a personality. It was not only her prettiness – she bubbled over in her personality. She was one of the girls I would have selected as having the potential to go to bigger and better things.'

Halle's mother accompanied her to Chicago, where they found the world of glamour and luxury Kay Mitchell had promised to be quite different. Judith Berry remembers the reality of the situation. 'There were 12 to 13 girls living in this apartment, trying to be models, camping out on the floor. I really hated to leave her there.'

Halle moved into the tiny one-bedroom apartment with other would-be mannequins and became a starving artist, almost literally. She remembers going to bars that featured 'happy hours' with free food, which often served as her only meal of the day. 'Me and my model friends hung out at a lot of happy hours eating fried drumsticks,' she says.

Halle loathed her cramped living situation, and with her typical efficiency quickly found a way out of Camp Beautiful. 'After a month, the whole "sardine" thing wasn't working for me anymore, so I got together with one of the other models, Susan, and we got our own one-bedroom apartment.'

Poverty also caused her first and only rift with her devoted mother, who practised a form of tough love that infuriated her daughter and kept the two from speaking for almost a year. After a rare modelling gig in Milwaukee, Halle returned to Chicago to find her roommate gone and the $1,200 rent due. Halle asked her mother for a loan and said, 'Mom, I really need like 50 dollars for food.' The happy-hour freebies were apparently providing insufficient nutrition. Her mother responded, 'You wanted to go [to Chicago and model]. Now you're seeing what it's like in the real world.'

Halle remembers her feelings at the time. 'When she said no, my world came crashing down. I thought how could my mom say no? I'm thinking, "Mom, I'm trying to eat here. You do not understand the state I'm in," and she still said no.'

Halle had another run-in with her mother over something less crucial than hunger. She needed to pay a photographer to put together a modelling portfolio, and Judith declined to help out again. 'She called and asked me for, I think, $500 to do her portfolio, and it was at a time when I didn't have that kind of money to send her,' Judith Berry said.

Halle didn't speak to her mother for 'a little over a year after that. Then my ego kicked in, and I said fine. I'll never ask you for another thing,' Halle said.

In retrospect, her original rage over her mother's refusal to support her career efforts gave way to a recognition of the wisdom of Judith's tough love. 'She made me realize I had to either sink or swim,' Halle says.

Her mother says, 'Now she tells me, and I think it's true, that that was the best thing I ever did because from that day on she became independent, never looked back and has been making it on her own.'

In retrospect, Halle agrees with her mother's assessment. 'What seemed like a really terrible thing at the moment was probably the best thing she could have ever done for me.' Halle says she eventually forgave her mother and vowed never to let something 'as frivolous as that' come between them again.

Halle is only five foot six (1.7 metres) and weighs a waiflike eight stone (51 kilograms or 112 pounds). The kindest thing one modelling agent could say about her was that she was 'petite', then added that there wasn't much work for little women in a world of models the height of basketball players.

Because of her diminutive frame and her height (although she does boast an impressive 34C cup chest), Halle never had the potential to become a major player in a business populated with Amazonian women. In fact, most of her work in Chicago consisted of lingerie ads. They can't tell how short you are in a print ad.

Nevertheless, she found a lot of work and appeared in the Land's End catalogue and Marshall Fields and Lord & Taylor ads. But Halle remained a realist who knew her limitations. 'I wasn't quite tall enough to do the really fabulous stuff,' she says. 'I did a lot of lingerie and hand modelling at one point – that's how desperate things got. I knew I was never going to be a supermodel.' Halle turned out to be wrong about her supermodel prospects because one day she would replace the *hyper*model Cindy Crawford as the 'face of Revlon'.

Halle was too smart and ambitious and became bored with modelling work, so she began taking acting classes. While her modelling career drifted, a powerful man was about to enter her life and have such a profound effect on her both personally and professionally that she would come to consider him a surrogate father – in fact, she would say he was the only father she had ever known.

2. LIVING HELL

New Yorker Vincent Cirrincione is a talent manager turned movie producer. He was looking for a black actress to audition for a specific role, and one of Halle's former rivals from her beauty-pageant days told Cirrincione about Halle. But, by the time he had tracked her down, the part had already been cast. Nevertheless, Cirrincione asked Halle to send him an audition tape. She sent him the tape of her *losing* the Miss Teen All American pageant, but her 'failure' did not deter Cirrincione, who was smitten by the image he saw on his TV.

'A month or so later, this tape comes in, and I put it into the machine, and she just lit up the screen,' Cirrincione recalls. At his invitation, she flew to New York to meet him, and Cirrincione offered to manage her career after only one meeting.

It took Halle three months to convince herself that she should abandon the cosy mediocrity of her Chicago modelling career and relocate to New York, where the serious modelling and, more importantly, acting opportunities lay.

When she finally arrived in Manhattan in 1989, the industrious Cirrincione found a possible modelling gig for her almost immediately, but Halle resisted the job because she had her eye on bigger things that required more than a surly, look-at-me pout as she sashayed down endless catwalks at interminable fashion shows or posed in her skivvies in magazine ads.

Cirrincione and his wife, Vera, became Halle's surrogate family to the point where they invited her to move in and sleep on their couch. Vera, however, played more than a maternal role. 'New York can be a dangerous place, so I went with her to auditions,' Vera Cirrincione recalled.

Halle still resisted the life of a mannequin and found a simple way to sabotage her modelling career.

'I'd find myself at auditions with all these black girls who all looked alike – big, curly long hair.' To separate herself from the pack, she cut most of her hair off. Then, she says, she went to see Cirrincione – 'and he about had a stroke. He said, "You're not going to work. You're not commercial anymore."'

Cirrincione says, 'I looked at that short crop and said, "Well, there goes your commercial career." And she said, "That's not why I'm here." '

Like so many models, Berry wanted to become an actress, and her new manager tried to satisfy that desire by getting her auditions for various projects that failed to land his client a job. Halle auditioned for the soap opera *Days of Our Lives* and an updated version of the 1970s phenomenon renamed *Charlie's Angels 1988*, which never aired.

While she was in Los Angeles to audition for the *Charlie's Angels* revival, the co-creator of the original series, Aaron Spelling, who has a track record of discovering future stars and reviving the careers of fading ones (Linda Evans, Joan Collins), felt he had found another winner and encouraged her to sign up with an A-list manager. With Cirrincione on her team, the industrious neophyte had already anticipated the starmaker's advice. Their relationship continues to this day, and Cirrincione also serves as executive producer on many of her film projects.

But Halle's beauty, once a blessing, now seemed, if not a curse, at least a handicap in her attempts to make the transition from modelling to acting. She described the prejudicial mindset she encountered during these failed auditions. 'When you're a model, they think you're stupid and they think, "Oh, you're beautiful, so you want to be in movies but you have no talent." '

Her pageant days also came back to haunt her reincarnation as a serious actress. 'Many times I would go to an audition and they'd say, "Oh yeah, ex-beauty queen. OK, read for me," and then they would turn their heads while I auditioned,' she said.

Halle recognized the blessing and curse her beauty created, and she realised that good looks would open doors, but only talent would allow her to step inside the world of acting. Or, as she said in 1993, 'Beauty can be used as a tool to draw people in. But, once you're in, you've got to be able to do something. I don't think I'm bad-looking, and I know my looks have made a difference in some situations. But I also see a lot of people around me who are much more beautiful than I am.'

Fortunately for Halle, her new manager was just as 'dogged' as his client. She has said, 'Vince is a bulldog. He'll try every angle to get me into the room to be seen. And getting in the room, especially if you're black, is the hardest part.'

Her beauty eventually turned out to be more blessing than curse and led to her first big break. But Halle attributed the coup to her new hairdo. 'Two weeks after [cutting her hair], I got my first acting job, and I think the haircut had a lot to do with it because I wasn't like all the other girls they had seen for the job,' Halle said.

Only two months after she had reluctantly relocated from Chicago to New York, she landed a role on a sitcom about something Halle already knew a great deal about: the world of modelling. 'Great stretch, huh?' Halle said with a laugh.

The show was the ABC sitcom *Living Dolls*, a spin-off of *Who's the Boss?*. The comedy revolved around the adventures of four aspiring models and their agent (*The Waltons*' Michael Learned), who serves as matriarch and mentor for this mini-clan of beautiful women.

Living Dolls was spun off the episode of *Who's the Boss?* in which Alyssa Milano's character went to New York to interview teenage models for her school paper. This paper-thin premise led to a sitcom about the models Milano interviewed.

The Complete Directory to Prime Time Network and Cable TV Shows was being generous when it described *Living Dolls* as a 'lightweight comedy'. Much like Halle's starving-model days in Chicago, the programme featured four beautiful teenage girls sharing a cramped apartment in Manhattan with their agent, a chaperone-mentor named Trish Carlin (Michael Learned), who heads the fictitious Carlin Agency. Each girl represented a 'type'. Martha Lambert (Alison Elliott) was the innocent one, Caroline Weldon (Deborah Tucker) was the narcissist, Charlie Brisco (Leah Remini) was a hard-boiled former street kid and Emily Franklin (Halle) was typecast as the smart one. Conflict and comic relief were provided by Trish's sixteen-year-old son, Rick (David Moscow), and his mother's attempts to keep his hands off her beautiful charges. Marion Ross, the mother from *Happy Days*, played Trish's sister, who pinch hit and supervised the girls when Learned's character went off on business trips.

Halle has said she was cast as the 'token Negro' on the show and was given nothing to do. The white writer-producers didn't know how to write for a black woman. To their credit, the writers designated Halle the brain of the bunch and provided a 'back story' that she was in the business only to save up enough money to pay for medical school. Her character was an overachiever, just like Halle.

The doomed sitcom debuted on 26 September 1989, to contemptuous reviews and ratings that hovered in the Nielsen's basement. Howard Rosenberg, the TV critic for the *Los Angeles Times*, wrote, '*Living Dolls* is bad enough when it tries to be funny, even worse when it tries not to be funny. As for the latter, it doesn't have to try.' The *Orange County Register*'s Ray Richmond wrote, 'The sit-com-by-numbers writing is numbingly bad, the acting horrendous, the pacing terrible. And those are the good points.'

The reviews might as well have been the show's obituary, because it was cancelled less than three months later after only thirteen episodes, the last show airing on 30 December 1989.

Halle wasn't crushed by the abrupt end of her TV stardom: she was relieved. 'I was happy to be making that kind of money, but I got pretty bored creatively, so when it was canceled I was happy.' She didn't work for six months after *Living Dolls* went off the air, but she was glad to have escaped an artistic environment she found stifling.

There were worse things than boredom that she encountered during her unhappy days as a reluctant sitcom star. The stress of working on a failing, stultifying show had terrible personal consequences for the young model turned actress.

In terms of Halle's life experiences, the only notable thing about the sitcom was that during taping she collapsed on the set and was rushed to the hospital in a diabetic coma. 'The doctors told me that all of the stress I'd been under probably brought the diabetes out early. Otherwise, it might not have surfaced until I was 50 or 60,' Halle has said.

When doctors tried to explain the disease to Halle, she focused only on its terrifying elements. 'All I heard [about] was shots [injections] every day and that I could lose my eyesight and my legs. I was scared to death.' Not only scared to death, but Halle literally thought she was dying! 'It was the first time I had to work

12 or 14 hours straight without a break to go to my usual vices –
a candy bar, a little nap, a glass of juice.'

After she came to in the hospital and was told she had diabetes,
she thought she was dying, 'because all I heard was disease. I
quickly learned all about insulin and how it is manageable.' But
there are still flare-ups, usually during stressful periods when 'my
blood sugar gets a little out of control. I get a little more sleepy
and lethargic. I can usually tell.'

Occasionally, the symptoms are worse than lethargy. 'Sometimes my blood sugar goes really high and I get really sick. Stress
has a lot to do with diabetes and there is a lot of it in this
business.'

Race, which had been so critical during her formative years,
even played a role in her new illness. Blacks have a much greater
incidence of diabetes. Two million African-Americans – one in ten
of the population – suffer from the chronic disease.

Halle confronted the reality of her condition. She would have
to take insulin injections three times a day for the rest of her life,
change her diet and exercise regularly to keep the life-threatening
disease at bay. She also had to have insulin with her at all times
in case of another attack.

At first, Halle tried to ignore her condition and didn't exercise
or change her diet – two of the most important ways to combat
diabetes. But, a few years after her diagnosis, she was 'scared
straight' when she temporarily lost the use of her right leg and
realised she had to adjust her lifestyle to her illness or face even
more serious consequences, such as blindness and amputation.

Halle has not since fallen into another diabetic coma because
she attacked her new illness with the determination and drive that
she has applied to her career. 'I've changed my diet. I exercise and
meditate to avoid stress. I need three square meals a day. I eat lots
of vegetables and make my own juices, always have some fruit and
avoid sugar and fried foods,' she says. She also installed a gym in
her home and hired a personal trainer to keep her pumping. She
discovered that in some ways that diabetes, as awful as it seemed
when first diagnosed, has had a beneficial effect on her life. 'I
notice a big difference in my attitude when I'm exercising. I'm
happier, more confident, less stressed,' she says. In fact, she

LE BERRY

became something of an exercise addict, pumping iron ninety minutes every day. And her disease gave her a new cause to fight for – working closely with the Juvenile Diabetes Foundation.

The six months of unemployment that followed the failure of *Living Dolls* may have made Halle feel that her career was over. It certainly was for the rest of the cast, as her co-stars Tucker, Elliott and Remini fell into the 'Whatever Happened to . . .?' category.

But Halle need not have worried. After half a year of idleness, she would get the career break of a lifetime.

3. THE BIG SCREEN AND THE BIG TIME

Nineteen ninety was a golden year for Halle Berry and her career. She would make three films and take risks that would help add longevity to a career that could easily have ended as the beautiful actress reached middle age (that's about 35 in youth-obsessed Hollywood) and was no longer typecast as the ingénue or attractive leading lady.

The film director Spike Lee at first couldn't see past the beauty of the woman who came to audition for *Jungle Fever*, in which he planned to cast her as his wife, a conventional role as a homemaker. (That part eventually went to another model, Veronica Webb.) Halle had other ideas. She wanted to be considered for a drastically different role in the film. 'I asked, "Do you think I could audition for the part of the crack whore?" I liked that part better. She was so screwed up. I could relate to that,' Halle said.

She knows her good looks have opened doors, but she's smart enough to realise that beauty also has its limitations. 'I love that no one believes that was me as the crack whore in *Jungle Fever*. Frankly, fighting against my looks has become a large part of my career as an actress. I mean, everyone should have such problems, but producers never consider me for anything that isn't glamorous,' she has said.

Playing a crack whore, she added, provided a great entrée to the film industry, allowing her to shed her physical self and play a character role. 'This gave me a chance to be seen by people in the industry as something other than a model [or] beauty queen.'

Halle wanted something on her résumé other than being a model and impersonating one on TV. Spike Lee ultimately managed to see past her beauty and cast her as the doomed crack addict and prostitute, but only after a withering assault and desperate deeds by Halle. She remembers her first meeting with Lee: 'All I was, up until that point, was a model. I asked him if I could read for the part of the crack kid in the movie and he let me do it, and he eventually offered me that part.'

Halle said that Lee 'eventually' gave her the role. But, even after she finally persuaded the director to let her play the addict, he had an eleventh-hour change of mind. Vera Cirrincione recalled, 'At the last moment Spike told her they'd pay her, but that she was too pretty for the role. She got on the phone and said, "Spike, give me a chance, give me a chance, and I will prove that I can do this. Give me a chance."' Vera estimates Halle spent an entire hour on the phone begging Lee.

The Times of London also claimed Halle spent an hour importuning the director, but he still refused. So Halle decided to show the director another side of herself, and it wasn't a pretty view. 'There's a hundred sides to every person, and I wanted to be taken seriously. So I'll take all the makeup off. I'll take off the tight dress, and I'll get downright gritty to prove I can do the dramatic roles,' she said.

Halle got much more than 'gritty' to make Lee change his mind. She resorted to not bathing for ten days, and returned for a second audition that literally stank. Only then did Lee change his mind and cast her as the drug addict.

Halle embraced the role with her usual determination – determined to live the creepy life of an addict just short of ingesting the drug that turned people into its slaves. She became a method actress with the ability to disappear into a role like such protean performers as Meryl Streep and Robert De Niro.

To research her role, she decided to live on the street. She also didn't shower or shave. 'I needed to feel grungy. The hair underneath my arms [grew] so long I could braid it,' she said. She also visited a real crack den in Washington, DC, accompanied by an undercover police officer, who insisted she wear a bulletproof vest. 'Things that today I doubt I would ever do, because it's too dangerous and it really doesn't make a lot of sense. But at that time, I was young and I was like, "I don't know anything about crack. I've got to go see."'

On the film, Halle became good friends with her co-star, Samuel L Jackson, who played her addict boyfriend, Gator. Jackson took the neophyte actress under his wing and became a mentor and tour guide to an underworld the perfectly coiffed and garbed former beauty queen couldn't even imagine – until she saw it in the flesh.

Jackson squired her around New York City, where they visited crack neighbourhoods. What she witnessed during her descent into hell's 'hood horrified this product of white, middle-class suburban Cleveland. 'I saw 12- and 13-year-old girls perform oral sex on men for a hit [a puff on a crack pipe]. There were automatic weapons and knives everywhere.'

She even toyed with the idea of trying the drug to see what all the fuss was about, but something deep inside warned her not to go *that* far. Something outside her also scared her off: the personal history of her mentor and co-star. 'Sam Jackson was my ace in the hole,' Halle said. 'I didn't know anything about crack addiction. He was very open about his drug addiction, so he was very supportive and very aware about the subject.'

Jackson was impressed with his protégée's fortitude and predicted big things for the tyro actress. 'When you look at Halle, you think ingénue. I told her, "This is the kind of role that will take that curse off you forever," ' Jackson said.

The theme of *Jungle Fever* is that interracial romances are doomed to failure, something Halle knew about first-hand from her parents' disastrous marriage. Annabella Sciorra plays an Italian secretary from Bensonhurt, New York, who falls in love with a rich black architect played by Wesley Snipes. Samuel Jackson's crack addict Gator is Snipes's brother in the film.

The first scene to feature Halle is a shocker. The erstwhile beauty queen is unrecognisable. She's wearing rags and Halle's usual *café au lait* perfect complexion has zits! *USA Weekend* magazine wasn't quite accurate when it said Halle wore no makeup in *Jungle Fever*. The makeup man on the movie had to paint acne on her face, and something that looks like a herpes sore appears on her lower lip. But even wearing rags and no beauty makeup, and sporting a hairdo that hasn't seen a comb in days, Halle doesn't look ugly, merely cute.

In her first scene, she and Jackson engage in an obscenity-fuelled argument in which they speak with the staccato tempo of crack addicts making their dialogue unintelligible. In another scene, based on an incident she witnessed in real life during her research on the streets, Halle's desperate addict offers Wesley Snipes's character a blow job for five dollars. When he turns her down, she offers to do it for three. It's impossible to imagine where Halle with her pristine past found the inspiration to play such utter degradation of a human being. But she did.

Despite her own parents' failed marriage, Halle strongly disagreed with Spike Lee's belief that interracial relationships are doomed; and, despite her position as a newcomer in the film business, she had the temerity to get into a shouting match with the powerful director on the subject. 'I remember having a big row with Spike Lee on the set of *Jungle Fever* because he said my parents divorced because black–white love can never work. I told Spike that that was just his warped and twisted point of view.' She told Lee her parents loved each other, but her father's drinking, not his skin colour, had doomed the marriage.

Rumours arose that, despite their philosophical differences, Halle and Lee became lovers during filming. Halle has categorically denied them, despite the fact that while making the movie she lived above his film-memorabilia store in Brooklyn. She apparently did have an affair with the star of *Jungle Fever*, Wesley Snipes, and their break-up in 1991 left her 'crying all the time', according to an interview in *People* magazine with a production assistant on Halle's next film, *Strictly Business*. In a rare case of kiss-and-tell for the actress, who usually refuses to discuss past bad relationships or badmouth ex-lovers, she said about Snipes in a *TV Guide* interview in 1998, 'He broke my spirit but not my heart.'

Jungle Fever was released in the US on 7 June 1991, and received mixed reviews. The *Chicago Sun-Times*'s film critic, Roger Ebert, found the supporting cast, including Halle, 'brilliant', but didn't believe the movie's primary plot, the interracial romance between the characters played by Snipes and Sciorra.

The *Washington Post*'s Desson Howe, like Ebert, found the treatment of the romance flawed: 'The most obvious problem occurs between Snipes and Sciorra. Lee's so interested in the ripple effect they cause, he almost forgets the affair itself.' The supporting cast, however, he found 'uniformly bright and appealing . . . Lee's stylistic touch is the ultimate star of the show. It's always there, even during those times when Lee can't see the jungle for all the trees.'

Jungle Fever was a modest commercial success, grossing only $32 million in the US; but, since the film cost only $14 million to make, it was considered a hit.

The year of *Jungle Fever*'s release, 1991, was fantasy-come-true time for Halle Berry and her career. In that same year, she appeared in two other films, *Strictly Business* and *The Last Boy Scout*, and found herself commuting from movie locations to the set of the hit TV series *Knots Landing*, where she played a production assistant, Debbie Porter, for two years (1991–2).

After only one year in the business she had three films and a night-time soap on her résumé. An impressive start, and it would only get better.

But it was marred by a personal tragedy that must have diminished the joy of her public success. A man she was dating (and whom to this day she refuses to identify) slapped her so hard she lost 80 per cent of the hearing in her left ear. Halle was not a codependent personality – at least not at this time in her life – and she ended the affair immediately. The young woman had learned one lesson from her mother's years of tolerating her father's abusive behaviour: you don't have to be a victim. Or, as Halle said of the alacrity with which she terminated the affair, 'The one thing my mother always told me, "If a man hits you, you leave smoke. You get goin'." So I got my stuff and got goin'. I left so fast there were skid marks.'

But she could console herself that, during that same year, she appeared in two big-budget films that came out in quick succession in November and December.

Strictly Business, which was released in the US on 8 November 1991, was a comedy and a change of pace after the nightmarish crack world Halle had inhabited in her first film. Kevin Hooks, the director who hired Halle to play *Strictly Business*'s femme fatale, had rejected her when she had read for an earlier project of his, *Heatwave*, a cable-TV movie. Even though Halle wasn't right for the first film, Hooks couldn't get the image of the beautiful woman who had auditioned for him out of his mind.

Hooks recalled his first impression of the young actress who had come to read for the role of the girlfriend in *Heatwave*. 'I was struck by a number of things. First of all she was gorgeous. We spoke. She wound up not getting that role, but you could tell that this was a girl who was very self-assured and self-confident and very humble and sweet. You meet so many people in Hollywood that have an angle who are cynical and manipulative. She's really an exception to that.'

The second time Halle read for Hooks, for *Strictly Business*, she got the role of Natalie, with whom the hero, an up-and-coming black business executive played by Joseph C Phillips – best known as the rigid son-in-law on *The Cosby Show* – is head over heels in lust. Phillips's character allies himself with a mailroom clerk (Tommy Davidson) who promises to help him woo Natalie in return for help in getting into the company's executive-management trainee programme. For *Heatwave*, Halle had been too beautiful. For *Strictly Business*, whose production notes describe Natalie as a 'mind-numbingly beautiful waitress', Halle seems typecast. But not according to the director. Two days into the shoot, the filmmakers decided that her mocha complexion was politically incorrect! 'They said they were tired of seeing black women perceived as beautiful because they are light-skinned, and I can appreciate that,' Halle said. 'But they should have thought about that before they hired me.' *Strictly Business* has the unique distinction of being the only film from which Halle was ever let go. This was only temporary, however, and two weeks later she was rehired.

As with many people's first impression of Halle as being preternaturally sweet, Hooks found there was a will of steel beneath the *gemütlich* exterior. Halle wasn't there only to act but to learn as much as she could about filmmaking.

During two days of rehearsals before filming began, Hooks remembered, Halle asked more questions than any other member of the cast. 'Almost as if she was putting it all on to a computer hard drive, so she could recall it when the moment felt right. That was the most impressive thing I saw with her at the time.'

Despite her seriousness between takes, once the cameras started to roll Halle demonstrated a protean immediacy that anticipated the diversity of her future roles.

Hooks said, 'Working with her during the film itself, she seemed to be very spontaneous. She was somewhat of a chameleon in different scenes and situations. So she even was, at that time with this comedy, preparing herself for those kinds of relationships in her film career.'

Although Halle didn't have a big part in *Strictly Business*, which was shot in Manhattan and Harlem, Hooks saw the beginning of the camera's love affair with the young actress. 'The truth is that Halle made the camera fall in love with her,' he said – just as in *Jungle Fever* her grotesque behaviour and slovenly appearance produced the opposite effect. 'I wish I could take credit that I had shot her in a specific way to get those results. But the reality is it's hard to make Halle look bad. In *Jungle Fever* she didn't go the glamorous route, but she's so radiant and the camera picks up on every ounce of that.'

Although she was appearing in a comedy, Halle took her role so seriously that she didn't seem to be acting – to the amused consternation of her co-star, Joseph C Phillips, who described their romantic scenes: 'She keeps kissing me for real. It's throwing me off.'

When *Strictly Business* opened in the US on 8 November 1991, it received mixed to poisonous reviews, with at least one critic complaining that perhaps the camera had fallen in love with Halle a bit too much.

Chris Hicks, film critic for Salt Lake City's *Deseret News*, complained that the camera had a voyeuristic, even fetishistic, obsession with the beautiful ingénue:

> The way the camera ogles Natalie [Halle], panning up in slow motion from her legs to her torso (attired in a low-cut, ultra-tight dress, of course) *Strictly Business* too often resembles a dozen other mediocre films . . . Poor Berry, who really shined in a very different role as a crack addict in Spike Lee's *Jungle Fever*, is used here merely as a sex object.

Although Roger Ebert of the *Chicago Sun-Times* found the plot 'routine', he praised the film for its subversive subtext:

> The movie questions the notion that black 'authenticity' is only to be found on the streets or in clubs, in rap music or

high-fives. There is a reality here in which young Bobby [Davidson's mailroom clerk] can indeed get a trainee position and start climbing the corporate ladder – and Bobby likes that idea. Cleverly and subtly, the movie undercuts the negativity of dozens of black movies, which taught that the only correct stance towards the white corporate world was to reject it.

Whether the movie was subversive or not, the public seemed to agree with Ebert that its plot was routine, and the movie grossed a disappointing $7.6 million in the US. But, with a budget under $4 million, the comedy made a small profit and its paltry box-office performance didn't hurt Halle's burgeoning career as a film actress.

At first glance, it's hard to figure out why Halle Berry chose as her next film such a dismal project as *The Last Boy Scout*, since her character is killed off early on and her part amounts to a glorified cameo. Maybe it was the heavy talent in front of and behind the camera and the fact that *The Last Boy Scout* would be her first big-budget movie that tempted Halle. The director was *Top Gun*'s Tony Scott and the writer the creator of the hugely successful *Lethal Weapon* franchise, Shane Black. The hottest actor in Hollywood at the time, the superstar Bruce Willis, was the name above the title. But, even though it wasn't much of a role, she threw herself into researching it with her usual method-actor zeal. She went to a strip club in Hollywood called Girls, Girls, Girls, and paid the owner $50 to let her strip on stage. But Halle let her research go only so far. 'I had to give the owner my tips,' she said, because she refused to remove not only her G-string but her bikini top as well. Nudity would be a recurring problem in her career, lessening as she grew older and more secure with her body and sexuality.

The Last Boy Scout is yet another 'buddy movie', a film genre so popular in Hollywood that an entire website (www.actionadventure.about.com/cs/buddymovies/pairing) is devoted to what can be a lucrative franchise for movie studios that love Roman numerals attached to their product. Buddy movies also allow typically liberal Hollywood filmmakers to put more black faces on the screen because the classic formula for these very formulaic movies pairs a white man (usually a cop or private eye) with a black man, and they start out hating each other owing to the clash of their contrasting personalities but ultimately learn to overcome their differences in order to provide a united front against the bad guys. *Lethal Weapon* and its three sequels represent classic buddy movies, with Mel Gibson's psycho cop tormenting his by-the-book partner (Danny Glover), who just wants to coast until his upcoming retirement, which in most buddy movies is only days or weeks away. Once in a while, a black actor is a big enough star that he gets to play the lead, eccentric buddy. (Eddie Murphy's voluble ex-con versus Nick Nolte's burned-out cop in *48 Hrs*, Wesley Snipes's US marshal paired with Gary Busey's skydiving aficionado in *Drop Zone*.)

In *The Last Boy Scout* Willis teams with the umpteenth black sidekick by playing a down-and-out private eye hired by a disgraced pro football star, Jimmy Dix (Damon Wayans), to protect his girlfriend, Cory, a stripper/prostitute played by Halle.

Willis's gumshoe (Joe Hallenbeck) and Wayans's ex-jock have both seen happier times. Willis's private eye was once a cracker-jack secret-service agent who saved President Jimmy Carter from an assassin's bullet, but found his government career cut short after antagonising a powerful politician. He's also dealing with his wife's infidelity. Wayans's character was a star NFL quarterback kicked off the team and out of the league because of dual addictions to gambling and Demerol, a highly addictive painkiller and a chemical cousin of heroin.

Besides being a buddy movie, *The Last Boy Scout* is also a conspiracy movie, with evil emanating from the top, in this case, the corrupt owner (Noble Willingham) of Jimmy Dix's former team who tries to bribe politicians into legalising gambling on pro football – ironically one of the things that destroyed the career of Wayans's character. The usual mayhem of action movies dominates the story with explosions, kidnappings, car crashes, graphic torture and, more troublingly, a foul-mouthed child (Danielle Harris), Hallenbeck's daughter, whose life is threatened. ('She doesn't just talk dirty,' the *Washington Post*'s Desson Howe complained, singling out the film's misogyny for special opprobrium. 'Large sods of earth roll from [Harris's] tongue. In *Scout*, if a woman isn't a slut or a bimbo, she's a bitch.')

Living up (or down) to his reputation as a loser, Willis's PI blows his current assignment when Halle's stripper is gunned down by gangsters early in the film.

Halle may have considered herself lucky: her role was so brief that the commercial and critical failure of *The Last Boy Scout* didn't rub off on her and tarnish her track record as a serious actress.

When *The Last Boy Scout* was released in the US on 13 December 1991, it was a major box-office disappointment, grossing only $59 million, lunch money for a production with a budget of $70 million.

The reviews were corrosive, and the film's hatred of women came in for special bashing by politically correct pundits. Roger Ebert summed up his love/hate relationship with the misogynist movie and predicted (inaccurately as it turned out) that, despite its major flaws, *The Last Boy Scout* would be a major commercial hit. He wrote:

> *The Last Boy Scout* is a superb example of what it is: a glossy, skillful, cynical, smart, utterly corrupt and vilely misogynistic thriller. How is the critic to respond? To give it a negative review would be dishonest, because it is such a skillful and well-crafted movie. To be positive is to seem to approve its sickness about women. I'll give it three stars. As for my thumb, I'll use it and my forefinger to hold my nose.

Halle's next role and film must have been a gratifying departure from the sleazy bit part she played in *The Last Boy Scout*. In 1992's *Boomerang*, she would receive third billing and enjoy an on-screen romance with the biggest black superstar of all time, Eddie Murphy, about whom *Playboy* magazine said in 1990, 'Few in Hollywood have ever achieved domination so quickly and completely.'

The actor was the biggest box-office draw of the 1980s. In 1985, ShoWest, the Las Vegas-based theatre owners' trade group, named him star of the year and in 1992 star of the decade. As of 2003, the *Movie Times* website (www.the-movie-times.com) ranked him No. 6 at the box office with his 27 films averaging a gross of $85 million per picture for a career total of $2.3 billion. (Interestingly, in an industry so often taken to task for its underemployment and negative portrayals of African-Americans, No. 1 on the list of box-office draws is Will Smith, with Cuba Gooding Jr at No. 14 and Halle's long-time mentor and friend, Samuel L Jackson, ranked 25.)

After the financial failure of 1990's *Another 48 Hrs.*, Murphy had decided to get out of the action-film business and reinvent himself as the black answer to Cary Grant in a romantic comedy about the world of wealthy African-Americans. In *Boomerang*, Murphy plays Marcus Graham, a womanising advertising executive who leaves a trail of broken hearts behind until he meets his match in the form of his boss, Jacqueline Broyer, a man-eating cosmetics executive played by Robin Givens. Broyer turns him into a whimpering 'Why haven't you called me?' lonely heart. For consolation, he becomes romantically involved with Broyer's sweet-tempered assistant, Angela Lewis, with the sweet-tempered Halle typecast in the role.

Murphy's contract stipulated that he was allowed to see numerous actresses before picking his leading lady or ladies. Before meeting Murphy, Halle auditioned for the producer–director brother team of Warrington (the producing half) and Reginald (the director) Hudlin, and both brothers instantly knew they had found the appropriate sweetness to play off Givens's viperish character. But the final decision would rest with the film's superstar.

As it turned out, Halle was the first actress to read for Murphy, and he immediately waived his right to see other actresses. In fact, he insisted on casting her.

Producer Warrington Hudlin described the blown-away enthusiasm both he and the star felt about Halle: 'She came in [to read without Murphy] and she was fabulous. She was unbelievable. But you have to give Eddie choices. He has approval of his co-stars. So Halle came in to basically do a scene with Eddie, the scene where she breaks up with him. And let me tell you, she came with fire. She blazed him so bad, at the end of the scene he just turned away and walked to the corner and put his head in the corner until she left.

'And then when the door shut, Eddie turned to me and my brother and said, "I don't want to see any other actors. She's got the part." I said, "But, Eddie, there are other people in the waiting room, waiting to come in." He said, "I told you, I don't want to see anybody else. She's got the part." Eddie actually caused me some ill will with some other actors who are talented. I had to go out to the waiting room and say, "Everyone else go home." But he just refused to see anyone else. She brought him to ground. The scene she did was unbelievable.'

Although she had made her film debut as a crack addict, Halle has said more than once that she did not want to be literally and figuratively 'ghettoised' in films about the 'hood. *Boomerang*'s glittery metropolis almost exclusively populated with rich black people is as far as you can get from the inner city.

Although *Boomerang* was a confection of a film, the chocolatey goo contained a hard core that many white critics couldn't find, but it was evident to its star. '*Boomerang* is a very political film,' Murphy told the *Los Angeles Times* in 1992. 'Because it is black and yet it's about nothing to do with being black and it cost $40 million. So, if it's successful, then it will prove that you can do movies about blacks that are not just set in the 'hood.'

Murphy's desire to stay out of the 'hood is understandable since he didn't grow up there, and neither did Halle after the age of ten. While money in her single-parent home was tight, Halle did not grow up in a slum, and Murphy grew up in a two-parent home in a solid middle-class neighbourhood, so neither of them ever felt the nostalgic pull to recreate their formative years in a ghetto in the safety of a studio backlot.

The fact that Murphy felt he was making a political statement in *Boomerang* didn't stop the expensive self-indulgences over which bean-counting executives at his home studio, Paramount, were tearing out their follicles. The trade paper *Daily Variety* had a mole on the set and reported that Murphy's tardiness and occasional no-shows 'drove the crew crazy and helped push the film over budget'.

En route to a location in Washington, DC, Murphy, according to *Variety*, decided to go for a walk and turned up so late that the director decided to shoot another scene that didn't require the leading man's participation. When Murphy finally appeared and learned that the crew were not ready for him, he walked off in a huff. The star developed wanderlust during another stroll to the set and decided to take in a movie on a Monday morning. Crew members twiddled their thumbs – and collected their hefty hourly wages – while Murphy sat through a two-hour-plus showing of *Cape Fear*. Murphy's apologists said he didn't show up for the exterior shoot because it was raining. When the sky cleared, Murphy appeared.

When the actor did another disappearing act in Atlanta, it was attributed to his fear of the riots that followed the acquittal of police officers on trial for the beating of Rodney King in 1991. His late arrivals were matched by early exits before the day's filming had wrapped.

Daily Variety also revealed the perks and power of the star, who nevertheless could be as passive-aggressive as any powerless subordinate. When Murphy's personal assistant ordered ten CDs for the stereo in his boss's trailer, Paramount refused to reimburse the assistant. Instead of throwing a fit, Murphy ordered thirty steak dinners from a pricey restaurant for his entourage's lunch, and Paramount was told to pay up or else. The studio didn't have the temerity to call his bluff and discover what 'or else' meant. The steaks and CDs were charged to the incredible inflatable budget.

Murphy also alienated the crew, said *Variety* – by ignoring them. The rough-edged, blue-collar types who work behind the camera can't abide a stuck-up star, even a billion-dollar-grossing one. No matter how big an actor is, it's not a good tactical move to tick off these 'below-the-line' folk, because they can sabotage your scenes and allow stunts to turn into 'accidents'. When Sharon Stone antagonised the crew of *King Solomon's Mines*, they surreptitiously urinated in a pond just before she shot a bathing scene in it.

A Murphy spokeswoman didn't deign to explain the star's aloofness, but she did address *Daily Variety*'s claim that he was often a no-show. Eddie wasn't being 'difficult': he was being a perfectionist. When a scene wasn't 'working', he would leave the set and return, refreshed – the next day!

Murphy must have felt a lot of scenes weren't working. His late arrivals, according to *Daily Variety*, totalled one hundred hours! The average cost of shooting on a studio backlot soundstage runs into six figures an hour – even more if you're on location and a swath of the nation's motorcade-riddled capital, where much of *Boomerang* was shot, has to be shut down. Murphy's tardiness cost the production an extra $1 million, *Daily Variety* reported.

While his spokespeople came up with creative excuses, Murphy didn't seem contrite about his unprofessional behaviour. 'Every time they write I'm late, they should also write that my movies have made $2 billion,' the superstar once said. *Boomerang's* producers didn't mind, either. The film's white producer, Brian Grazer, a champion schmoozer to the stars, said, 'Eddie might show up two hours late, but he contributes to rewriting the script and does brilliant things.' *Boomerang's* other producer, Warrington Hudlin, added, 'We'd rather have a comic genius like Eddie late than another actor on time.'

Halle's behaviour on the set provided a huge contrast to her co-star's. While it may have been politically expedient for Warrington Hudlin to excuse Murphy's expensive capriciousness, the producer seems to have genuinely fallen in love (platonically) with *Boomerang's* second leading lady. Typically, between takes, stars hide out in their trailers. But Halle, Hudlin said, 'would eat with the crew. She would sit down with the grips and the faggers. She is such a regular down-to-earth accessible person. It just shocked me how sweet she was. But then you meet her mother, and she's so sweet and down-to-earth, you go, "OK, that's where it came from." '

While a powerful producer like Brian Grazer with a string of hits (*Splash*, *Kindergarten Cop* and who later went on to *The Nutty Professor* and the Oscar-winning *A Beautiful Mind*) was still afraid of antagonising Murphy and made excuses for his tardiness, a newcomer like Halle, despite the sweetness almost everyone who meets her feels compelled to comment on, felt no compunction about publicly taking to task an overindulged movie star.

In 1993, Halle said, 'Eddie is a star and lives the big-star life, which was really interesting because that's totally not my thing.

All the bodyguards and the whole star trip is not my scene. It was the first time I was exposed to that.' (She must not have had much contact with Bruce Willis during the filming of *The Last Boy Scout*.) 'I found it interesting rather than funny because I did see situations where maybe Eddie needed those five bodyguards because sometimes women would just come up, mobs of them, and try to attack him. But he had all these people living in his house, and I felt it would be a drag.'

Although she didn't get to know Murphy well, she thought he seemed bitter and unhappy, despite his success, she told the UK's *Daily Mail* a year after *Boomerang*'s release.

It was probably beneficial that Halle was not superstarstruck by Murphy because she had to strike him in their final scene together after her character learns that he has spent the night with his ex-girlfriend (played by Robin Givens). It's much easier to smack around a fellow actor than a superstar whose films have grossed two billion dollars.

Boomerang debuted in the US on 1 July 1992, and in the UK on 30 October 1992. The comedy turned out to be a middling hit for Murphy, grossing $131 million worldwide. The critics, however, didn't share the public's enthusiasm for Murphy's riff on Cary Grant in blackface.

The *Los Angeles Times*'s critic, Kenneth Turan, criticised *Boomerang*'s affirmative-action approach to casting because of the nearly all-black cast. *Boomerang*, Turan wrote, 'takes pains to create a reverse universe where white people are invisible, except when comic relief is called for'. Only seven white people appeared in the film, Turan noted, and he objected to the attempt to create an alternate black universe on film, calling it 'silly and arbitrary and not dramatically motivated'.

Murphy and the director Reginald Hudlin were so irritated by the charge of reverse racism that each man (or more likely each man's press agent) penned a rebuttal for the *Los Angeles Times*'s op-ed page. Hudlin made a telling point when he noted that *Boomerang*'s seven white actors outnumbered the blacks who had appeared in *all* of Woody Allen's films combined, despite the fact that blacks and Latinos outnumber whites in Allen's beloved Manhattan.

To other critics' objections that *Boomerang* had created a fantasy world, Murphy suggested that the scenes in the film depicting white racism were more documentary than fantasy. An episode in a clothing store, where the white clerk suspects that the Murphy character and his buddies are shoplifters, was based on the real-life experiences of Oprah Winfrey and her friend, the Oscar-winning choreographer and producer Debbie Allen (*Amistad*), both of whom Murphy said had been turned away from posh stores. Warrington Hudlin, he added, has found it hard to get a cab in New York City, a problem that seems endemic among blacks no matter how well dressed they are. As for the film's other alleged fantasy, a world of co-opped and coutured black people, Murphy, in that *LA Times* op-ed piece, quoted a trade magazine for 'buppies' (black urban professionals) that said the top five black-owned companies on *Black Enterprise* magazine's annual Top 100 list raked in more than $2 billion in 1991. Murphy's million-dollar co-op and Givens's designer duds in *Boomerang* weren't fantasy: they were just a glimpse of a socioeconomic group usually ignored by white filmmakers who focus on the black underclass of pimps and junkies. *Boomerang*, ironically, reflected a less opulent version of Murphy's own reality, where 'crack' refers to the minced pepper sprinkled on top of gourmet dishes.

Halle's role in *Boomerang* didn't escape controversy and charges of racism. In one scene, her character lapses into a foreign language and then translates for her date. 'It's Korean for "I'm so sorry I shot you, but I thought you were robbing my store" ' – a reference to the tense relationship between the Korean-American merchants who operate stores and other small businesses in the black ghetto, and their customers.

During the 1992 Rodney King riots in Los Angeles, TV cameras showed Korean-American businessmen festooned with more firepower than Rambo, standing on the roofs of their establishments, a visible deterrent to would-be looters.

Despite her acidic crack about trigger-happy Koreans, *Rolling Stone*'s film critic Peter Travers objected to Halle's typecasting as Murphy's sweet young thing. 'Berry, so good as the crack addict in *Jungle Fever*, is saddled with the sappiest role. Virtuous, compliant and family-oriented, she's just the thing for Marcus

[Murphy] when he's ready to make love instead of doing the nasty.'

Perhaps Halle consoled herself with the fact that *Rolling Stone* was even less enthused with her leading man's performance. 'Murphy is performing in a vacuum these days . . . What Murphy's doing isn't acting: it's masturbation.' Ouch!

Regardless of the critical carping, Halle revelled in the deluxe world depicted in *Boomerang* and considered it a needed antidote to Hollywood's obsession with blacks at the other end of the socioeconomic spectrum, in which she refused to participate. Even at this early stage in her career, she had turned down a role in *Menace II Society*, which was set in South Central Los Angeles' black ghetto, even though it eventually won kudos from the critics – white critics.

Halle had left the inner city years ago, and she saw no reason to return to its cinematic incarnation. 'We've got *Boyz N the Hood* and *New Jack City*, and those are definitely stories we've got to tell. But we as black people have many more stories. I'm hoping they find other life experiences just as interesting.' Halle would do the same as her career progressed and she achieved more clout to get her out of the screen ghetto.

In fact, the ghettoisation of blacks in Hollywood was politicising the actress, and her famed sweetness disappeared when she deplored the fact that things hadn't changed all that much since the notorious 'blaxploitation' films of the 1970s. 'It's not only no different from the *Shaft* [1971] era: it's even worse now,' she said. 'The nature of these movies is that they're so violent; they deal with such negative subject matter [that] we're not willing to pay money to see them. Just turn on the news.'

Despite the controversy created by *Boomerang*, the film refused to exploit white stereotypes of black people, and Halle felt the comedy represented a step forward in her career and gave her enough power to play the lead in her next project, a production that no one would accuse of trafficking in stereotypes.

Halle's acting career was taking off. And so was her love life. Or so it seemed.

4. WHITE ROOTS

Nineteen ninety-three was a better year for Halle's career than the previous year had been, and in the romance department it was even better. She would star in a miniseries based on Alex Haley's blockbuster novel *Roots*, appear in three feature films – and fall madly in love (or was it lust?) with a handsome jock more famous than she was.

What more could a girl ask for? As a woman, Halle would eventually get more than she asked for or wanted from this liaison.

But her career just kept getting bigger and better. Her next project would be the first one in which she was the lead and had to carry the production. No more supporting or co-starring roles. The project was *Queen*, an $18 million, three-part, six-hour miniseries that aired in February 1993 on CBS and was based on a book that Alex Haley was finishing when he died of a heart attack on 10 February 1992.

'*Queen* was the first time I was the star of the show, and not just a movie – it was an eight-hour miniseries that I sort of had resting on my shoulders,' she said. (It was actually only six hours long, but the arduous role must have made the miniseries seem longer to her.)

While *Roots* had told the black, out-of-Africa side of Alex Haley's family history, *Queen* focused on his white antecedents, whose origins the author traced back to nineteenth-century Ireland and his great-great-grandfather, a sea captain named James Jackson. Jackson emigrated to America and had a son, also named James, played in the miniseries by Tim Daly from the hit American sitcom *Wings*. Daly's character, a white plantation owner, has a long affair with one of his slaves and fathers a child named Queen, Haley's paternal grandmother.

Alex Haley had the bizarre practice of writing all his bestsellers while travelling to nowhere in particular on a tramp steamer. When I interviewed him on the Burbank, California, set of *Roots: The Gift*, a 1988 Christmas-themed TV movie based on an incident in *Roots*, the novel, he explained that the ship's isolation allowed him to avoid distractions. But when it came to writing *Queen* he decided to bring along the screenwriter David Stevens (*Breaker Morant*) on a three-month voyage to Ecuador. It was a lucky break for the project. Haley died before he could complete his book, and Stevens not only completed the work, but went on to write the teleplay for the miniseries.

Queen was a project that had special resonance for Halle, since, like the title character, she was biracial. 'Being interracial myself, it hit me harder because I realized that, had I been born a hundred years ago, this could be my story,' she said. 'Queen's life could have been my life. And that was horrifying.'

Although the part was especially compelling for Halle because of the racial issue, it was not an autobiographical role at all. Queen remains confused about her racial identity for most of her life – calling herself 'Little Miss In-Between' – and tries to pass for white. Halle has never questioned her racial identity ever since that pivotal day in her childhood when her mother had sat her in front of the mirror and told her that people would see what *she* saw in the mirror: a black woman.

Queen Haley was a delectably meaty role after a series of fairly frothy feature films. '*Queen* is much more meaningful to me than a *Strictly Business* or a *Boomerang* or a *Last Boy Scout*,' she said. 'It's a big responsibility to black people and just people in general. It's the most challenging thing I've ever done and probably will ever do as an actress.' As it turned out, this was inaccurate.

No one has ever accused the actress of lacking self-confidence. In fact, for almost every role she's landed she has had to fight against all sorts of preconceptions, most notably the charge that she's too beautiful to play unglamorous roles. The producers of *Queen* at first refused to let her read for the part because of her looks and youth; but, with typical can-do fortitude, she paid for her own plane ticket to Los Angeles and convinced the producers she could become Queen Haley. Repeating the by now monotonous refrain, the miniseries' producer, David Wolper, said, 'We loved her acting, but we thought she was *too* beautiful, too young. We thought her skin was too tight, too perfect to make her age to a 72-year-old. And we didn't know how someone so innocent could muster the maturity to play someone so old.'

Heavy prostheses would eventually provide the right amount of sag, along with contact lenses that gave her the clouded eyes of an old woman and dyes that blackened her perfect teeth. Interestingly, Halle apparently was not as light-skinned as Alex Haley's grandmother, and her skin had to be lightened for the part.

Halle quickly won over Wolper with the ferocity of her desire to essay the role – and a certain amount of crazy financial extravagance. 'She had balls,' Wolper recalled. 'She said she would pay for her airfare, hotel, car, makeup artist, and overtime for the crew. I've never had an actor push so strongly for a role.' And she got it.

But then, for the first time in her career, Halle found herself consumed by self-doubt, terrified by the realisation that she would be carrying the project as the title character who appeared in almost every scene. After informing her she had landed the part, her manager told her the director, John Erman, wanted to meet her immediately. 'I broke down in tears and said, "I don't want to go, I'm scared, I don't want to go!" For the first time the pressure of carrying a six-hour movie sort of hit me. I didn't quite know how to get through it,' Halle remembered.

In the course of those six hours, Queen Haley is rejected by the white side of the family (something that happened to Halle and her mother). Erman, who felt Halle brought her own painful history to the project, said, 'Her story and Queen's story – it's the same story, isn't it?'

Not quite.

At one point in the miniseries, Queen passes for white and is raped and beaten by her white lover when he learns she is part black. She becomes pregnant as a result of the rape, and spinster aunts on the white side of the family try to abduct the child and raise it as their own. Queen becomes homeless, and her lover is lynched, which causes her descent into madness until, towards the end of her life, she finds love (and regains her sanity) with a sweet-souled man (Danny Glover).

Queen was largely shot on location in Hollywood, South Carolina, near Charleston. It was a nightmarish shoot. Early on, Halle fell off a horse and seriously injured her coccyx. While she recuperated, the project had to be shut down for a very expensive two weeks. The delay wasn't just at a financial cost, however, as her co-star Danny Glover had a commitment to another project that he needed to fulfil. Halle, therefore, forced herself to return to work earlier than she should have – with a little pharmaceutical help.

Despite so much medication that she feared becoming an addict ('I've had to get cortisone shots and shots of Novocain, pain pills. I'll be a drug addict by the time this over,' she said), some days she was in such agony that an ambulance had to deliver her to the set.

As much as anything else, though, Halle Berry is a trouper. The four-hour daily makeover that aged her skin and blackened her teeth began to wear Halle down – not only because of the tedium of the makeup ritual, but also because of the pain. 'After the horseback accident it was a challenge just to walk. So, after that accident, I really can't be honest about what was hard because everything was hard after that,' she said.

The pain and the furnace-like heat of a South Carolina summer eventually took its toll on the actress, but there were also things going on in her private life that would ultimately cause more pain than the fall from the horse. Much as she loved *Queen*'s script, she found reliving Queen's life on screen almost unbearable, and the famously sweet-tempered actress by her own admission became a nasty diva after one slap too many in front of the camera.

(Bruce Willis once told me that punches in movies can be faked by careful positioning of the camera, which hides the fact that the punch glides past the victim's face. But slaps can't be faked with cinematographic trickery. When you see actors being slapped hard on screen, they really are being walloped. Willis told me it drove him crazy when he had to beat up his then real-life wife Demi Moore in 1991's *Mortal Thoughts*.)

Halle eventually got tired of being the project's punch bag. 'Towards the end [of the shoot], I was such a wreck that no one wanted to be around me. I was a bitch. I was biting everybody's head off,' she said. She played Queen from the age of fifteen to seventy-two and acted out scenes of physical and sexual abuse.

'I really felt the injustice, and I was called nigger just one time too many times on screen. It was all too much . . . It's difficult not to let some of those tears be real,' she said in an interview with the UK's *Daily Mail*.

Eventually, all her pain and suffering would seem worthwhile when the miniseries debuted on 14 February 1993, and earned Halle some of the best reviews of her career. *USA Today*'s Matt Roush wrote, 'The role will make Berry a star . . . *Queen* will be remembered for Berry's electrifying arrival as a major actress.' The *Baltimore Sun*'s David Zurawik was even more enthusiastic:

> Just as Vivien Leigh became a household name as Scarlett O'Hara in 1939, the same will probably happen to Halle Berry as Queen. Berry brings a radiance to the role that makes you want to watch and watch and watch . . . an actress you can't take your eyes off.

It was during her interview with the *Daily Mail* to promote *Queen* that Halle volunteered information the reporter didn't pick up on – information that would later make international headlines when Halle elaborated on this throwaway line: 'I was being slapped around and raped on screen, *but I was going through my own torment off-screen as well.*' [Emphasis added.]

Ironically, her torment began when she fell in love while shooting *Queen*. During a break in filming, she was watching an MTV programme called *Rock 'n' Jock*, and one of the participants on the show was David Justice, an African-American outfielder for the Atlanta Braves. Halle later described the effect the television image had on her. 'I had cardiac arrest, he was so gorgeous.'

A few weeks later, a journalist asked Halle for a favour. 'A friend of [Justice's] was interviewing me, and David had asked for my autograph. I had seen him on television . . . so I knew who he was. So I said to the interviewer "Here's the autograph and give him my telephone number as well." He rang within the hour.'

They spent four hours on the phone. 'We found out how much we had in common. And two weeks after that we met, and I knew the minute I saw him face-to-face that I was going to marry him,' she said.

Vera Cirrincione, the wife of Halle's manager, didn't feel the new couple had much in common: 'I didn't think they were made for each other,' she said. Vera pointed out that Halle had an artistic bent. Her house was overflowing with works of art, but her new love didn't share her aesthetic interests.

Love or lust is blind, and Halle wasn't put off by Justice's shock-jock wardrobe when they first met. Justice affected the pimpish attire favoured by some professional athletes. The handsome jock was decorated like a Christmas tree with necklaces, earrings and bracelets. Every finger sported a ring.

But Halle saw past the jock stereotype and tacky garb and felt she had found the man destined to take a leading role in the rest of her life. That didn't stop her, however, from being upfront and telling him he was wearing too much jewellery.

In 1993, while she still had on her rose-tinted glasses, Halle said, 'I recognized a gentle quality in David, and I said the next man has got to have some real tender qualities because I didn't want to fear that he was going to hit me.' Halle was obviously still traumatised by her run-in with the guy who had caused her hearing loss, which is not surprising since the incident had occurred only a year before she met Justice.

While they were still in the honeymoon stage of their mutual infatuation, Halle brought up Justice whenever she was interviewed, and he did the same with his new love. She told the *Cleveland Plain Dealer* in 1993, 'The minute I met Dave Justice my life was over.' She meant that in a good way at the time, but later events would demonstrate the chilly irony of her romantic optimism. Justice was equally smitten at first: 'I tell Halle, "I thank God every day for giving you to me." '

Before they met and she learned something about the man who had so caught her fancy on MTV, Halle worried that Justice might have a pro-athlete-size ego and libido to match because of all the groupies who throw themselves at men of fame and power. 'I was afraid he might be a jock-type guy in love with his looks, but I found that he had just had an eight-year relationship and that he skipped two grades in junior high and was real smart.'

Halle was determined to see something in her new love that would turn out to be missing once the blindness of ardour disappeared. 'He seemed like the prince on the white horse with this gorgeous big smile and his massive shoulders,' she said. And she couldn't resist invidious comparisons to past disasters in her love life. 'My previous boyfriends were never friends, like David is. In the past I was attracted to jealous, dominating guys.'

Justice was finally the one to break this pattern of seeking out Mr Wrong, she said, characterising herself as a classic codependent personality until Mr Right mended her masochistic ways. 'Before David, I always picked guys who needed to be rescued. I would baby them and take care of them instead of being an equal and a partner. When I came into their lives, they needed somebody to help them and to get them through a rough time.' After Halle had helped them through their various crises, they would walk out on her, she said. 'And I'd be stuck holding their baggage plus whatever I'd acquired from knowing them. I was the one who always ended up getting hurt in the process.'

She also found a new openness missing from past relationships. 'There are no secrets. From the beginning, we decided to tell each other everything, even if it was painful. I didn't think I'd find somebody who had the same values and was brought up the same way as I was.'

Once she peeled away the bad jewellery and accessed the man beneath, she discovered something else about her new love that charmed her. Justice was a mummy's boy who had tattooed his mother's name on his biceps. Later, Halle would take a cue from Justice and have his name tattooed at the base of her spine.

Justice was equally infatuated with the beautiful young actress and, like her, felt they were fated to be together. A year into their relationship, when white-hot passion has usually evolved into the smouldering variety, he gushed to *Sports Illustrated* in 1994, 'I knew when I first saw her that I was going to marry her. It's like I heard a voice. "This is going to be your wife." '

He told *People* magazine, 'When we finally met face to face, it was love at first sight for me.' He compared their first meeting to another momentous event in his life, although it was just the opposite of the joyous one he was now experiencing. 'Like when I was fifteen coming home from school. I put my hand through a door window and cut my wrist right there.' Justice severed a tendon, and his doctor told him if the gash had been a half-inch deeper the athlete would have lost the use of his hand for two years. And, if the wound had been only half an inch to the right, his main artery would have been severed, and he would have died instantly. 'But it didn't happen like that. And you know why it didn't? It wasn't meant to be.' He and Halle *were* meant to be.

Justice's childhood had parallels with Halle's. Like her father, his left when he was four years old, and he was raised by his mother, Nettie, a maid in a rich white household. Despite his mother's modest position, and unlike Halle's childhood, where money and luxuries were scarce, Justice never felt deprived of material things during his youth. 'I grew up great and had everything I wanted,' he told *Sports Illustrated*, including athletic gear, expensive sneakers and even a moped.

Like Halle, Justice was at the top of his class and probably even smarter than his future wife. He had a genius-level IQ over 140, had skipped two grades and graduated from Covington High School in Kentucky when he was only sixteen.

He dropped out of Thomas More College in Crestview Hills, Kentucky, and was drafted by the Atlanta Braves as an outfielder in 1985 and sent to a farm team, where he laboured in obscurity for five years. In 1990, he moved up to the Braves, where the muscular, six-foot-tall, 200-pound slugger hit 28 home runs, earning him the National League title of Rookie of the Year.

It took him a year in the majors before he started wearing his furs and jewellery. His Mercedes sported a self-congratulatory vanity licence plate that trumpeted his athletic prowess: 'Sweet Swing.'

Halle 'attacked' her new love with the same fierce determination she displayed when seeking out acting roles. *She* proposed to *him* about a year after their first phone conversation. The woman whose name was tattooed on her son's biceps was delighted with his choice of wife – or, more accurately, his future wife's choice of her son as husband. 'We couldn't have found a better bride if we had ordered one from Sears and Roebuck,' Nettie Justice told *Sports Illustrated*.

Halle shared her new mother-in-law's enthusiasm for the union. 'People say, "Oh, you're too young, and you have this great career",' she said, 'but when you find that someone special, what's too young?' Halle was only 24 at the time.

'It was like Marilyn Monroe and Joe Dimaggio,' she said, exaggerating the prominence of both of them and ignoring the disastrous end of that famous match of the ultimate movie star and the all-American sports hero.

Halle Berry and David Justice were married in Atlanta at the stroke of midnight on New Year's Day 1993 and spent their honeymoon in the Caribbean. Although Halle would later say that the first year of their marriage was 'one of the best years in my life', there was trouble in paradise almost from the start.

Less than a month after the wedding, Halle was already describing pet peeves she had about her new husband. 'When I'm trying to sleep, he's in bed watching *Sports Center*. I have to get up early, and he sleeps until midday.' They also seemed to have an *Odd Couple* attitude towards neatness, with Halle playing Felix Ungar opposite Justice's Oscar Madison. 'David can throw his dirty socks on the floor, leave the toilet seat up and leave the cap off the toothpaste,' she said.

And, while Justice may have grown up a mummy's boy, Halle wasn't equipped to play the mother in their marriage. 'His mom spoiled him and gave him breakfast in bed every day growing up. But he does love home-cooked meals, and I need to work on that. I grew up on Hamburger Helper,' she said.

At this point in the relationship, two months into the marriage, Justice also seemed to be playing the sensitive male – when he volunteered for culinary duties in the Berry-Justice household. 'I want to go to cooking school. I'll be the gourmet cook of the family,' he said.

Even during this infatuation phase of the marriage, Halle still kept one eye on her career and saw her husband as her saviour only when and if her career faltered. 'I'm not always going to be the young, young star,' she said the week *Queen* aired on CBS, 'and having a stable force like David in my life really helps.'

But their careers seemed designed to cause problems in the marriage. Conflicting schedules kept them apart, sometimes for as long as three months. Ten months into the marriage, she tried to put a positive spin on these separations and told the *Los Angeles Daily News*, 'It's always like the first date when we do get together, but I really get lonely sometimes.'

When they did manage to spend time together, they discovered they didn't have a lot in common. Halle had no interest in sport, but forced herself to become a baseball fan. 'I don't care about football, basketball, golf or tennis, but I am into baseball because of David. I need to be a part of his life. I need to be able to talk to him about what's important to him – just like he's had to learn about moviemaking.'

She revealed that her interest in baseball didn't come naturally to her and found she had a limited attention span for the slow-moving game. 'I had to make a real effort at first. But once I started to learn about the game – the intricate parts of it, the pitches, the plays, how to keep score – that made the time go by. Now I can sit through a three-hour game and think, "Wow! Where did the time go?" '

Halle also didn't care much for Atlanta, despite the fact that they lived in the stylish suburb of Sandy Springs in a three-storey, six-bedroom mansion, which she decorated. 'I like things simple, so it won't be overfurnished,' she said. She also didn't care for Atlanta because her husband was such a huge celebrity there, and she felt their every move was being watched and commented on in what she described as their 'fishbowl existence'. She also noticed that whereas she was always the gracious movie star with fans, lavishly doling out autographs, her husband was less extroverted in his dealings with his admirers.

Although Halle didn't like Atlanta, her husband, fortunately, loved LA, and the couple bought a Mediterranean-style home in the Hollywood Hills, where their neighbours included Sharon Stone and Jerry Seinfeld. Justice enjoyed the relative anonymity provided by LA, a town with so many celebrities he felt like a small fish in a big pond, which was fine with him. 'Believe it or not, you feel like more of a normal person. I can go anywhere I want, do anything I want. In LA they are so used to seeing so many so-called celebrities that they are just used to it. It is nothing to them,' he said in 1993. Justice loved the freedom to go rollerblading almost every day with his wife without having baseballs shoved in his face to be autographed.

Much as he enjoyed LA's low-key lifestyle compared with the fishbowl of Atlanta, Atlanta was his place of business, and he ended up spending most of his time there.

'A year into our marriage, I would say things weren't so good anymore. We stayed married four years, so it was three years of struggle,' she said in 1998.

Things weren't so good because Halle was just as career-obsessed as her husband, and she couldn't work on her career in Atlanta. 'I didn't want to be without my husband, but I wanted to work. So one day I went to my husband and said, "I know why we're so miserable . . . because *I'm* miserable. I need to get back to my career and start getting my identity back. I've become David's wife. I've lost myself." '

Halle returned – alone – to LA with her husband's blessing, but the decision turned out to be a curse for their marriage. 'I started doing movies again,' she said. 'That created more separation. Our relationship started to fizzle. I became a madwoman trying to save it. Blaming myself a lot – if I'd never left, if I were a better wife . . . I know now had I never left I would have died. Faded away.'

And, although Justice had encouraged his wife to return to LA and work, it's possible he secretly resented her decision to choose career over him. 'David felt like his wife wasn't around as much as the other guys' wives,' she said.

Although she missed her husband and feared the effects of their being so far apart, Halle didn't give up a lifetime of being an overachiever just because she was now also a wife. During the first year of their marriage, she appeared in three films, further exacerbating the couple's geographical and emotional separation.

A month after *Queen* aired, Halle did a cameo, playing herself, in *CB4*, a parody of rock documentaries, except that the band in the movie's title, which was short for 'Cell Block 4', was a rap, not a rock, group. The farce, which came out in the US on 12 March 1993, was a vehicle for the stand-up comedian Chris Rock, but Halle found herself in superstar company with other celebrities such as the basketball star Shaquille O'Neal and the rapper Ice Cube, who were so famous they could also play themselves in the film.

By this point in her career, Halle, at only 25, was a big enough star to play herself on film. *CB4* received poisonous reviews. (The

Internet film critic James Berardinelli, who called *CB4* a cross between *Wayne's World* and the classic rockumentary spoof *This Is Spinal Tap*, wrote, 'In the final analysis, despite the occasional laugh or two, this is yet another moderate failure to heap on the discarded parody pile.'

CB4 disappeared from cinemas after a disappointing gross of only $17 million. But *CB4* was not a 'Halle Berry film' the way *Queen* had been, and its failure didn't tarnish her sterling box-office record.

Halle didn't have to carry her next film, *Father Hood*, either, but she had second billing and some of the film's failure did rub off on her. Released on 27 August 1993 in the US, *Father Hood* reworks the theme of Steven Spielberg's debut feature film, *The Sugarland Express*, and told the story of a father who is also a small-time crook (father-hood, get it?), played by Patrick Swayze, who kidnaps his children after losing custody of them because he believes they are being abused in foster care. Halle played a newspaper reporter, her original real-life career goal, who covers Swayze's run from the law with his two kids in tow and publicises his escapades in her newspaper.

The *Chicago Sun-Times*'s film critic Roger Ebert felt pity rather than pique for Halle. 'Her role is not only the most thankless one in this movie, but the most thankless role in any film I have seen this year.' Almost all of her scenes, Ebert noted sympathetically, have her on the phone with the runaway dad. 'It must have been lonely on the set,' Ebert said of these solo scenes. While he roasted *Father Hood*, Ebert couldn't resist praising its co-star, even though she was in such a turkey of a film:

> Since Berry is potentially one of the hottest actresses in Hollywood right now, after work in *Strictly Business*, *Boomerang* and *The Last Boy Scout* and her countless fashion and personality layouts in magazines, there is only one explanation for her appearance in this worthless role: Her agent should have been fired. Life is too short and fame too fleeting for an actress on the move to waste time in nothing roles.

Savvy reporter and critic that Ebert is, he apparently didn't realise the limited options for actresses of colour, and sometimes the only jobs they can choose from are these 'nothing roles'.

Father Hood was never even released in New York and some other major markets, so Halle's public embarrassment, like the film's release, was also limited. The film grossed an anaemic $3.4 million in the US.

While Roger Ebert gave *Father Hood* only one star, he awarded Halle's next film, *The Program*, which was released a month later on 24 September 1993, three. He also continued his journalistic 'love affair' with Berry by twice in his review referring to her as a 'beauty' and 'beautiful'. As with *Father Hood*, Halle also got second billing after the male lead, further enhancing her pecking order among the competition, even though she seemed to be her own harshest critic when she told a journalist at the time that her career was 'just OK'.

The Program had an impressive pedigree. It was directed and co-written by David S Ward, most famous as the Oscar-winning screenwriter of *The Sting*. It was a drama about troubled college football players. Typecast yet again as a 'beautiful' upper-class woman, Halle plays a character who tutors a dumb jock, a freshman running back played by Omar Epps. Epps's Darnell Jefferson needs to improve his grades or risk getting cut from the team, but, as the film progresses, what most motivates this reluctant scholar is the belief that if his grade point average rises he will win the love of – and here comes that word again – the 'beautiful' Autumn (Berry).

Halle was refreshingly upfront about the fact that she had no interest in sport – except for the Atlanta Braves because of her marriage. She agreed to co-star in *The Program* because her role was socially significant and allowed her to play a person whose socioeconomic background was 180 degrees away from her own upbringing. 'I thought [*The Program*] had a real positive portrayal of a black woman. It was very different for me, this real collegiate type of character from an affluent family.'

She liked the class conflict and the character's relationship with Darnell Jefferson. 'Though he was a street kid, he still was smart enough to know that he wasn't smart enough,' she said. 'He wanted to better himself, and he did listen when people talked to him.'

Although only in her mid-twenties at the time, Halle Berry felt the welcome burden of being a role model when she chose and also rejected film projects. 'That's sort of my way of giving back,' she said. 'I'm so lucky that I'm able to work in this industry, so I don't take it lightly. Black youth today desperately need positive images and role models. So I won't do certain movies.'

In an industry where one of the most critical commandments is 'Thou shalt not badmouth other filmmakers because thou mayst one day want to work with them', Halle ignored the commandment and didn't hesitate to name names of films she felt did not provide a picture of black people that wasn't stuck, literally and metaphorically, in the ghetto of ghetto-themed films. 'I won't do *Boyz N the Hood* or *Menace II Society*,' she said. 'You can turn on the television and get the honest depiction of what's going on in inner city communities today. We don't need to saturate our entertainment with that too.'

The Program's leafy college setting was about as far away from the 'hood as you can get, and yet it was anything but a fantasy depiction of college sport. Steroid abuse, alcoholism (the star quarterback played by Craig Sheffer is a suicidal lush) and plagiarism (a bright student takes an exam for a quarterback who's failing, and both are expelled) are all dramatised, or, as Halle said, '*The Program* isn't uplifting. It takes issues, busts them wide open, exposes them and offers some sort of solution to these problems. And it doesn't just revolve around people shooting up each other and taking drugs.'

As a sign of things and problems to come, when Halle said this in October 1993, her husband David Justice had yet to see *The Program*. While she was promoting the film in LA, he was preoccupied by the Atlanta Braves' tight pennant race three thousand miles away.

Justice also couldn't help her research her role because, as she made clear, their sports crowd didn't have the drug and alcohol problems suffered by the jocks in *The Program*. 'Nobody that I know, that we are friends with, is that way. They wouldn't be friends of ours because we don't live that way,' she said.

Then in an eerie non sequitur that turned out to be a premonition she couldn't have imagined coming true at the time, she added, 'These movies are not important enough to make me suicidal.' Movies – of course not. But a failed marriage would be more than enough to push the actress over the edge less than three years after she had dismissed suicide out of hand.

The year 1993 would turn out to be one of mixed blessings and a definite curse. Or, as one journalist wrote in 1998, 'Berry's love life reads like a Danielle Steele novel.'

The year began with her marrying a hunky jock on the beach and ended with a financial scandal that mortified her.

Between these two events, Halle would find herself fleeing one of the tackiest events of 1993, if not the entire decade. On 8 October 1993, the Friars Club 'honoured' – if that's the correct term – Whoopi Goldberg at its annual celebrity luncheon at the Hilton Hotel in New York City. Goldberg was getting a lot of publicity at the time because of her very public romance with the *Cheers* star Ted Danson, who served as MC at the event. In front of 2,000-plus guests, Danson appeared in blackface with exaggerated white lips painted on in a latter-day version of minstrel-show makeup. It got worse. According to an eyewitness report in the *New York Observer*, Danson said during his speech at the lunch that, earlier in the day as he was shaving, Goldberg had performed oral sex on him and he told her, 'Come on, Whoop, don't nigger-lip it.'

Other 'highlights' from his speech included the revelation that the couple had been so busy with their careers that, 'we haven't seen each other in a coon's age', and a description of his girlfriend's vagina as 'wider than South Africa and twice as inflamed'. There was even a watermelon joke.

The only problem was that no one was laughing – except Goldberg, who told the horrified audience, 'It takes a whole lot of fucking courage to come out in blackface in front of 3,000 [*sic*] fucking people. I don't care if you don't like it. I do.'

The then mayor of New York, David Dinkins, a black man, walked out of the room, leading an exodus of other prominent people, including Halle, who a year later explained the reason for her departure – not that she really needed to. 'I couldn't laugh. I didn't find it funny . . . as a black woman who struggles with racism every day, who has white men tell me to my face they won't see me for a role because I'm black, I couldn't find it in myself to sit there and pretend to find it funny.'

Halle had waited a year before speaking out because she said the last thing she wanted to do was tear down another black woman. But she found it impossible to ignore the embarrassment she felt at the luncheon. 'Just as I respect Whoopi as a black woman, I have to respect myself as a black woman. And that means standing up for what I believe to be right. That night, I said what's right for me is to get the hell out of here.'

The Times of London once wrote that Halle 'has managed to sidestep the pitfalls of racial militancy', preferring 'evolution over revolution', which is simply not the case. Halle is very militant about endemic racism in Hollywood casting; she's just not a *strident* militant, like Spike Lee, who, it has been noted – despite his jeremiads against 'The Man' – when he decided to open a clothing store, he chose as its location the stylish (and mostly white) Westside of Los Angeles rather than mostly black South Central LA.

Halle's is a genteel militancy, preferring persuasion over stridency. She will argue a director or producer into exhaustion when he declines to hire her solely because of her race rather than legitimate objections such as her age or, most often, her beauty. She fights her battles on a case-by-case, film-by-film, basis, rather than taking out ads in the Hollywood trade papers denouncing underrepresentation of minorities in the entertainment industry.

The Times in the UK also said Halle has no trace of an African-American accent, which is simply not accurate. An American ear can definitely hear just a *soupçon* of the Old South in her voice, no doubt a product of her early years growing up in Cleveland's predominantly black inner city before moving to the white 'burbs of Cleveland.

A much more embarrassing incident occurred two months after Ted Danson's grotesquely un-PC minstrel show-and-tell from hell at the Friars Club lunch.

In December 1993, a Chicago dentist, Dr John Ronan, sued Halle in the US District Court for $80,000, a loan he claimed he had made to her to launch her career when she left Chicago's dead-end modelling jobs for a fresh start with her manager Vincent Cirrincione in New York.

Though the case was later dismissed, Ronan stated in the suit that 'between the inclusive dates of March of 1989 and October of 1991 the Plaintiff loaned to the Defendant the sum of $80,000'. Ronan admitted he had lent her only $50,000, but he wanted the extra $30,000 for legal fees and 5 per cent annual interest.

'Basically, he wanted to be repaid for all the things any boyfriend does for his girlfriend,' Halle says. For fifty grand, Ronan must have done a lot for this girlfriend. Halle was by now a happily married woman, and Ronan told the press that they had been lovers when he lent her the money.

Not only did Ronan tell the press about the loan, but he also sold explicit stories detailing their love life to the tabloids, claiming they had had sex on the beach, on a yacht and in his dentist's chair. Halle said of the dentist's venal tabloid trafficking, 'That was the worst thing you can do – making up lies about sexual encounters that got very explicit, very low down and dirty. It was just the lowest of the low.'

The dentist also claimed he had asked her to repay the loan and she had refused. 'We started seeing each other in 1989,' Ronan told *Jet* magazine in 1993. 'I told her, "If you really want to be an actress, I'll help you." I committed to her financially for three years, regardless of what happened to our relationship.' The dentist helpfully supplied journalists with photos of the two in romantic although hardly X-rated settings such as candlelit dinners in restaurants.

Ronan said he didn't start pressing his ex-girlfriend for repayment until he read that Halle had been paid $125,000 to co-star in *Boomerang* and felt she now had the wherewithal to repay him. 'I started trying to collect my money in 1991,' he told *Jet*, somewhat undercutting his argument, since *Boomerang* came out a year later. Halle 'said I started [the lawsuit] because she married someone and was jealous; but I had no other choice but to litigate,' Ronan said.

The embarrassing subtext of the ugly suit was that Halle had been a kept woman. What Ronan neglected to mention in his press interviews, but was reported in *Jet* and *People* magazines, was that a year before filing suit against Halle he had filed for bankruptcy.

Halle insisted that the dentist's largesse was just that – a gift, not a loan. The US tabloid, the *Star*, claimed Halle gave it an interview (movie stars in the US simply do not talk to such publications as the *Star* and the *National Enquirer*), in which she said of her ex-lover, 'He bought me a lot of things. He's a very wealthy man, and he's just trying to hurt me.'

The *Star* claimed that Ronan had treated her to lavish vacations in Las Vegas and Hawaii, but his attorney, Edward Margolis, insisted they were business trips! 'It was a simple business deal,' the *Star* quoted Margolis as saying. 'He expected to get paid back. The money was associated with building her career.' (In Hawaii?) 'It's cut and dried: he loaned money. He wants it back,' the attorney said, adding that Halle would be embarrassed if the case went to court, where his client 'would present much more revealing evidence'.

If she actually did deign to talk to the *Star*, Halle made some valid points rebutting the dentist's claim that his generosity had bankrolled her career: during their romance, Halle had more than enough of her own money and was not a kept woman. 'I made $90,000 from [the TV series] *Living Dolls*. I didn't work for six months, but I could have lived on that money for two or three years. There are people who support whole families on that kind of money, and I was a single person with no dependants.

'There was never any agreement to pay him back. This is just a man scorned. He is just saying these things to hurt me and embarrass me publicly.'

If that was, in fact, her jilted lover's intention, he failed to do so. At least not embarrass her in front of the only person besides her mother she truly cared about. Halle was relieved that her husband was supportive throughout the ordeal and didn't mind that his wife's past love life and financial woes received such a public airing.

'I was worried,' she said, 'but not for myself. My concern was David. I thought, "What is he going to think? How is this going to affect him?" '

Her worries turned out to be unfounded. Before she could call her husband to brace him for the expected blast of bad publicity, her husband called her. He had tracked her down in Morocco, where she was shooting the Showtime cable-TV movie *Solomon & Sheba*, and told her over the phone, 'Baby, don't even worry. This guy can't touch you.'

Halle said of her husband's reaction, 'He was so supportive, so loving. He didn't question me about it. He didn't say is this or that true? All that mattered was that I was OK. He said, "Halle, this man is really sad. I don't want you worrying." ' Halle said that, after that phone call, she stopped worrying about the lawsuit and considered it nothing more than a 'nuisance'.

But it was an expensive nuisance. Halle has fought all her life, whether it was grabbing a role originally designed for a white actress or convincing her high school faculty that she hadn't committed voter fraud, and she refused to settle with the dentist, despite the fact that her legal fees ended up totalling far more than the dentist sought from her. It was money well spent, she felt. 'I work hard for my money, and I can't think of a better way to spend it than to protect my character,' she said.

Typically, Halle found the silver lining in this ugly dark cloud. 'As bad as it was, I think a lot of good has come out of it for me. I've learned to stand up for myself,' she said in a 1998 TV documentary, pointing out that she could have made the suit go away by writing a cheque. 'I could have settled with [Ronan]. God knows David and I had the money to pay him eighty thousand dollars. It cost me a hundred and fifty thousand to defend myself and win rather than give this guy eighty.'

A judge sided with Halle, and in 1994 dismissed Ronan's suit because he had failed to list her as a debtor when he filed for bankruptcy.

Despite her husband's voluble support during her legal night-mare, she later felt he still had doubts and that the case had contributed to their deteriorating relationship. In a 1998 inter-view, she recalled her husband's attitude at the time of the lawsuit: 'David wanted to know, "Why is this guy making all this up?" ' Halle's response was simple: 'Because he's nuts.'

'David could never grasp the idea that this guys was nuts. I think he half believed him.'

But towards the end of 1993 the actress had more important tasks than shooing away nuisance lawsuits and voting with her feet at politically incorrect Friars Club luncheons. She was about to integrate Bedrock.

5. INTEGRATING BEDROCK

Maybe it's overcompensation for being only half black, and she feels a need to prove her African-American 'credentials', but sometimes Halle Berry's racial trailblazing in Hollywood can verge on self-parody. Or maybe it's because she's had to fight so hard and long in an industry that largely ignores black actresses that every battle for her seems as critical as D-Day and General MacArthur's landing at Inchon during the Korean War combined.

When Halle auditioned for *The Flintstones*, to her the feature film wasn't just an animated cartoon come to life, but an opportunity for all the 'sistuhs' she felt she represented in the movie business. Or, as Halle described her crusade in Fred Flintstone's prehistoric hometown, 'Bedrock needed to be integrated.'

The Flintstones was a live-action re-creation of the hit animated series seen on millions of television sets on both sides of the Atlantic. Its witty send-up of modern suburban life set in a Stone Age where dinosaurs served as everything from construction-lot cranes to vacuum cleaners made this kiddies' show a hit with adults as well.

Halle auditioned for the role of Sharon Stone, a sexpot secretary who works for Fred Flintstone (John Goodman) after a mistake on scoring an IQ test leads to his promotion from the stone quarry where he operates a 'dino-crane' to the executive suite. Halle was never even considered for the secretary's role, and as usual, practically had to fight her way into the casting room.

'As a black woman, the industry doesn't know what to do with you. You have to fight for roles that aren't specifically "black" roles – like *The Flintstones*,' she said. And, when she finally got a chance to audition, she was going after 'sloppy seconds', since, according to the director Brian Levant, the role of Sharon Stone was written with the real Sharon Stone in mind. Fat chance that superstar Stone would have agreed to play such a small part. But the executive producer, Steven Spielberg, thinks big, and Levant claimed Spielberg 'envisioned it that way. [Sharon Stone] made a very poor decision and took a film the title of which I can't even remember and I'm sure I'm not alone in that.' Sharon Stone's decision to pass on Bedrock, Levant added, 'opened the door for a lot of people'. He reran a compilation tape of everyone who had auditioned for the part, 'and it was only then that she [Berry] totally blew us away'.

Halle tells a contradictory story about her involvement in *The Flintstones*. First of all, the part was never intended for the real Sharon Stone. The character's name was just a pun on all the other Stone Age anachronisms that made the TV series such a hoot. (Like using a parrot as a telephone receiver and a goat for garbage disposal.)

'Let me clear this up. Sharon Stone was never in the film. They told me that the script was written before Sharon Stone *was* "Sharon Stone" – before *Basic Instinct* made her a household name,' Halle insisted.

So, even if Sharon Stone was never up for the part, Halle didn't even make the original shortlist of actresses considered for the midriff-baring, sarong-clad secretary who makes Fred Flintstone's tie curl up cartoonishly (not to mention phallically) with sexual symbolism at the sight of her.

'This is the '90s,' she said at the time of the film's release in 1994. 'And we're a whole lot different today. That was one of the reasons I went to my agent when I heard they were having a hard time casting this role. They had seen a lot of white actresses and nobody got the role. I said to my agent, "This is a comedy. Can they take a joke? Will they see me?" And he said he would try.

'People don't really, really seek me out. Even with *The Flintstones*, I had to hear about it. They didn't ask to see me. But when I read [the script], I thought I could play this,' she said.

When Halle read for Levant, she tried to break the ice with a joke and yet refused to ignore the race issue under the guise of levity. Levant recalled, 'The first thing that Halle said when she came in to read for us is, "I didn't know there were black people in Bedrock." ' Levant joined in on the gag and said, 'Hey, we know where life started – in Africa. So there better be black people in Bedrock.'

Halle obviously agreed: 'How can you make a children's movie in the '90s and not have any black people in the cast? When I met with him, I told him I thought [*The Flintstones*] should be integrated.'

Levant didn't really need to be convinced. Even before Halle's impassioned speech, he didn't like the idea of a lily-white Bedrock. 'We wanted to create a more racially balanced world,' said Levant, who noted that he had minored in black history in college, where he learned humans first emerged from Africa. The director thought it was ridiculous that in 1960, when the TV cartoon series debuted, the show presented a totally white world. 'We have all these different cultures existing today, and I wanted to see it in the film,' Levant said.

Even so, the decision to hire Halle was not a case of affirmative casting, with guilt-ridden, bleeding-heart, liberal white film-makers hiring her to meet some imaginary quota system like the preferential treatment sometimes given to law- and medical-school applicants of colour. Her reading just blew away the director and executive producer Spielberg, who gave up any fantasy he might have had that the real Sharon Stone would play the supporting role. Levant said, 'It has been cited many times as color-blind casting, and that's partially true. The fact that she shone so brightly in the audition allowed us to add some ethnic diversity, which we wanted to do. But it wasn't the driving force [behind her being hired]. Her performance was the driving force. We took the tape [of her audition] over to [Spielberg's headquarters] Amblin and showed it to Spielberg, and he knew Halle because she's participated in some sort of program where they bring writers in and actors to perform their scenes. He's seen her work up close and thought it was a great choice.'

Halle was delighted when she learned she had been given the role. 'I was the symbol of black beauty [in the movie]. Me, a black woman.' But what most thrilled Halle about the project – which she has said was a milestone in her career even though *The Flintstones* was not 'an important movie' – was that, for the first time, she was able to play a race-neutral role. It was the first time she wasn't cast in a part only a black woman could play.

As the devious Sharon Stone, Berry conspires with an embezzl-ing executive (Kyle MacLachlan) to defraud Slate & Company,

Fred Flintstone's prehistoric employer. When Fred starts to uncover the scheme, Stone is assigned as his secretary and seductress to distract him from exposing the embezzlement.

For all her feistiness about integrating Bedrock, once she got the role she admitted being intimidated by working with so much established comic talent. 'We've got really huge comedians on this show, and I was the last one cast, and I knew who all the players were going to be. And I knew I fought to get the role. And when I got it, I thought, "How am I going to hold my own with all these comedians?" So I was a little worried. Luckily, my part wasn't supposed to be a "yuck it" kind of role. It was a little more subtle. I didn't have to worry about pushing jokes and worrying about the timing.'

To make up for her lack of experience as a comedian, she studied tapes of Mae West movies, although the final performance that emerges is more Marilyn than Mae.

Coming off the very dramatic miniseries *Queen* and about to play yet another crack addict in the upcoming feature *Losing Isaiah*, Halle was thought by some friends and handlers to have made a career blunder by appearing in a live-action cartoon – not to mention the fact that she received only sixth billing, although she *was* cast just above Elizabeth Taylor at seventh.

Well intentioned though such concerns about her career were, Halle played them down somewhat, although, as she defended her decision, one could still detect the high school senior who felt she might not have been beautiful enough to become prom queen. 'It's amazing how people can be so negative. Some people have said to me, "*The Flintstones*? That's a cartoon. I thought you wanted to be a serious actress. You just did *Queen*. I mean, Halle!" But not everything's going to be *Queen* or *Malcolm X*. This film is really important to me because to be a black woman and be the object of everybody else's desire in this movie is such a coup. The fact that these executives at the studio, who are all white males, took the risk to have a black woman as this character says a lot as to where we're going. No, we don't want to be just sex objects or be just beautiful. But the level of consciousness is being raised, and that's important to me. We're starting to be seen a little bit differently.'

But not quite the same. And not everyone's consciousness was raised to the same level – among the merchandising there was no doll for Halle's character. For once, she refused to rise to the bait and denounce the cutthroat world of toymakers. 'I don't think they intentionally slighted me,' she said. 'It's not something that most people think about if you're not black.' She did note, however, that, as a black child, she could never find a doll that shared her skin colour.

Levant offered conflicting stories to the press for the lack of the doll. 'As I understand it,' he said, 'you usually have the bad guys and the good guys, so the kids can hold them in each hand and fight. What would you do with a Halle Berry doll?'

Levant blamed Spielberg for Halle's slight by Mattel. She was neither a bad guy nor a good guy but somewhere in between, hence unsuitable for duelling-doll contests. As originally conceived, Sharon Stone was a villain. Perhaps out of bleeding-heart liberal guilt, Spielberg insisted that the Stone character eventually be rehabilitated, according to Levant. 'That was [Spielberg's] influence; he thought she should be redeemed at the end. I had originally fought it, to tell you the truth, but finally I think it worked out great. People liked her so much they didn't want her to be bad. [Spielberg] just had a feeling that there shouldn't be more than one bad guy in a *Flintstones* movie. I thought that was a little easy. But it worked out well for the film.'

On another occasion, though, Levant contradicted himself and claimed he had fought for a Halle doll. He also contradicted Halle's claim that she didn't mind not becoming a piece of Hollywood merchandise. 'Although we had cautioned the toy-makers at Mattel, that, for instance, in *Jurassic Park* I don't think they had any black characters in their toys,' he said, 'we warned them on *The Flintstones*: "You really should make a Halle Berry doll" – but they didn't want to make that many. So they made an arbitrary cut there, and I think she was a little upset by that. They didn't make a Halle Berry doll and they should have. I saw that she had been disappointed that there weren't toys of her. They had Fred, Wilma, Barney, Betty, Kyle [MacLachlan], who was the villain, and Dino. Even Dino. And they were not successful sellers I might add.'

It's not surprising that Halle's villain underwent a metamorphosis to good girl during the convoluted evolution of the script. The amusing scandal surrounding the project was that no fewer than 32 uncredited writers worked on the screenplay. It was more than screenwriting by committee and more like screenwriting on an assembly line. During one story meeting, which may be apocryphal, a battalion of writers sat around a conference table and injected gags into the witless script.

The Flintstones was released in the US on 27 May 1994 and in the UK on 22 July the same year. With the relatively modest budget of $45 million – especially for a film packed with special effects – it turned out to be a solid commercial hit, earning $130 million in the US and another £19 million in the UK.

And, despite the cut-and-paste quality of the script, the reviews were not as vitriolic as might have been expected. In fact, *The Austin Chronicle* in Texas wrote:

> Thirty-two writers reportedly had a hand in writing *The Flintstones*, which would seem to bode ill for the plot, but it still turns out to be a surprisingly watchable spectacle, thanks mainly to a gargantuan budget [sic] and a free rein on set design and art direction.

Movieline magazine's Stephen Farber was not so enthusiastic:

> Thirty-two writers came up with this? Live-action cartoons always seem precious and labored and about 85 minutes too long. But you can't really fault the casting or the special effects or even the lackluster direction by Brian Levant. The witless script is the one and only culprit.

Worldwide, *The Flintstones* grossed a whopping $358 million and became Halle's first $100-million-plus hit. That statistic on her résumé must have made up for being ignored by Mattel's merchandising department.

For those who thought Halle had handicapped her career by appearing in a cartoon come to life, she would demonstrate in her next two projects that a single film could not define her entire career, and she had no difficulty returning to much more substantial fare.

6. LOSING ISAIAH, REGAINING RESPECT

For someone who refused to appear in films she felt ghettoised black people and presented a one-sided, negative portrait of people of colour, Halle Berry has, over the course of her career, played not one but two crack addicts on screen.

But her next film, *Losing Isaiah*, was no *Menace II Society* or *Boyz N the Hood*, glamorising the black underclass or revelling in its violence. In fact, *Losing Isaiah* was a serious film about a woman who tries to escape the desolate world of the inner city and her crack-addicted past.

In the harrowing drama, Halle is Khaila Richards, a crack addict vegetating on the mean streets of Chicago's South Side, where the film shot for an exhausting three months of eighteen-hour days. Khaila is the mother of an infant, and, in a scene that's painful to watch, she absent-mindedly deposits her baby in a garbage dumpster in an alley while she goes in search of her next crack score. In the meantime, in another sequence that's even harder to watch, a garbage truck pulls up to the dumpster and empties out its contents, including the baby! When the child's mother finally returns, the dumpster is empty and the baby gone.

Almost as if to punish herself for such a grotesque act of parental neglect, Halle's crack addict brazenly shoplifts at a convenience store, perhaps hoping to be arrested and sent to rehab, both of which happen. She also receives a prison sentence.

The abandoned baby is found and lands in the intensive-care unit of a hospital, where Margaret Lewin, a social worker played by Jessica Lange, falls in love with the tiny lost soul and decides to adopt him. In one heart-wrenching scene, Lange picks up the baby and gently rocks him while he's still attached to a snarl of intravenous feeding tubes, monitors and other emergency-ward gadgetry.

And so the baby grows up in a loving family with a father and an older sibling, the social worker's biological daughter. Three years later, Halle's crack addict shows up. She's been rehabilitated, is now drug-free and even has a job.

And she wants her child back. The custody battle climaxes with a powerful courtroom scene.

After playing a crack addict in *Jungle Fever*, Halle would have seemed like a natural for *Losing Isaiah*, but as usual she found she had to fight for this role, and this time her race was not a problem or an issue. This was definitely not a white or race-neutral part.

Losing Isaiah's director, Stephen Gyllenhaal, admitted that he didn't even want to see Halle. 'It was mostly courtesy,' he said, explaining why he finally let her read for the role. 'I figured, "Let's get this over with – *quick*." ' But, in the course of a gruelling two-hour audition, Halle made all the director's misgivings evaporate. Even so, she still had to do a screen test to convince the studio brass, and the scene chosen required her to cry hysterically – for 50 takes. On the 51st take, her eyes rebelled. 'They felt as if someone was sticking knives in them,' she said. Her manager stopped the screen test and insisted on getting her medical treatment. The doctor's diagnosis: she had scratched her cornea. His prognosis: anaesthetic eye drops couldn't be used because they might permanently scratch the cornea and for the next 48 hours she would experience the worst pain in her life. The doctor was not exaggerating. 'He told me there was no pain greater than the one I was going to endure that I could live to talk about,' she said. 'He was right.'

By now, Halle wasn't even surprised or fazed that she had to fight for the job. 'I knew there was a lot of skepticism. And I had to be honest with myself and realize why. My career is very new; I haven't proven myself in many ways – I haven't had the opportunity,' she said in 1995, inexplicably dismissing or discounting her impressive work in *Jungle Fever* and *Queen*. 'And I understood that this was a big movie for Paramount, and a big deal for [Gyllenhaal] as a director. I understood all that, but I think what it did was it just sort of lit a fire under my butt to prove myself!'

In the custody battle played out in the courtroom, Samuel L Jackson plays her lawyer, Kadar Lewis, and argues that a black child should be with his black mother, even if the mother is an ex-crack addict. On the stand, Jessica Lange's adoptive mother undergoes a withering cross-examination by Jackson's attorney, who gets her to admit she has no black friends, has no black children's books for her son and hasn't taught him anything about his roots or black history. It is the lawyer's contention that a black child cannot be raised by a white family with his racial identity fostered or intact.

Halle said she could 'definitely relate' to the movie's theme: 'The issues that are brought up, especially in court scenes, were really important. Can this white family give this little black child the history, the culture, that he needs to have? And can they do things like comb his hair? You know, knowing the differences in texture between a black person's hair and a white person's hair. The different products that black people use in their hair. I mean, little things like that seem really minute, but in the scheme of things they can become really important things.'

Ironically, Halle's rehabilitated addict was arguing a case that Halle's own childhood contradicted. A black (or biracial) child can be successfully raised – black consciousness intact – by a white parent.

But it's not an easy load to tow. 'Isaiah grows up in an all-white family and they treat him like he was just like they are,' Halle said. 'I mean, that's lovely. We would all hope the whole world could be like that. But, when that child leaves that home, somebody's going to tell him, "You're black, you're different and you're not equal to white people." And, when that happens, is he going to be prepared to deal with that?'

Halle wasn't. By the time she was six, kids were taunting her. 'I got the name calling. I had a rough childhood.' It became so bad that Halle began to think she had been adopted. 'When enough little kids tell you that she can't possibly be your mother because she's white, and you're like six, what they say means a lot to you.'

Unlike the movie's social worker, who ignores her adopted black son's heritage and history, Halle's mother made sure her daughter recognised and accepted her roots. 'The great thing about my mother is that, even though she was white, she was really concerned about what would happen to me as I grew up as a black woman in this country. She taught me a lot about my history, where I came from and how to maybe deal with racism: don't get mad about it, don't get militant about it, but make quiet change, you know. Live a good life and work hard at whatever I decide to do. And that's the best revenge,' she said, perhaps recalling the prom-queen fiasco in high school. 'To succeed in this country where maybe people don't want to see us as a race succeed.'

She also praised her mother in an interview with the syndicated columnist Marilyn Beck:

> My mother went out of her way to put me in touch with my culture and made me aware that I am a black woman. She prepared me for the world and all the discrimination and things I was going to have to deal with.
>
> If white parents adopting a black child go the extra mile to incorporate that child's heritage and history into their lives, then it's OK. But I don't agree with white families who say, 'We're going to adopt a black baby, raise it with our family and it will see no color.' They're doing the child a disservice. That might be fine while the child is at home. But when he gets out in the real world, someone's going to say, 'Hey, you're black' or call him the 'N' word and he'll realize he's different. He won't be prepared.

Halle seems to have taken her role home with her and brought it along on press interviews.

Although they played nemeses in the courtroom in *Losing Isaiah*, Jessica Lange served as a role model for Halle because they shared a similar career trajectory and both overcame stereotyping as mannequins wonderful to look at but incapable of acting.

Halle said, 'I remember when Jessica was in King Kong's hand and she was just a "model", and people gave her a hard time too! I was so proud to be working with her, and in a way I'm proud of her accomplishment, just as a woman that she overcame all that [stereotyping as a model]. It's a great incentive to me, and it's proof that it can be done.'

Lange was not only a role model, but her career served as both a cautionary tale and a fairy tale with a happy ending. Lange's career missteps showed Halle that choosing the wrong role can kill a career just as it's getting started. Lange made her film debut in the disastrous 1976 remake of *King Kong*, with the soft-spoken actress forced to recreate Fay Wray's screaming hysterics in the 1933 original. Critics dismissed Lange as yet another model turned wannabe actress, and reviews of her performance in *King Kong*, coupled with its poor box-office performance, made it impossible for her to find work for three years after the film's release. The film historian Leonard Maltin wrote of *King Kong's* reception, 'The ensuing debacle nearly ended her career before it started; both the picture and her performance were trashed by critics, and she languished in obscurity for three years before making another picture.' That picture was *All That Jazz*, whose director, Bob Fosse, was a friend of Lange's and Maltin suggested the small part Fosse gave her as the Angel of Death represented a form of mercy casting, helping out a friend who was down on her luck and career.

Halle's modelling career had never achieved Lange's level of success, and her film debut, *Jungle Fever*, was much more auspicious than Lange's. Lange eventually gained respect and regained her career momentum by playing a tortured movie star, Frances Farmer, in 1982's *Frances*, and Halle would also earn some of the best reviews of her career playing another doomed actress, Dorothy Dandridge. Both Lange and Halle would prevail and disprove naysayers' claims that they were just pretty faces in search of a body of work.

Unfortunately, although she admired Lange and her achievements, Halle wasn't allowed to hang out with her co-star between takes because the director didn't want their adversarial on-screen relationship to be softened by an off-screen friendship, so Halle found herself admiring her role model from afar.

Halle explained, 'We thought the uncomfortable feeling that two strangers have when they meet would work for these characters. And we wanted to preserve that, so we didn't spend time together. In the rehearsal period, we were talking to each other through Stephen [Gyllenhaal, the director], so we really had no contact at first. And through him we decided that it's best we look the other way and we don't have lunch, we don't socialize.'

Without Lange as a mentor, it was lonely on the set for Halle, and, even after her character gets off crack and rehabilitates herself, playing someone who had to regain custody of a child she lost through her own criminally irresponsible behaviour drove her to the brink of madness. 'To evoke the kind of emotion I needed for this part, I had to dig up my own pain and relive the things that have hurt me so deeply in my life. That was a very vulnerable place to be. There were days I felt like I was right on the edge of sanity and insanity,' she said.

For some reason, during two weeks of reshooting, the actresses were allowed to get to know each other, which delighted Halle. 'I would hate to walk away from this experience thinking, "I have learned nothing about Jessica Lange, this woman who I admire so much!" '

Halle had done enough research for *Jungle Fever*, so didn't feel compelled to visit any crack houses this time around, but she did find herself relying on a cast member from *Jungle Fever*, Samuel L Jackson, her attorney in *Losing Isaiah*. On both films, Jackson served as her mentor.

'On my first film, he kind of taught me the ropes and took me in and helped me. He would even come to the set on days he wasn't working and I was doing things by myself, to support me,' she said.

Halle's relationship with the crew was not as happy as her interaction with Jackson. She was also beginning to worry about being typecast – now, not as a brain-dead former model and beauty queen but as an actress who specialised in playing inner-city scum. And she felt she still wasn't getting a crack at A-list scripts. She poured out her rage on all these issues when she said a year after *Losing Isaiah*'s release, 'I say thank you and please, and I expect the same in return. But when I was called a bitch by [a crew member], I went off. Don't try to make me feel lucky to be here, because I've worked damn hard and I've got the goods. I still have to convince managers and agents that they should send me out for the next level of scripts. I don't want to abandon black filmmakers, but I don't want to keep doing "girls in the 'hood" either.'

Losing Isaiah was released in the US on 17 March 1995. However, in the UK it went straight to video in June 1996 with no cinema release, and this may have reflected the $17 million film's poor critical reception and paltry box-office take of only $7 million in the US and $900,000 overseas.

Although Halle was nominated for a National Association for the Advancement of Colored People Image Award as an outstanding lead actress in a motion picture, the critics did not share the NAACP's enthusiasm for her performance. The *San Francisco Chronicle*'s critic, Edward Guthmann, wrote, 'Halle Berry, best known for her title role in the TV miniseries *Queen*, gets her first meaty film role.' What about *Jungle Fever*? And, though on television, if *Queen* wasn't 'meaty', what is? Guthmann damned Halle with faint praise, in Pope's phrase, by adding:

> Berry, whose talents are competent, makes the transition
> from ghetto crackhead to reformed citizen a bit too neatly.
> Like Audrey Hepburn, who segued from sewer rat to sleek
> princess in *My Fair Lady*, [Berry] is a lot more convincing as
> the made-over, scrubbed-down Khaila than she is as an edgy,
> bleary-eyed addict.

The *Washington Post*'s Rita Kempley, however, compared the performances of Jessica Lange and Halle, and it was an invidious comparison that accused the more experienced actress of chewing up the scenery while the relative newcomer noshed politely on her role:

> Lange . . . has never looked worse. Tears spill from her tired
> eyes and stringy locks frame her lined, puffy face. She grinds
> her teeth to show her barely contained rage, her Big Scene
> ready to pour out in a passionate, babbling cascade. Berry . . .
> is more controlled in her transformation from defeated addict
> to determined young striver.

Halle didn't have much time to brood about *Losing Isaiah*'s critical and financial failure. Soon after the film wrapped, she found herself half a world away in Morocco, and, instead of playing a crack addict on the bottom rung of society, she was at its very pinnacle, playing a real-life queen.

7. BLACK QUEEN TAKES WHITE KING

Career advisers and friends all told Halle not to take on her next project, playing a biblical queen opposite *NYPD Blue*'s Jimmy Smits as the King of Israel, in the American cable channel Showtime's *Solomon & Sheba*.

'So many people told me, "You can't do TV if you expect to be a movie actress." I said, "Listen, the same rules that apply to Julia Roberts don't apply to me." Black actresses don't have the same choices as white actresses.'

And even if cable TV was a step down from feature films, Halle felt she would again be blazing the way for actresses of colour because the biblical queen, who many historians believe was black, had always been played by white women in the past.

'The Queen of Sheba was Ethiopian, yet this is the first time a person of color has ever played the lead in a major Biblical production,' she said. 'Anytime it's something where a black woman wouldn't be the obvious choice, I really go after it.' It would seem, however, that the obvious choice to play an Ethiopian would be a black person.

In 1959, Hollywood mounted a lavish feature-film production of the same name with Yul Brynner as the wise ruler of Israel and Gina Lollobrigida as Sheba's queen. In those days, an interracial romance on screen was out of the question. 'The way I see it, when Gina Lollobrigida did the movie the first time, it was an injustice,' Halle said.

Shot on location at Morocco's Atlas Studios, the TV version of the saga must have appealed to Halle because the Queen of Sheba is one tough lady – a female Rambo as powerful out of bed as she is tempting in it.

Halle's character doesn't start out as a queen. She's a beautiful woman coveted by the King of Sheba. When her father tries to stop the king from raping his daughter, the king stabs him, but then Halle's character goes into Rambo mode, seizes the king's sword and kills him. Having eliminated the ruler of Sheba, she is proclaimed its queen, but that's just the beginning of the adventures and dangers facing the uneasy head that wears this crown.

Sheba is a tiny country in this version, but it's rich in one of the most coveted spices in the ancient world, frankincense, and the spice is coveted by the King of Israel, who in a fit of biblical imperialism decides to annex Sheba and gain control of its spice trade.

Halle's queen travels incognito to Israel and appears at Solomon's court dressed as a man. The queen (like the actress who portrays her) is too beautiful to fool anybody, and soon Sheba gets Solomon's mind off annexing her country by seducing him. Lust for a beautiful woman replaces Solomon's lust for territory, and Sheba's kingdom seems safe from encroachment by Israel until the queen is falsely accused of conspiring to assassinate the King of Israel. Another roll in the hay convinces Solomon of Sheba's fidelity, and her execution for treason is cancelled.

Despite their mutual infatuation, duty prevails, and the two lovers reluctantly agree to return to their respective kingdoms and make laws, not love.

Solomon & Sheba debuted on American television on 26 February 1995, and its hoary rehash and fictionalisation of the biblical story were met with derision by the critics. The American *People* magazine wrote:

> In a tale from the Old Testament, the Queen of Sheba (Halle Berry) plights her destiny with the wise and often shirtless King Solomon of Israel (a buffed up Jimmy Smits) . . . Shot in Morocco, this is a beautiful, burnished costume epic, even if it moves along at the pace of a camel caravan caught in a sandstorm.

The magazine gave it a 'B' grade.

Contrary to her friends' fears, the epic didn't hurt Halle's career, and the distant movie location even taught her a new skill. She had grown up, as she's said many times, considering Hamburger Helper an entrée, but out of boredom she allowed Italian members of the film crew to teach her how to cook. It turned out to be a labour of love – love for her husband. 'I'm gonna come home and know how to cook something! He'll be really impressed,' she said on the set.

8. INJUSTICE

Nineteen ninety-six was a very busy year for Halle Berry – personally and professionally. Like the period of the 'two cities' in Dickens's tale, 1996 would also be the best of times and the worst of times for the actress. She would appear in four feature films – and her fabled romance with the Atlanta Slugger would play itself out like the saga of Marilyn Monroe and Joe Dimaggio with an all-black cast.

None of these 1996 films would prove as memorable or challenging for her as *Losing Isaiah*, and all of them would be eclipsed by the mutual mudslinging during her rancorous divorce from David Justice.

By 1996, Halle and her husband were living on opposite sides of the country and barely saw each other. That her work ethic was bordering on workaholism made the geographical and emotional distance mandatory. During one busy month in the spring of 1996, two of her films came out in the US over the same weekend, and the actress ended up competing against herself at the box office. Her films that year would also be the first time she got first billing, and her star was so in the ascendant that even in one of the films, where she played herself in a tiny cameo, one critic nevertheless chose to headline his review, ' . . . starring Halle Berry'.

Halle began the year with a huge box-office hit, *Executive Decision*, which was released in the US on 15 March and in the UK on 10 May 1996. The big budget ($55 million) thriller grossed $69 million in the US, £2.5 million in the UK and $65 million in the rest of the world, yet another solid hit on Halle's résumé. It also allowed her to break a record for black actresses in general and enrich her in particular when she became the first woman of colour to earn $1 million for a film, according to the *Hollywood Reporter*.

'I always wanted to buy my mother a nice house,' Halle has said, and one of the first things she did with her newfound wealth was to buy more than merely a 'nice house', a lavish, two-storey white-clapboard home in one of the priciest enclaves in the Cleveland area, at the water's edge on Lake Erie. Her mother was so touched she wiped away a tear when she said in a 1998 TV documentary, 'She's a wonderful daughter. She made a dream come true for me. I never expected to live in a place like this.' (One wonders if in retrospect Judith might have felt any guilt about not being able to send her daughter money for food and a modelling portfolio during Halle's starving-artist days in Chicago.)

Halle attributed her record-breaking salary to the generosity of the film's producer, Joel Silver, and said, 'He calls me his million-dollar baby.' In return for this largesse, Silver would later extract his pound of flesh when she appeared in another of his productions, *Swordfish*, in 2001.

In *Executive Decision*, which one critic called *Die Hard in the Ozone*, Arab terrorists commandeer a 747 and threaten to blow up both the plane and its cargo of nerve gas over Washington, DC, which will allegedly kill half the people on the eastern seaboard of the USA. Steven Seagal is a military expert and Kurt Russell plays the civilian scientist, and both are assigned to board the plane in midair and take out the bad guys. Halle Berry got third billing as a plucky flight attendant, Jean. (A trivia note: another flight attendant is played by the former Mrs Donald Trump, Marla Maples, in a cameo.)

The *San Francisco Chronicle*'s Mick LaSalle wrote, 'She does what she has to do – act brave and look scared.' The *Chronicle* panned the rest of the film, complaining that it 'goes on for a long 135 minutes – at least 35 minutes more than necessary'.

The *Hollywood Reporter*'s reviewer sounded more like a fan than a critic when he wrote, 'Halle Berry . . . has the audience hanging on her every movement as a brave flight attendant.' The *New York Times*'s Janet Maslin actually enjoyed *Executive Decision* and called it a 'good, taut movie for red-meat action audiences', but she wasn't as kind to Halle, whom she dismissed as 'window dressing' and called Marla Maples's stewardess 'Skyjack Barbie, cowering decoratively'.

Halle made at least one new fan from *Executive Decision*, co-star Kurt Russell, who has said, 'She's in that rarefied atmosphere of human beings who are fortunate enough to be probably the most beautiful people on the planet.' (*People* magazine would agree and place her on its '50 Most Beautiful' list seven times.)

For the first time in her career, Halle Berry achieved first billing in her next film – and had more to do. *Race the Sun* came out in the US on 22 March 1996, but went straight to video in the UK owing to its poor box office – only $1.7 million – on the other side of the Atlantic.

Based on a true story, *Race the Sun* casts Halle as a new teacher at a high school on the Big Island of Hawaii where most of the students come from poor families and lack academic motivation. Although she's supposed to be teaching English, her speciality, Halle ends up assigned to a science class. To motivate her students, who are so dejected they call themselves 'lolos' (meaning low lifes), she concocts a science project in which the class will build a solar-powered car and race it in a local contest. The students win and get an invitation to compete against teams from around the world in a race between Sydney and Melbourne.

The *Los Angeles Times* called the movie, even though it was based on the real-life exploits of students at Konawaena High in Hawaii, a derivative rip-off of other fish-out-of-water sports flicks such as *Cool Runnings* (about a Jamaican bobsled team at the Olympics). The *Los Angeles Times*'s John Anderson wrote:

> As if to emphasize that there is no paradise on Earth, *Race the Sun* takes the shtick about a dedicated teacher who meets surly but soon-to-be-inspired students, flies it to Hawaii and shows how cultural diversity and fresh plot lines are both endangered species in this country.

Peter Stack of the *San Francisco Chronicle* had a marginally better time in the cinema: he called *Race the Sun* 'a lively spectacle' and praised its depiction of

> kids learning to set aside their differences and insecurities to bond as a team. It's not a soaring, transcendent film experience – mostly it's corny and predictable. But it has a certain sunny charm and a few winning gags to keep it in the winning column.

(The reviewer couldn't know at this time that *Race the Sun* would end up in the losing 'column' when the box-office results came in, and the film grossed less than $2 million in the US.)

Girl 6 debuted in the US the same week as *Race the Sun* (and on 7 June 1996 in the UK), but Halle had only a cameo in the film about a starving actress who takes a job working a phone-sex line, so she wasn't really competing against herself at the box office.

But by now, Halle was famous enough to play herself in this Spike Lee film, and, although she's listed 36th in the credits (Madonna's cameo earned her the 25th spot), her prominence in the film industry was by now such that *Rolling Stone* magazine headlined its review '. . . starring Halle Berry, Spike Lee and Quentin Tarantino . . .'

The real star, or lead at least, in *Girl 6* is the title character (the numerical designation is her ID as a phone-sex operator), played by Theresa Randle. Her job is to bring callers to orgasm by talking dirty to them on the phone. But soon she finds herself becoming a sex addict and joins her customers in their orgasmic phone adventures. She's such a good actress (or addict?) that she's no longer faking her orgasms on the phone.

Rolling Stone didn't do Halle much of a favour by calling her the star of the film because it begins its review by saying, 'It's hard to say exactly at what point during *Girl 6* it will hit you that this peek into the world of phone boning is the worst movie Spike Lee has ever made.' Lee also appears on camera as Girl 6's buddy, and *Rolling Stone* calls him and co-star Quentin Tarantino 'the most despised pseudoactors in the movies'. Mercifully, despite her headline credit, *Rolling Stone*'s Peter Travers fails to mention Halle in his review.

In a sign of things to come in Halle's own career, there's a dream sequence with Randle's Girl 6, in which she imagines herself as Dorothy Dandridge becoming the first African-American to receive a Best Actress Oscar nomination. In another dream sequence, she imagines herself as Pam Grier in the 1970s blaxploitation flick, *Foxy Brown*, a role Halle intends to reprise (for real) in the future.

Although the *Los Angeles Times*'s Kenneth Turan praised Theresa Randle's hapless phone-sex operator for her 'warmth, vulnerability and sensitivity', he found the film 'baffling, sketchy and unsatisfying'. Happily, Halle fails to make an appearance in this review, just as she was spared by *Rolling Stone*.

Moviegoers shared the critics' opinion of *Girl 6*, and it achieved only $4.9 million in ticket sales in the US.

Unlike in *Girl 6*, Halle did have the title role in her next film, *The Rich Man's Wife*, which debuted in the US on 13 September 1996, and unfortunately shared *Race the Sun*'s fate in the UK, where it was released only on video. And again, as a sign of her ascendancy in the film business, Halle got top billing in addition to the title role.

Just before principal photography began, Halle admitted that star billing was a major reason she agreed to appear in the project, plus the fact that she couldn't resist such a histrionic role as a femme fatale. 'There aren't many scripts that have such a strong central female character as the driving force of the movie, and it gave me something new to do, an opportunity to be the leading lady,' she said. 'This movie allowed me to do something different from other roles I've played. It's a murder mystery, *film noir* kind of movie, which I've wanted to do for a long time.' The usually super-self-confident actress confessed, however, to some trepidation about having to carry the movie. 'It's satisfying but I'm also scared to death! I'd be lying if I said that I didn't feel pressure, but I also know why I'm doing what I'm doing, and I'm really doing this because I love to act. And I love to be in front of the camera. It's what I get the most pleasure from.'

Halle had been fighting for crumbs for so long that, when she was finally offered a sumptuous cinematic banquet, she wondered about the old saying: if it *looks* too good to be true, it probably is. After the film's release, she said, 'Well, I thought honestly, "They're offering it to me – what's wrong with it?" It's not often that I just get offered good scripts.' Movie critics and the public would ultimately prove Halle's suspicions correct, but at the outset she couldn't possibly have known that she was about to get star billing in one of 1996's biggest flops.

Besides having her name above the title, Halle was intrigued by the idea of working with a female director. *The Rich Man's Wife* was written and directed by Amy Holden Jones, who had written such blockbusters as *Indecent Proposal* and the movie that made an unknown actress named Julia Roberts a star, *Mystic Pizza*. (The offer to star in *The Rich Man's Wife* must have been especially gratifying to Halle since she had auditioned and been rejected for the role of Diana Murphy in *Indecent Proposal*, which went to Demi Moore.)

Jones has confessed that the decision to cast Halle in *The Rich Man's Wife* was not a difficult one because she had been a fan of the actress for years. 'I'm friends with [the director] Stephen Gyllenhaal, so I had seen her work in *Losing Isaiah*, and I thought she really did a great job in it,' Jones said in 2002 after Halle's Oscar triumph. 'It was made for Joe Roth when he was interested in making thrillers or genre movies without, at the time, huge stars. Halle was not a huge star at that time. She was breaking in as opposed to being established as she is now. She seemed like a great choice, and I ran it by them and [the producer] Roger Birnbaum felt it was a great idea and we went to her and she wanted to do it. It was a pretty clear choice right from the beginning.'

The Rich Man's Wife reworks the ingenious plot of Alfred Hitchcock's classic *Strangers on a Train* without that 1953's film brilliant results. It's also the dark side of the Cinderella fairy tale, where Cinderella discovers that Prince Charming is no prince and anything but charming.

Halle's Josie is a destitute seventeen-year-old convenience-store clerk when her 'prince,' a wealthy, older TV executive named Tony Potenza (Christopher McDonald), sweeps into her store and sweeps her off her feet en route to the altar. Flash forward seven years, and Prince Charming has turned into a nasty, abusive drunk who had the foresight to make his bride sign a prenuptial agreement that will leave her with nothing if she leaves him. Jodie has become used to the good life, which includes a hunky lover (Clive Owen) on the sly, and she just can't bring herself to leave her husband from hell.

Over drinks with a stranger, played by Peter Greene, she confides in him her homicidal fantasy about how her husband's death would free her from the prenuptial agreement and leave her a wealthy widow. To Josie, it's just a fantasy, but, like Robert Walker's psychotic mummy's boy in *Strangers on a Train*, her confidant decides to act out her fantasy and kills her husband, leaving her the prime suspect with a terrific motive for getting rid of the jerk.

The *Los Angeles Times*'s Kenneth Turan hated the film, but even he couldn't ignore Halle's beautiful presence in an ugly movie: 'Only those who enjoy seeing Halle Berry in numerous chic designer outfits will come away satisfied.'

The *San Francisco Examiner*'s Barbara Shulgasser wrote that Halle's character does so many stupid things in the movie that members of one preview audience seemed to have taken a proprietary interest in her survival and would scream out warnings in the middle of the movie such as, 'Don't touch the murder weapon.'

Unfortunately, movie audiences in general did not have the same proprietary interest in the film itself and not enough people were willing to pay to see Halle model haute couture, with the result that *The Rich Man's Wife* earned an impoverished $8.5 million in the US.

Halle didn't care that *The Rich Man's Wife* was a commercial and critical failure. For her, it was a personal triumph since she got to essay a rare race-neutral role. (The actor who played her husband is white.) She was also happy to be taking direction from a woman for a change. 'I worked with a woman director, which was important to me, and I got be colorless for three months and feel what white leading ladies feel every time out.'

Appearing in a colour-blind movie may not seem like that big a deal until you learn how sensitised Halle has become to being rejected for so many jobs just because of the colour of her skin. Often, she's been turned away because the character she wants to be play has a white brother, and it would be hard to explain why he has a black sister. (Apparently, Hollywood's casting people haven't heard of stepsisters.) And sometimes the logic of her rejection went beyond racism and became simply unfathomable.

Halle once mentioned an unidentified project where they wouldn't even let her audition for the part of a forest ranger. 'The producer didn't think a forest ranger could be black!' she said.

The sulphurous reviews and commercial failure of some of her films in 1996 must have seemed like a minor distraction, a sideshow compared with the nightmare her real life had become that year.

There had apparently been problems at home for a long time. Back in 1993, an acquaintance suggested that her performance in *Queen* had been slammed by the critics because of her problems in her marriage. (The acquaintance may have been right about that, wrong about Halle's performance, since most critics had raved about her work in the miniseries.) A few, however, had been unkind about her work in *Queen*, and Halle blamed reviewers' barbs for her depression at the time, which included her first but not last contemplation of suicide and led her to seek counselling.

'I was bitter and just mad at people when I got through the TV series. So I got some therapy after the show just to get me back in touch. The therapist helped me work through all those emotions and helped me understand what it all meant. He told me to scream and get all the anger I felt out of my system. I had gone to him thinking I was going to give up acting and become a full-time civil rights activist. It took me two months to get myself back to reality, if you can call Los Angeles reality.'

Three years later, it would become clear that it wasn't the failure of *Queen* but the failure of her marriage that had Halle lying on a shrink's couch and screaming out her anger. Therapy helped up to a point, but Halle said she didn't feel whole again until 'I learned to live with myself by myself. I had to face all the demons I've been trying to push under a rug my whole life. And in my darkest hour, I realized that I couldn't run from them any more. The time had come for me to face them, embrace them, and get on with the business of living my life. It was the hardest thing I've ever had to do.'

Her journey of self-discovery made her take a metaphorical look in the mirror, and she didn't like what she saw staring back at her. 'It was hard for me to look in the mirror and admit I was living a superficial existence and really take ownership for that. When you're a so-called celebrity, it's very easy not to deal with yourself because everybody is loving you, everybody is giving you things, everybody is doing so much for you that you don't have to do anything for yourself.'

Another lesson she learned from the mess of her marriage was that she used relationships to repress uncomfortable feelings about herself and her worth. 'I knew there was a deep spiritual being inside me, but I was afraid to let that be seen for fear of rejection, fear of judgment, fear of not being this person the public had made me out to be. So I live up to "her". That's why, when my marriage was falling apart, I was saying, "We're the happiest couple in the world." I should have said a lot sooner that, not only was my marriage not perfect, I was miserable.'

As their marriage fell apart, Justice was unable to put on the kind of happy face his wife did. He blamed their estrangement on Halle's unwarranted jealousy and differences. He is quoted in *People* magazine of May 1996:

> She wasn't the same person I was with before we got married. She'd get mad when I watched ESPN [the television sports network]. And every time she saw a picture of me with a woman, any woman who might have been standing by my side, she thought I was cheating. She carried a lot of baggage from her previous relationships. She was always suspicious. I've never known a girl who could throw a tantrum like she does.

Justice failed to mention that the 'baggage' she carried from her previous relationships included a punctured eardrum.

Beautiful women often gravitate towards famous athletes, and Justice's claim that he was the innocent victim of groupies' unwanted attention might have seemed valid and his wife's jealousy paranoid. On the other hand, Henry Kissinger once famously said that even paranoid people have enemies. And, as it turned out, Halle's jealousy was not misplaced or imagined.

On 18 February 1996, a few hours before her husband was scheduled to report for spring training in West Palm Beach, Florida, police in nearby Riviera Beach spotted a late-model Lexus parked in a seedy area of the city known for drug dealing and prostitution. Deputies also saw a man walk up to the car, but he fled when the officers approached. The police found money spread out on the passenger's side of the car. And behind the wheel was David Justice. The police detained him, but, after finding no drugs in the vehicle or on his person, they let him go.

That would have been the end of the incident, had the officers not decided to release a statement to the press that identified the famous jock behind the wheel. No crime was committed or alleged, so why did the police notify the press? Their 'explanation' was that Justice was famous.

Whatever the reason for his presence in a red-light drug district, Justice was traumatised by his run-in with the police, and, in the light of law enforcement's past treatment of people of colour, he had good reason to fear, if not for his life, at least his hide. He told *USA Today* in 1996, 'All I could think about was Rodney King. I rolled all my windows down. I turned out all the lights. I put my hands out the window.'

After the police publicised the incident, *People* magazine asked Justice if he had ever cheated on his wife, and he said, 'Absolutely not.' In the same article, Halle seemed to believe her husband and said, 'If anything was going on, I didn't know about it.' (In the 5 April 2002 issue of *Us Weekly*, however, and though it was never proven, the magazine claimed that her ex cheated on her with 'strippers and every twinkie walking by with a skirt'.)

Less than a month after her husband had been questioned by the police, though, Halle filed for divorce in California while Justice filed in Georgia. It was a move Halle did not want to make despite her excellent instincts that it was the right move, however painful and regrettable. 'I heard that David had gotten into that "trouble" on the news,' she said after the incident in the red-light district. 'Part of you thinks, "That's my husband!" ' Even so, she said she realised by then that the marriage was irreparable.

'I called David and said, "What's going on?" He said it wasn't like the reports said. It really didn't matter at that point. I really realized our marriage was over, and I just really wanted to know if he was OK. A real explanation wasn't really what I was in search of. I think all I wanted to hear – and this is how emotionally I wasn't ready to let him go – I wanted to hear him say, "I love you. I'm sorry. I shouldn't have been there." '

Intellectually, rationally, she knew they weren't suited to each other, but emotionally she was still bound to her partner. He was not. 'I didn't want the divorce. David very clearly said he didn't want to be married at this time in his life. He said, "Maybe I got married too young."'

Typical of so many celebrity splits, the divorce played itself out in court and in the press as well. The principals' contradictory revelations in interviews suggested there were two different marriages going on at the same time in the Berry-Justice household.

With 20/20 hindsight, which seems to be the opposite of rose-tinted glasses when it comes to vicious divorces, Justice claimed the marriage was a disaster almost from the start – and he blamed his wife. 'When we were in Bermuda for our [third-year] anniversary, we both agreed we'd made a mistake with our marriage. I was unhappy. She was unhappy. I always felt I was walking on eggshells with her. Everything I did was wrong.'

Halle's recollection of the Bermuda trip contradicted her husband's. She said in 1997, 'I knew the reality of being public people and both of us having such demanding careers had started to take its toll on our relationship. But we had gone to Bermuda on our three-year anniversary trip and said all the right things to each other – we were going to go home and really give it a try; how the marriage could work if we both wanted it to. I believed that.'

Halle was even willing to put her all-important career on hold for the sake of her marriage. 'I passed up a movie so I could go to spring training with David and try to invest the time in *us*. And then one day he came home and said, "I don't want to be married."'

Halle did, however, and suggested they seek professional help to save the marriage, but Justice remained adamant about divorce. With the same tenacity she has pursued acting jobs, Halle tried to hold on to the point of self-humiliation. 'I was begging and pleading with him [to reconsider] because I always thought my marriage would be for life. I said, "Can't we get some counseling?" But David didn't want to hear counseling. He wanted a divorce,' she said.

'When I realized he was really serious and there was nothing I could do, the next day I packed my things, and I went back to my home in LA.'

She spent the next two months in a fog of denial. 'I was walking around in a daze. I didn't know how I was going to function. I would wake up in the middle of the night and think this is just a bad dream. I kept saying, "No, this isn't really real. David's just on a road trip." '

At first, Halle tried to be diplomatic and circumspect, refusing to play out the divorce in the press. About the time she filed for divorce in February 1996, she told *People* magazine that she was not prepared to discuss the reasons for the break-up. That may have been because she didn't know why they were separating. 'It's something I'm still struggling to understand. Every day wasn't bliss, but I didn't see our problems were so great we'd be divorcing,' she said after her initial refusal to discuss the end of the relationship.

Unlike his wife, Justice blabbed from the beginning, at first blaming the rupture on conflicting careers and geography: 'We were bicoastal and didn't get a chance to spend a lot of time together.' A friend of Halle's backed up her husband's explanation for the divorce. 'She's madly in love with him, but David wanted a wife, and she was always off making movies,' the unidentified friend told the 11 March 1996 issue of *People*. To which Halle retorted, 'What am I supposed to do? Say, "By the way, can I have this week off? My husband is in the World Series." '

At that juncture, things were still fairly civil between the two. But, with each successive press interview, crueller things were said and even worse acts committed.

On 11 September 1996, in a pre-trial deposition, Justice demanded that Halle reveal alleged past affairs with Wesley Snipes and Eddie Murphy, among other co-stars.

Halle got a revenge of sorts by serving her husband with divorce papers while he was in the middle of a game against the San Diego Padres, which must have rattled him and probably ruined his performance that day. But this kind of petty revenge provided no solace and failed to diminish the rage she felt, which she decided to transfer to her father.

Halle hadn't spoken to Jerome Berry in more than a decade, and it wasn't a coincidence that she contacted him the same day she began divorce proceedings. 'I had to track him down because I hadn't talked with him in years,' she recalled. 'I was filled with pain and rage. I got him on the phone and unleashed all this anger. I released it. I told him how much he had hurt me by abandoning our family, by not being in my life when I was a child. At the end of the conversation, I think he said, "I'm sorry." '

That was one of only three contacts, all by phone, that she had with her father since he left the family a second time when she was ten. 'Some of those phone conversations weren't so pleasant because he has a way of trying to turn the guilt around and leave it on me,' Halle said.

In 1993, she told the *Los Angeles Daily News* that her father was homeless, living on the streets of Cleveland, and dismissed a reporter's suggestion that since she was a rich movie star she might help him out financially. 'I don't know him and I don't owe him. When we needed him most, he bailed out. It would hurt my mother if I gave him money now. I would do it if he got help . . . I don't deny that he's my father, but I don't want him to be a part of my life.'

The final, rage-fuelled phone call she made during her divorce from Justice was the last time she spoke to Berry. 'I have no contact with my father,' she told the *New York Times Magazine* in December 2001. 'A few years ago, he sold a story to *The Star* about me for a six-pack of beer. I thought, "If you're going to sell the damn story, then at least make some real money." '

Actually, Jerome Berry gave an exclusive interview to the *National Enquirer*, which neglected to mention his fee, if any, for the interview, which had the usual lurid tabloid headline: HALLE BERRY'S SECRET TORMENT: DYING DAD BEGGING HER FOR FORGIVENESS BEFORE IT'S TOO LATE. The story quotes her father addressing his daughter directly: 'Halle, please forgive me and visit me before it's too late.' Berry adds that his doctors tell him he 'may' be dying, and he says his last wish is to see, or failing that talk on the phone to, his 'darling daughter'. The interview – which had him on death's doorstep but ran in 1998, five years before he died – also claims that he and his daughter were on speaking terms until she abruptly cut him off in 1996, contradicting Halle's claim that they hadn't spoken in ten years.

The rage Halle felt towards her father had been brewing for a long time, long before the disintegration of her marriage exacerbated that fury. She revealed in an interview with the black-orientated *Essence* magazine that she had already been in therapy for a year before the separation. 'It took me a long time to identify my father as the source of my pain. I used to think that it didn't bother me that he wasn't around. Now I know that I missed a lot because he wasn't there for me.'

The absence of a father during her formative years left her ill equipped to deal with adult relationships. The magazine quoted her as saying:

> I used to think not having a father was no big deal. You don't really miss what you've never had. But as I've gotten older I realize I *have* missed the influence of a father in my life and I think that's why I haven't dealt with relationships with men very well because I was never sure how to.

She clearly thought the opposite sex were not of this earth when she said, 'Men are like creatures from another planet.'

Her anger over the divorce was compounded by interviews her husband gave to the press during this desolate period in her life. The reputable *Us Weekly* claimed that Justice was suing his wife for alimony and even quoted him as saying, 'I figured since she wants to take all of my money, I should turn around and do the same to her.' *Jet* magazine also appeared to quote him on the subject of money: 'Halle wants a financial settlement to divorce me . . . it's in the range of a million.' He also allegedly accused his wife of being a cheapskate while they were together. 'In this marriage she never paid for one bill . . . I was good to this girl and she knows that . . . now she wants me to pay her money to get rid of her.'

In a letter to the editor published in *Ebony* magazine in May 1997, Justice denied the magazine's claim in its March 1997 issue that he sought money from his wife:

> As for the facts of our break-up, some of the points made in your article are incorrect and misleading . . . I am not seeking

alimony from Halle. Halle refuses to grant me a divorce until I grant her a financial settlement which is why our divorce process has taken so long. Our divorce could be finalized if we both just took what is ours and moved on, but unfortunately, this is not the case.

It got even uglier as monetary issues were replaced with accusations of physical violence and intimidation. On 1 October 1996 in Los Angeles Superior Court Halle successfully sought a restraining order against her husband that stipulated he stay 500 yards away from their home in Los Angeles.

The order was the result of two incidents that occurred in June and September 1996, when Justice turned up at their home to pick up some personal belongings. The incidents were described in ugly detail in Halle's request for the restraining order:

Approximately three months ago, Respondent [Justice] appeared at my home and demanded to come into the home. I contacted private security who came to the home and, without police intervention, both security individuals persuaded the Respondent to vacate the premises and to make arrangements, through his attorneys, to pick up whatever personal belongings he had left in the home.

The Respondent is a member of the Atlanta Braves baseball team. Although he is currently injured and not playing, he travels with the team. The team is in Los Angeles. Today, Monday, September 30, 1996, at approximately 9:30 a.m., Respondent again appeared at my home and demanded entry to the house allegedly to pick up some of his personal belongings. I was present and did not wish to see the Respondent. I arranged to have private security come to the home, my agent came to the home, my attorney came to the home and the police were summoned. Respondent's personal belongings are not at my home. All of his personal clothing and other items have been boxed and/or in the garage. There is absolutely no need whatsoever for Respondent to enter the house. He is more than welcome to have his personal belongings which are, as mentioned, in the garage.

It was my further hope that Respondent would act like a gentleman and arrange to come to the home at a mutually agreeable time to pick up his personal things. Unfortunately, Respondent did not see it that way. I personally heard the Respondent state to an unknown party on a cell phone if he is not given access to the home, he would 'break everyone of the fucking windows in the home and break the door down to get in because it was his home.'

As a result of the intervention of the Los Angeles Police Department, Respondent entered the garage under police supervision and was allowed to remove his personal items. He did not take all of the items which were then available for him to take.

I am in fear of my personal safety and well-being [emphasis added]. I live in an area that is rather isolated and secluded and on a very narrow street. I do not have personal security with me at all times. The Respondent has kept guns in the home in the past and I do not know if there are any in the home which he left since our separation.

There is absolutely no reason whatsoever that the Respondent should be allowed to come to my home for any reason. As indicated, I am more than willing to arrange a mutually agreeable time for Respondent to come to the home and remove the remaining personal items which he has there and which are already boxed and available for him to take.

For all the foregoing reasons, I respectfully request that the Court order that Respondent stay at least 500 yards from my residence at all times. For the record, I have no objections to those orders being made mutual in connection with our homes in Atlanta.

Reading the lengthy request for a restraining order, one can detect a combination of terror and anger on Halle's part. The terror may have been worsened by what psychologists call post-traumatic stress disorder. The possible presence of firearms in the house and Justice's alleged threat to break the windows in their home may have dredged up memories of the violent movie star who damaged her hearing and of her father hurling the family pet against the wall. In post-traumatic stress disorder, victims of past violent attacks often become supersensitive to new assaults or even the threat of one, and they relive the original trauma when the next one occurs.

A year later, Halle still felt traumatised by the incident that required a restraining order and incredibly enough revealed that she was still in love with the man who had caused her suffering. 'I think that was the lowest point. When I had to call the police and seek protection from a man I loved so much – that I still love – I thought, "This is rock bottom." ' When a magazine reporter expressed incredulity that Halle was still in love with Justice, she explained, 'I think once you really love someone, a little piece of you always will. So some part of me will love David until the day I die. That's just a fact.'

The frightening details of the restraining order quickly made it into the press, and Justice dismissed his estranged wife's fears and accusations. 'I pose absolutely no threat to Halle,' he said in a press statement.

(In March 2001, Justice's ex-girlfriend, Nicole Foster, filed a $5 million paternity suit against him and accused the baseball player of battering her, which Halle felt validated her own fears and justified her earlier request for a restraining order. In a lawsuit filed in Los Angeles Superior Court by a palimony attorney, Foster alleged assault that included striking her 'in the back of the head with a cordless phone, causing a large knot'. On another occasion, the suit alleged, Justice 'pushed her down onto their bed and held her down while choking her'. Foster was pregnant during the first attack, and later miscarried. Foster's suit also alleged that Justice had fathered her son, one-year-old David Justice Jr. At the time of writing it was unclear what the conclusion of the suit was.

(Now, and on the record, Halle wasn't the only woman to have felt the wrath of David Justice. 'I always worry that the world thinks I'm crazy,' she told the *New York Times Magazine*. 'It was nice to see that I wasn't,' she said, referring to the palimony suit's allegations.)

Although less traumatising than Justice's home invasions, the details of the divorce proceedings were just as ugly. Seemingly for no reason other than to embarrass Halle, Justice tried, unsuccessfully, to drag Wesley Snipes to a pre-trial deposition hearing in a desperate attempt to smear his wife with details of her romance with Snipes, all of which were irrelevant since the alleged affair with the actor had ended long before she had met Justice. On another quest, attorneys for Justice demanded that Halle surrender all correspondence with Spike Lee, Eddie Murphy and the musician Christopher Williams, all of whom were alleged to have been former lovers of his wife. Was Justice trying to paint his wife as a promiscuous adulteress? If so, there was no legal justification for the demands since in California, which has no-fault divorce laws, adultery, which Justice never accused his wife of committing, is not required to get a divorce.

Halle knew exactly what her soon-to-be-ex-husband was up to. In a pre-trial deposition, she said, 'I believe my husband, David Justice, is attempting to create a smear campaign.' The demands for her correspondence with various alleged past boyfriends she labelled 'a fishing expedition to support plaintiff's contention that she involves herself with certain men so that she may financially gain'.

The cold legalese of her response to her husband's attempt to pry into her prior love lives didn't reveal the underlying pain she felt about the accusation that she had been unfaithful. 'I think that hurt me the most,' she told *Ebony* magazine in 1997. 'Because if there is one thing I am about, it's monogamy.'

Examining Halle's life at this time, everyone but the totally heartless can't help but feel pity for the much-put-upon actress. While she was being terrorised at home by her husband, the behaviour of one of her co-stars on the set of *The Rich Man's Wife* may have been magnified by the post-traumatic stress syndrome she possibly endured since her sense of hearing had been beaten out of her, or by her earlier experiences of her abusive father.

In an industry where people rarely knock colleagues – because they may have to work together again in the future – Amy Holden Jones, the director of *The Rich Man's Wife*, said that Halle was a charming workaholic and another actor, Peter Greene, who played Halle's psychotic nemesis in the film, had an extreme style of method acting.

Jones said, 'Of course, she's stunningly beautiful. But the first day of shooting, what was probably most impressive, was how spectacularly well prepared she was. How professional she was, how meticulous she was. She still remains one of the hardest working, most professional actresses I've ever worked with. I think you might expect a diva of some kind with that much beauty. But she was every inch the hardworking professional trying to get the movie to be as good as it could possibly be. I don't think there was ever a single moment when she wasn't there on time, wasn't prepared.

'And it was a difficult picture for her in many ways. It was a hard point in her life. She was beginning to have problems with David Justice, and Peter Greene was quite difficult to work with for all of us, but Halle was right face to face with him all the time in the scenes with him where he's playing a violent character threatening her. It was certainly hardest on her.'

Greene, whose character volunteers to act out Halle's character's fantasy of getting rid of her abusive, alcoholic husband, is a method actor. According to Jones, he 'became very volatile whenever the cameras were rolling, such that occasionally Halle [seemed] actually physically afraid of him ... So here we have someone with less of a reputation and less of a name, luckier to get the part, who was constantly demanding more attention, time, care, to get him on the spot doing what he was supposed to do, than Halle who was always right there, doing anything she could. It really wasn't terribly fair to her.'

As if she didn't have enough on her emotional plate at the time with a violent husband and a threatening co-star, Halle's physical health by now had also deteriorated, Jones recalled. 'It was a very vigorous shoot. She had health issues that required her to really rest when she was not working and [limited] a little bit the hours she could work. So you had to be pretty sensitive about her privacy for those reasons. She really has to take care of herself to feel her best.'

Jones had no idea about the turmoil Halle was facing at home or that her marriage was falling apart. In fact, Halle and Justice still appeared to be very much in love. 'I really only realized that it was difficult later,' Jones said. 'She and David obviously loved each other. He came to the set several times. I was in her trailer when he hit a home run that won a game in the World Series, and she was so excited. They were such an extraordinarily beautiful couple. And he's a fascinating man, extraordinarily interesting to talk to. At the time I simply thought how wonderful that these two amazing people have each other. But you also always had to wonder how they could deal with so much separation. They were quite private about it – as far as I could tell they were dealing with it. It was only after they broke up that I realized she'd been coping with this stuff herself, behind the scenes.'

Halle herself commented: 'I wasn't good at being a baseball wife. I was lonely and really depressed and I wasn't a sports fan. David wanted me at the games with the other wives, so I went, but I had never watched baseball before, and, since we got divorced, I haven't watched a single game,' she said in 2001. In 1998, she complained that she was forced to learn about 'a game that to me was like watching grass grow'.

She had further exorcised her husband from her life by having his name, which she had had tattooed on her backside, trans-formed into a sunflower. 'I thought about it for a long time because I wanted my new tattoo to be reflective of where I've been, where I'm going, who I want to be,' she said in 1997. 'That's why I chose a sunflower. A sunflower opens and closes. Sunflowers go through the dark times and the bright times and through it all they always reach for the sky. I think that's what my life is going to be about. I don't expect things to always be sunny. Sometimes I am going to have to weather the storms. Sometimes I'm going to have to close up and go inward and deal with whatever is happening. But I know that the sun is always going to come, and when it does, like the sunflower, I'll open again and continue to grow.'

Turning Justice's name into a sunflower was also a symbolic way of convincing herself that the marriage really was over – 'Something that would help me get closure,' she said – when part of her still wanted the relationship to continue. 'For a long time I thought David and I had a chance of getting back together,' she said a year after their divorce. 'I'd be lying if I said there were not times when I didn't hope that David would wake up one day and say, "Let me go get my wife back." When I realized it wasn't going to happen, and maybe it was best for both of us that it didn't, I knew I had to do something that would help me say goodbye. Something that would help me get closure.' Getting David's name off her buttock seemed like a great way to close the deal. But it was easier to have a tattoo artist obliterate her husband's name than it was for her to get him and the failure of their marriage out of her mind. She began to obsess about the relationship, and obsession led not as in the past to thoughts about committing suicide, but to actually attempting it.

'When you go through a divorce, especially when you're not really the one trying to leave, you can feel worthless. I'd been used to succeeding. I thought I could not go on. After everybody said, "OK, she's fine" and went back to their lives and I was alone, that's when those thoughts came. I thought nobody is here, now I can do it.'

Those thoughts of hopelessness led to her garage, where she came close to taking her life. She described the incident with amazing candour in a 1997 interview with *Ebony* magazine:

I took my dogs, and I went in the garage and sat in the car. For two or three hours, I just cried and I cried. I thought, 'I can't face it.' I think that's the weakest I have ever been in my life. That's what the breakup of my marriage did to me. It took away my self-esteem. It beat me down to the lowest of lows – the gum on the bottom of David's shoe – that's what I felt like.

In 2000, Halle revealed that she did more than just sit in the car and contemplate suicide. She turned the key in the ignition and, as she told *In Style* magazine, 'I sat there for a while and I could smell the fumes.'

Without her husband, she felt like nothing. Six years later, she had enough clarity and distance to be even more upfront about her motivation for contemplating taking her life. 'I think I was still using men and my mate to identify who I was. And, when that was gone, then I was nothing,' she told the TV interviewer Barbara Walters in 2002.

But the same strength and steeliness that had made her career prosper stopped her from going out in a toxic blue cloud of carbon monoxide. 'Somewhere in my heart, I think I knew I didn't really want to end my life. I just wanted to end the pain.'

The deciding factor, however, was her selflessness and concern for others, in particular her mother. She told Walters, 'It's almost like I had a flash of, you know, that good angel and the bad angel on my shoulder . . . And something was telling on the right side of my brain, "Girl, don't do it! Girl, don't do it! Think of your mother . . ." I couldn't do that to her. So I got out [of the car].'

Vera Cirrincione provided a succinct postmortem on the divorce and its aftereffects: 'I liked David very much. I think he was very hurt by the divorce, but Halle was devastated.'

Vera's husband, Halle's manager and surrogate father Vince, played his paternal role and was alarmed enough by the devastation his wife described that he phoned Halle's mother in Cleveland, even though he said he didn't know Judith Berry very well, and said, 'I think Halle really needs you right now.' Recalling this in 1998, Vince said, 'And she came right away. This girl was in pain, and she needed someone close.'

Her mother's ministrations may have had a curative effect, because eventually Halle's enmity towards her husband turned to civility, and, after all the nasty pre-trial deposition mud slinging about past lovers, when the time finally arrived to come to terms, both principals behaved decently. 'We came to our own settlement,' Halle said. 'We had our lawyers leave the room, and we hashed it out together . . . and that conversation will remain private till the day I die.'

Although Halle Berry had been harassed by her husband and worried by a crazed co-star in 1996, the year wasn't a total disaster. In March, it was announced that Revlon was replacing its long-time 'spokesmodel', Cindy Crawford, with Halle. Her first commercial for the cosmetics firm aired during the Oscars ceremony that year. Halle had resisted hawking beauty products for years for two reasons. Until the Revlon offer came along, she had been asked to advertise cosmetics only for black women. Just as she wanted to play race-neutral roles in films, she didn't want to get stuck in the ghetto of black beauty products. Then there was the whole issue of fashion models and ex-beauty queens not being taken seriously as actresses.

But by 1996, Halle felt she had paid her dues and established enough credibility as a serious actress in more than fifteen films and TV projects that she could take the risk and trade on her beauty. Or, as she put it, she had by now overcome the 'stigma' of her beauty-queen past.

'I've been offered so many times to do this by cosmetic companies,' she said in 1996. 'And for so long I was trying to dispel my beauty-pageant model image to be taken seriously as an actress.' But, after playing crackheads with bad complexions and unfortunate bodily hygiene in *Jungle Fever* and *Losing Isaiah*, Halle was certain people knew she was more than just another pretty face. Because of those roles 'where I've shed the makeup and gotten some respect, I've gotten back to glamour and beauty and fashion. That's as much a part of me as anything else. That's just another side.

'Other companies wanted me for their black line of cosmetics, which is something I didn't want to do.' Revlon was the first firm that 'wanted me to be their spokesperson across the board, which is saying that black women are included in their major lines. We don't need a special line just for us. That's making us too different.'

At least one press critic felt Revlon hadn't made Halle 'different' enough from its previous – white – spokesmodels. Michael Musto, a columnist for the *Village Voice*, an alternative weekly newspaper in New York City, accused Revlon of lightening Halle's skin in its ads. 'They've made her even lighter than Ava Gardner in *Show Boat*,' Musto wrote, referring to the biracial character Gardner played in the 1951 film version of the Broadway musical. (Strangely, a few years later, when Halle appeared on the cover of *Vogue*, the editors for unfathomable reasons made her look much darker.)

The cliché that it never rains but it pours needs to be changed in Halle's case to 'when it rains on everyone else, a tsunami engulfs her'. As if she didn't have enough nightmares to wake up from at this time in her life, after surviving her husband, a scary co-star and a suicide attempt, Halle fell victim to a mugger. In mid-1997, she had gone on a shopping spree alone at the Beverly Center, a big grey elephant of a shopping mall between Beverly Hills and West Hollywood, California. It was closing time, late at night, as she walked towards her car in the catacomb-like garage, her arms overflowing with packages. She sensed but couldn't see someone following her. Then she felt this invisible stalker's breath on her back. Was she just imagining things? Had David Justice's violent intimidation made her paranoid, suspecting danger where it didn't exist?

Halle wasn't hallucinating. Her hunch turned out to be correct. Just as she reached her car, something sharp was pressed into her ribs. She would never know if it was a knife or a gun or a Keystone Mugger's finger, and she didn't really care. Wisely, she complied with her assailant's demand and gave him what he wanted: her packages, her handbag and all her jewellery. She even volunteered her car as a getaway vehicle, but the mugger, despite all the spoils that weighed him down, disappeared on foot.

Could 1997 get any worse? Yes, it could. In May, two of her four Maltese terriers, fifteen-year-old Bumper and nine-year-old Petey, were devoured by coyotes while they played in the backyard of Halle's home in the Hollywood Hills. Coyotes inhabit the lush vegetation of the hills that separate the Los Angeles basin from the San Fernando Valley, and rarely intrude on their human neighbours except when drought drives them down the hillsides in search of water. If a light snack like a toy terrier makes itself available, the famished carnivores won't pass it up.

Halle's pets had been outside for only a few moments when she looked out of the window and saw their eviscerated corpses. The *Star* reported that Halle was devastated by the fate of her dogs, one of whom she had had for twelve years. Quoting the usual all-purpose 'friend', *The Star* had Halle wailing, 'Oh, my poor, helpless babies! How will I survive without them? This is the worst thing that's ever happened to me!' *The Star* claimed she sobbed this lament to a friend, apparently unaware that much worse things had happened to her that year.

The Star also reported that her mother had flown in to comfort her daughter after the loss of Bumper and Petey. (As with most tabloid reportage, there was a kernel of truth amid all the journalistic fiction. Judith Berry had come to LA about this time, but it was to console Halle during her divorce, not the death of her dogs.)

The Times in London confirmed the tabloid report about Halle's terriers' untimely demise, but seemed disdainful of her pain. 'She was devastated when she found her two devoted dogs torn apart by coyotes. She has all the makings of a lifelong soap opera to rival Liz Taylor's.'

The divorce from David Justice became final in July 1997, and the fact that the ex-couple issued a joint press release suggests that the earlier rancour had evolved into a semblance of civility, although the terseness of the statement didn't reflect the anger and violence that had preceded it: 'Miss Berry and Mr Justice each have the highest respect for the other personally and professionally, and they both deeply regret that the marriage was not a successful one. They express their hope that they will remain good friends.'

Whether or not they were able to maintain a friendship after the restraining order and Justice's public criticism of his tantrum-prone ex-wife, Halle refused to criticise her former husband, and, when a reporter asked her if Justice had ever physically abused her, she was reluctant to say any more than, 'I like to think that he was a good guy. Just not right for me.'

Halle went back into therapy, and, less than a year after she had contemplated taking her life, she was again optimistic about her prospects. 'Today, I wouldn't even think about sitting in a garage with the car on. I know it sounds clichéd, but you have to find a way to hold on because time really does heal all wounds.'

Time and work. To heal her wounds and take her mind off morbid thoughts about the failure of her marriage, Halle threw herself into a mindless farce. Maybe laughing on the outside would somehow help her not to cry on the inside.

9. DEMOTED TO PRINCESS

Halle seemed to have realised that her next film, *B.A.P.S*, would provide an antidote to her poisonous mood after her divorce when she said in 1997, 'Doing a big broad comedy like this comes at an odd time of my life. Probably it's the best medicine I could ask for.'

B.A.P.S may have been medicinal for her spirits, but it was treated like poison by most of the critics. The *New York Post* described it as a *Dumb and Dumber*-style farce without having seen the film, and the newspaper was being kind compared with what other critics would call the comedy.

The term 'white trash' has been around for years, if not centuries, but if there is such a phenomenon as 'black trash' that's what Halle and her co-star Natalie Desselle play in the film, whose acronym stands for 'black American princesses', which at the beginning of the film they most definitely are not, although by film's end they become more than that.

Halle is Nisi, a Decatur, Georgia, waitress who hates her dead-end job and ne'er-do-well, perennially unemployed boyfriend. But she and her hairdresser friend Mickey (Desselle) share a dream of opening a combination restaurant and beauty parlour. The problem is that they have no money to make their dream a reality. Then they learn of a contest in Los Angeles to choose a dancer in a video by the rapper Heavy D with a prize of $10,000 – enough, these unrealistic dreamers believe, to bankroll their hybrid food-and-hair emporium. The running visual joke in *B.A.P.S* is that these two women are clueless fashion victims (the *LA Times* called them 'walking fashion crises), who have gold teeth that set off airport metal detectors, bouffant hairdos (Halle's is platinum white) so high that Roger Ebert of the *Chicago Sun-Times* said they 'pass beyond satire and into cruelty and appear to have things living' in them) and prehensile fingernails so long they could fish out that last, recalcitrant olive at the bottom of a tall bottle. Their couture would give the fashion designer Mr Blackwell palpitations so life-threatening he might retire the worst-dressed list he publishes every year after giving Nisi and Natalie a lifetime-achievement award.

When they arrive in Los Angeles, the girls become sidetracked from auditioning for the video by what seems like a much surer bet to acquire the seed money for their hash house/salon. The nephew (Jonathan Fried) of a dying millionaire (Martin Landau in a career-killing role) offers the girls $10,000 if they will make his dying uncle's last days on earth pleasant. No sex, just a walk down memory lane for the millionaire, who once had a rapturous affair with the family's black maid. The family made him dump the servant, a decision he's regretted ever since. Halle's character's job is to pretend to be the maid's granddaughter, which for some inexplicable reason will make the old man happy. The scheme, of course, turns out to be a scam by his nephew, but he in turn is outsmarted by these two supposed bimbos whose morality trumps the evil nephew's plans.

Halle hinted that she had misgivings about her role and the movie, but B.A.P.S was better than killing herself in the garage. 'In the beginning,' she said, 'I thought the characters were extreme. But then I went to a few places and discovered that this really wasn't all that extreme. These women do exist. And I think we were always mindful of not making fun of these women, by showing you how much fun they are. We wanted to show you how much they enjoy life and how free they are, who they are and their sense of style. It was a compliment for me to be allowed to portray one of these women, because we're sort of introducing them to people who didn't even know they're out there.'

Halle was only half joking when she implied in an interview with Roger Ebert that B.A.P.S may have saved her life. 'I hear about [the awfulness of] B.A.P.S all the time. Well, I'll tell you what. That came at a particular time in my life, right after the divorce. And it was either go to work in that movie, or hang myself with the shower curtain.'

In another interview, Halle suggested the real reason she agreed to participate in such inanity. She's a workaholic, and she needed a fix for her addiction. She hadn't come this far by resting on her laurels or taking time off even in the middle of a heartbreaking marital implosion. 'I thought, after doing three back-to-back projects, "Well, I need a break now." But after two weeks I got bored ... *B.A.P.S* is a big broad comedy for women, kind of like *Dumb and Dumber*, that slapstick type.'

The critical reaction to *B.A.P.S* made the critically reviled Jim Carrey vehicle *Dumb and Dumber* seem like a Feydeau farce by comparison when in debuted in the US on 28 March 1997. (It came out in the UK on 1 August of that year.)

But, while the critics were vitriolic, they seemed unable to resist Halle's beauty, which shone through her drag-queen hair and makeup, and some even praised her acting talent in a movie they felt unworthy of her.

The *New York Times*'s Janet Maslin called her 'one of the film's main comic assets. *B.A.P.S* [shows] that the star can be as funny as she is gorgeous (very). But it's still a weak and condescending comedy.' The industry trade magazine, *Box Office*, seemed almost blinded by Halle's beauty, but not blinded enough to accept the trash her gorgeousness was mired in: 'Halle Berry is very pretty. Even with gold teeth, prehensile fingernails, whipped cream blonde hair and a squeeze-tight orange plastic jumpsuit, she's still absolutely beautiful. Beyond that, *B.A.P.S* ... is bad, amateur, poor and silly.'

The usually kind Roger Ebert, who is married to a black woman and even likes black exploitation films, denounced *B.A.P.S* and awarded it zero stars, a rarity for the genial dean of American film criticism: '*B.A.P.S* is jaw-droppingly bad, a movie so misconceived I wonder why anyone involved wanted to make it.' (Ebert maybe hadn't been following Halle's messy love life and didn't realise the comedy was the cinematic equivalent of Prozac for the despairing actress.) Although it was directed by a black man (the comedian Robert Townsend) and written by a black woman (Troy Beyer), Ebert also found the film politically incorrect, an equal-opportunities despoiler for all races. 'My guess,' Ebert wrote, 'is that African-Americans will be offended by the movie and whites will be embarrassed. The movie will bring us all together, I imagine, in paralyzing boredom.'

Forewarned, the moviegoing public escaped boredom by staying away from the film, which grossed only $7 million in the US, but Halle got what she needed from the endeavour –

therapy. 'It's a comedy, and I wasn't feeling very funny [at the time], so I wasn't confident that I would be able to be in that space. But it turned out to be therapeutic. I could laugh and be silly and let go of all that negative energy,' she said.

B.A.P.S's surreal take on black people provided a distraction from the very real depression that had taken hold at this time in her life. 'I was just feeling like doing something, fun, big and broad, but then I thought it might be difficult for me to do this when I was going through a lot of pain and a lot of sadness in my life. It was helpful to go to a job where I laughed all day long. It was the best medicine.'

And, although 1997 was not a memorable year in her professional life, Halle got some good news at this time. She was able to stop injecting insulin due to a new diet that banned sugar.

She could also console herself that she would soon be starring in an ultra-sophisticated political satire with a screen legend, as well as a TV project produced by a mentor, best friend and the most powerful black woman in the world, Oprah Winfrey.

10. FRIENDS AND MENTORS

By 1998, at the ripe young age of 32, Halle Berry had nineteen films on her résumé – a bona fide movie star who could command $1 million per picture.

Except when they do a cameo or play themselves on a favourite soap opera or primetime series like *Friends*, movie stars almost never condescend to appear on TV. In Hollywood's rigid pecking order, film actors are several steps up the food chain from TV stars, and it's not a good career move, the conventional wisdom goes, to squeeze your big-screen persona on to the confines of the small screen.

Unless, of course, you're black, and especially if you're a black female. Then you grab whatever great role comes along and ignore the medium because you never know when the next quality script will be offered and you never know when you may get turned down for the forest-ranger part because there are no forest rangers of colour.

That was part of Halle's thinking when she deigned to do her second miniseries, *The Wedding*, which aired on 22 and 23 February 1998 on ABC. After being rejected as a forest ranger the year before, Halle wondered if she would be condemned to playing negative racial stereotypes. 'What can black actors be? Just drug dealers, pimps, prostitutes?' she asked one interviewer. 'Which is why *The Wedding* is so important. This little step helps dispel the stereotypes.' The miniseries depicted the antithesis of media stereotypes – a wealthy black family. Even the sulphurous reviews hurled at her last TV venture, *Solomon & Sheba*, hadn't soured the medium for Halle.

The other reason Halle didn't care whether or not television represented a step down was the name of the woman above the title. This time it wasn't Halle's. The full title of the multigenerational miniseries – primarily set in 1953 – was *Oprah Winfrey Presents: The Wedding*.

Winfrey, the American TV talk-show host and human conglomerate, officially served as executive producer on the project and unofficially did double duty as Halle's adviser, dear friend and a shoulder she cried on a lot during her break-up with David Justice and after the deaths of Bumper and Petey.

Halle has used the term 'mentor' to describe their relationship, but Winfrey felt the bond was stronger and familial and said she thought of the actress as her kid sister. 'I think she's one of the most genuine, sincere, committed and sweetest women I've ever met,' Winfrey said. And perhaps one of the most talented. Halle didn't even have to audition for the role. Winfrey's shortlist had only one name on it: 'Halle was it. I never considered anybody else,' Winfrey said, citing the actress's vulnerability as the deciding factor in giving her the part.

Although she played a wannabe princess in B.A.P.S. with a minuscule chance of ever becoming one, in *The Wedding*, Halle's Shelby Coles is as close to being a real BAP as anyone could get in 1950s New England: a member of a tiny minority of *haute* black bourgeoisie who managed to overcome the crippling prejudice of the time and prosper economically. Shelby is about to marry a white jazz pianist (Eric Thai) in a lavish wedding ceremony at a ritzy black enclave on Martha's Vineyard when a black man (Carl Lumbly) falls in love with her and tries to persuade the bride to jilt her bridegroom. In a refreshing rejection of stereotype, the white pianist is poor, while the black Coleses are rich.

Maybe it's just a bit of trivia or maybe it explains why Halle returned to TV, but *The Wedding* marked the first time Halle's character reflected her own racial background. The Coleses are light-skinned blacks, and they want to keep the family's complexion that way, so they welcome their daughter's white bridegroom into the family while being horrified by the black interloper who's trying to woo her away. Shirley Knight, a white actress, plays the Coleses' 98-year-old matriarch, the biracial daughter of a slave owner obsessed with keeping the black Coleses as white as they can possibly be.

The critics felt *The Wedding* was more than about skin colour, with *USA Today*'s Matt Roush writing, 'Love is anything but color-blind in *The Wedding* . . . but this ambitious multi-generational saga of interracial romance [goes] beyond a swoony skin-deep surface to address long-festering psychological issues worthy of an *Ordinary People*.' (The reference was to 1980's Best Picture Oscar winner.) And, as usual, the critic couldn't help but fall a little bit in love with the star of the show. 'Halle Berry is simply radiant as Shelby Coles, the pampered princess of an affluent mixed-race family in the Oval, an exclusive [and fictitious] minority enclave on the resort island [of Martha's Vineyard].'

Another reason movie stars avoid TV is that they fear that, once they appear on the small screen, they may never get out alive, or at least not escape with their film careers intact. It's almost a truism (with some exceptions like Jennifer Aniston and Tim Allen) that the public will not pay to see an actor in a cinema when they can watch him or her for free at home on TV.

In 1998, that was not a concern of Halle's, since right after *The Wedding* she returned to the big screen in a big-budget, high-concept political farce, *Bulworth*, starring opposite the screen icon Warren Beatty.

Beatty had the title role as California's Senator Jay Billington Bulworth, a bleeding-heart liberal running for re-election. Beatty's politician is a burned-out case, a man on the verge of a nervous breakdown. He feels he has sold out his political ideals to please the fat cats who finance his campaigns. In despair, he takes out a huge life-insurance policy, then hires a hit man to put him out of his misery.

The contract killing has a liberating effect on the senator, who decides that, since his days are numbered, he might as well start telling the truth on the campaign trail – poll numbers be damned. So, at one fundraiser, he asks wealthy members of the film industry how such 'smart Jews' can make such stupid movies. (This is as edgy and satirical the film is willing to be about the still taboo subject of Jewish influence in the entertainment business.) At a church in the Los Angeles ghetto, he tells his black audience that they will never achieve real political power unless they give more money to candidates. As his depression turns into a full-blown nervous collapse, the senator delivers campaign speeches using rap lyrics and wearing hip-hop couture – baggy clothes and a stocking cap.

At the black church, he meets a beautiful aspiring rap artist (Halle, typecast as the gorgeous one again), and they fall in love.

(Don't read the rest of this paragraph if you haven't seen *Bulworth* and plan to rent it on video or DVD.) Halle's rap persona turns out to be a front. She's really the hit 'man' hired to execute the contract the senator has taken out on his own life.

Beatty, who also directed and produced the film, explained why he cast Halle. 'I had seen her in a number of things and liked her very much,' he said. 'Bulworth was a guy who was depressed and took out a hit on his own life for insurance money, and he ran into somebody who changed his mind. She comes with that kind of firepower. She's a combination of a formidable actress with a sense of social fairness, genuine humility and she has a big sense of humor about herself. She crosses a lot of sectors and there is an inherent equilibrium about her that makes people gravitate towards her.' Her rapturous leading man predicted a long and flourishing career for his co-star.

Visitors to the set of *Bulworth* asked Halle the inevitable question about the fabled lady killer Beatty who if he, like Halle and her David Justice tattoo, had inscribed all his girlfriends' names on his backside, would have to hire a body double to accommodate the spillover or gain a lot of weight down there for a broader billboard.

Laughing, Halle told the *Los Angeles Daily News*, 'Whew! No, he didn't hit on me.' And that makes her the member of one of the most exclusive sororities in Hollywood – a beautiful woman Beatty hasn't made the move on. That didn't mean he wasn't immune to her charms. 'When people walk into a room and see Halle, they always laugh,' the actor said. 'They don't know how else to react. They're not used to seeing someone that beautiful.'

Although Beatty didn't become her lover, he has remained her career *consigliere*, someone she turns to – often the first one she turns to – in a crisis. 'Warren has stayed in my life,' she said in 2001. 'He's been a confidant. Any question I have he's got the answer.'

Although she had played inhabitants of the ghetto before, *Bulworth* was the first time she essayed rap. 'I'm just a glutton for punishment,' she said during an interview on the set of *Bulworth*. 'I just love doing different things, and that's the challenge of it. This was a lot of fun for me, another different character.' And a new hairdo, another first for the actress. 'I've got dreadlocks, up there rappin' like you wouldn't think I would be doing. And I found I had a little aptitude for it, though I couldn't make a living at it and better not quit my day job.'

There are no cows in *Bulworth* deemed too sacred for cinematic slaughter. The film lampoons rich Jews and poor black folk. Certain members of the black community were not amused by *Bulworth*'s lavish use of the 'N' word. At the end of the film, Halle's hit woman decides not to kill the senator because she's fallen in love with him and coos, 'You're my nigga.'

Despite language like that and the psychotic senator's allegation that poor black people are responsible for their economic misery, Halle was shocked that some African-Americans lambasted the lampoon. 'I thought black people would applaud this effort. But so many black people got offended by the movie or felt it aided in their oppression. I was baffled. My response was, "Lighten up and look at the message and don't get caught up in the stereotypes," ' she said.

Not all blacks were offended, however. The National Association for the Advancement of Colored People (NAACP) nominated Halle for its Image Award, which is bestowed for positive screen portrayals of African-Americans.

The critics and the rest of the public didn't share the NAACP's enthusiasm. *Bulworth* got mixed to poisonous reviews, and the $30 million production grossed only $26 million in the US after its release on 15 May 1998 and another £377,939 in the UK, where it debuted on 22 January 1999.

Writing in the Internet magazine *Slate*, David Edelstein said:

The years of [then President] Clinton's double talk have primed us all for *Bulworth*, but Beatty is peddling his own less flagrant brand of bull . . . [Senator] Bulworth might be white, but at heart he's supposed to be a *real nigger*. The movie's satirical vision never extends to its hero.

The *Los Angeles Times*'s critic dismissed *Bulworth* as an 'undisciplined . . . vanity project' mounted by the superstar, but Kenneth Turan couldn't resist describing Halle's rapper-turned-assassin as 'stunning', even with her dreadful dreadlocks and no makeup.

Salon.com called *Bulworth* an 'embarrassingly bad picture,' while the *New York Times*'s Janet Maslin expressed the minority opinion by raving, '*Bulworth* works, with both urbanity and *chutzpah*, by viewing political puppeteering with an all-purpose jaundiced eye.' Although the reviewer found Halle's role horribly underwritten, she couldn't avoid left-handedly praising the star's beauty. Janet Maslin felt that the script failed to explain the senator's attraction to the hit woman, but Halle's mug provided a paraphrasing of the adage that one picture is worth a thousand words – or in this case, one beautiful face is worth a thousand lines of pillow talk: 'In an otherwise sketchy and ambiguous role, Ms. Berry's Nina catches the Senator's eye . . . and he needs no further invitation to leap into Nina's world.' Dialogue wasn't necessary: Halle's expressive face said it all.

For her next project, Halle Berry chose a weird hybrid of a film – part biopic, part courtroom drama and part buddy movie, although in the case of *Why Do Fools Fall in Love*, the buddies were three black women, not the usual white cop/black cop Hollywood loves to pair.

Why Do Fools Fall in Love is the story of the fifties doowop singer Frankie Lymon (Larenz Tate) as well as the title of his one and only hit record, which the precocious but troubled black youth wrote and recorded in 1955 at the age of thirteen. Like too many other black recording artists, Lymon was ripped off by his white producer, Morris Levy (played by director Paul Mazursky), and saw very little of the money his solitary smash made.

In 1968, broke and only 26 years old, Lymon died of a heroin overdose, but during his short life he married three women without bothering to divorce one before marrying the next – or so they claimed.

In 1981, Diana Ross rerecorded 'Why Do Fools Fall in Love?' and turned it into a huge hit a second time. The film begins four years later with all three Mrs Lymons suing Morris Levy for the royalties they feel are due them as his wife and heir.

During the ensuing courtroom battle, Lymon's life is recounted in flashbacks dramatising this literally shooting star's career, the marital chaos he left in his wake, a stint in the army and finally the sad closure and peace of sorts he found at the end of a syringe.

Halle plays Zola Taylor, the lead singer of the fifties group the Platters and the first Mrs Lymon. Her relationship with the other two 'wives' – the sometime hooker Elizabeth Waters (Vivica A Fox, whom Halle would later praise and thank in her 2002 Oscar acceptance speech), the ultimate codependent who sells her body to pay for her husband's stay in rehab; and Emira Eagle (Lela Rochon), a virtuous waitress who marries Lymon during his army days – starts out as adversarial, since they all want a piece of their dead husband's royalties, but by the film's end the women bond and discover they have more in common than a messy marriage and greed.

Even though she wasn't the subject of the biopic, Halle received first billing. As usual, while panning the rest of the film, critics couldn't resist commenting on how terrific she looks, with one (the *San Francisco Chronicle*) calling her 'glamour queen Zola Taylor' and another (the *New York Times*) describing her as 'Zola Taylor, the glamorous lead singer of the Platters'.

Halle's looks were the only thing the critics found commendable about the production. The courtroom drama, which provides the movie's structure, doesn't contain much drama, or, as Roger Ebert said, 'By the end of the film, we're not even left with anyone to root for; we realize with a little astonishment, waiting for the court verdict, that we don't care who wins.'

The public didn't care, either, and, after its 28 August 1998 release in the US, *Why Do Fools Fall in Love* quickly disappeared from cinemas after grossing only $12.4 million. The movie proved even more evanescent than its subject's life and career.

Despite the failure of the Lymon saga, the biopic bug had bitten Halle, and her next project would recreate the story of another tragic singer whose life was also lost to drugs, but at least this time Halle would be the subject of the film. And it would receive a lot more attention and praise than the story of an obscure, one-hit wonder whose record remains more famous than he was.

11. INTRODUCING . . . ERIC BENÉT

Nineteen ninety-eight was a disappointing albeit busy year in Halle Berry's career, with two film flops and some arguable slumming on TV, but it was a pivotal year in her personal life.

This was the year that she met a handsome R&B singer with several hit records to his credit, Eric Benét. How they met depends on whom you talk to, including the two principals, who offer contradictory accounts.

Having been humiliated in the press during her break-up with David Justice, Halle had become inhibited about discussing her love life in public, which may explain why her recollection of her meeting Benét differs from his.

'I met him through a friend and she introduced us,' Halle told the UK's *Daily Mirror* three years after their introduction. She was apparently still hurting from the divorce and in no mood to be caught on the rebound by another man. 'We became mates and talked on the Internet a lot,' she said of the relationship, which began as a platonic one. But her intrinsically romantic nature – the mindset that prompted her to volunteer her phone number when all David Justice had asked for was an autograph – got the better of her common sense and wounded heart. And again Halle would become if not the pursuer at least the initiator of what turned into romance. 'There weren't any sparks or that mad passionate attraction in the beginning. Then one day I turned to him and said, "You know what? I think I love you." Eric's a very earthy, spiritual guy. I was also a fan of his music, so that helped. I've been on that [romantic high] before, thinking, "Oh, he's the one," and then a year later, I've realized he's not.'

In Benét's version of how they met, her romantic inclinations are even stronger. 'We used to go to the same LA mall,' Benét said. 'And she'd often come up and say hi. From there, we just began hanging out, and before you know it we were an item. Or make that *she* was the item. I was just the guy that the press would refer to as "Berry and her escort, an aspiring R&B singer." It was weird at first. Here I was used to getting most of the attention in whatever scene I happened to be involved in. But now I was dating a woman whose profile was 10 times bigger.'

(*Ebony* magazine offered yet a third version of how they met: backstage at one of his concerts in Los Angeles in 1998. The magazine said Halle was already a fan of his music even before they met.)

Benét was being modest and exaggerating Halle's prominence vis-à-vis his own impressive professional accomplishments. By the time he met Halle – whether it was at the mall or through a friend, he had released two hit albums, 1996's *True to Myself*, which went gold (half a million copies sold), and a year after they met he came out with an even bigger hit, *A Day in the Life*, which went platinum (a million copies). He had had less success as a member of a band named Benét, which included his cousin George and his sister Lisa, whose 1992 self-titled CD sold only 70,000 units.

Born Eric Benét Jordan in 1967 in Milwaukee, Wisconsin, the future singer had quite a different upbringing from the woman he would later woo and win. He was raised as one of four children by both parents in a middle-class household where music was part of everyday life. His father was a police officer with a taste for classical music and his mother liked to sing around the house.

Like Halle, he would experience some culture or racial shock when he transferred to an all-white grade school on Milwaukee's West Side; but, unlike Halle, he was never taunted by classmates because of his race. The easy-going youth seems to have got along with most people regardless of colour. 'I'd make friends with all sorts of kids: black, white and Asian. But back in my neighborhood people would see me with friends from school – some white or Asian – and be like, "Um, what's this about?" '

He was also something of a ladies' man early on, although Benét modestly insists he's not sexy. Women begged to differ. Benét claimed women were interested in him only because of his fashion sense. He favoured vintage clothes from the forties, a style he still effects today, and his sartorial image and conversational flair proved an attraction to many women. Benét neglected to mention the fact that he's also quite handsome. 'If you knew me back then, you would think it was hilarious,' he said, referring to his vintage duds. 'Girls always thought I was interesting and fun to talk to.' Still, there was no denying he was attractive enough to engage a stunner like Halle. 'If there is something about my exterior that brings people in to take a closer look at my interior, then it's a good thing.'

Overall, Benét encountered no major setbacks in his life until 1992, when all the bad things seemed to strike around the same time. After the relative failure of the Benét family album, he lost his record company contract. His father, to whom he had been very close, died of cancer. And his former girlfriend, Tami Stauff, died after five days in a coma following a car crash, leaving him to raise their thirteen-month-old daughter India, born in 1991, alone.

Crushed by multiple losses, Benét sank into a paralysing depression that made it impossible for him to pursue his recording career. To make ends meet and support his daughter, he took a dead-end job at UPS, the parcel-delivery service. Reflecting on that difficult year, he said, 'It was really the hardest thing I've ever gone through. Even losing my father, as traumatic as that was, didn't hurt as much because we at least knew he was dying. We all – my mom, my two sisters, my brother – got the chance to say goodbye. Tami and I weren't actually together at the time she died – I was seeing India every weekend – but the feelings of guilt, remorse, bereavement, depression just took over. Hearing India call my name when I came home from work at the end of the day felt like all I had to hang on to.'

His depression eventually lifted, and Benét returned to the recording studio, then hit the road performing his works. While on tour, he would leave India with his mother, but always with regret and a longing to return to his daughter. 'I love traveling all over the world, but nothing compares to hanging out at home with my daughter and family,' he said.

Perhaps because of her own fractured family, including the estrangement from her sister Heidi, Halle was ready to be absorbed by Benét's clan. She was even willing to play the role of India's mother. 'When I came into her life, India was seven,' Halle said. 'At that time girls start to need a mother, and not that Eric wasn't doing everything wonderfully, but he's still a man, so it's been a great thing for both of us.' She played the role so convincingly, India was soon calling her father's new girlfriend 'Mommy'.

India's appearance at this period in Halle's life was a case of perfect timing. 'When India came along, I was aching to be a mother. To love someone like that – she's just a joy.'

Cynics might say Benét caught Halle on the rebound from David Justice – and that such 'romances' have more to do with filling an emotional vacuum than providing a fulfilling and genuine relationship. Later events would prove the cynics might have been at least partially correct, but, at that moment, Halle had a handsome new man in her life, an adored and adoring surrogate daughter, and a career just as rich and about to get even richer.

By 1999, Halle seemed to have it all. Just the opposite might have been said about the person whose life she next chose to portray.

It took Halle seven years to bring the life of the fifties movie star Dorothy Dandridge to the screen, but she had been obsessed with the late actress's life even before then, ever since she first saw her on TV during a broadcast of the 1954 feature film *Carmen Jones*, which earned Dandridge a Best Actress Oscar nomination, making her the first African-American ever accorded that honour. (Dandridge didn't win the Oscar, which went to Grace Kelly for playing against type as a frumpy celebrity wife in *The Country Girl*.)

More than two decades after catching *Carmen Jones* on TV, Halle could still recall in detail the mesmerising impression Dandridge's image on the small screen made on her. 'I was in awe of her beauty, her talent, her charisma and the fact that she was a black woman,' Halle said.

'And there were other black people in an all-black musical. I'd never seen that growing up in an all-white suburb outside of Cleveland. I was fascinated by that.' Halle even credited Dandridge with infecting her with the acting bug. 'I knew I wanted to be an actress just because of her and how she jumped off the screen,' she said.

It's indicative of how few quality roles there are for black actresses that Halle had to beat a virtual chorus line of other prominent women, some with much more clout and money than she had in 1999, in order to play the title role in what would become the cable-TV movie *Introducing Dorothy Dandridge*.

When Halle asked her manager Vincent Cirrincione to buy the rights to *Dorothy Dandridge: A Portrait in Black*, written by Dandridge's manager, Earl Mills, she learned the book had already been optioned. When the film historian Donald Bogle's definitive biography came out in 1997, Whitney Houston's much deeper pockets bought up the rights before Halle could even engage in a bidding war that she no doubt would have lost anyway.

Another deep-pocketed pop star, Janet Jackson, was also developing a Dandridge biopic. Four others who wanted to play the doomed actress were the Oscar nominee Angela Bassett, who had proved she could do tortured black women to perfection as Tina Turner in the feature film *What's Love Got to Do With It*; the former Miss America Vanessa Williams; Jada Pinkett, who had special clout as Mrs Will Smith; and Jasmine Guy from TV's Cosby spin-off, *A Different World*.

But, as she had with everything else in her life and career, Halle kept on fighting, and, when the option on Mills's biography ran out in 1996, Halle was there, chequebook in hand. That was just the first of many hurdles she would successfully jump, including giving up her dream of turning Dandridge's life into a feature film and even giving up her salary when the project went over budget.

Then there was the question: Dorothy *Who*? While every black actress in Hollywood had heard of Dandridge, the white suits who dominate the movie business considered the subject matter too obscure, uncommercial and, considering the ending, literally and figuratively a downer. Halle described the importance of Dandridge among blacks and her relative unfamiliarity among whites when she said, 'So many people don't know about her. She was our Marilyn Monroe.'

(When Dandridge died in 1965 at the age of 42, the official cause of death was listed as a blood clot, although suicide or an accidental overdose of barbiturates may have been the real reason for her demise. Whatever killed Dandridge, after earning more than a million dollars during her three-decade career, she had exactly $2.14 in her bank account when she died. Friends have ruled out suicide because, at the time of her death, she was about to make a comeback singing at a prestigious nightclub in New York City. Despite the ups and downs of her career, Dandridge had everything to live for when she died.)

For seven years, Halle held meetings with studio executives and received a variation on the same rejection: 'Everyone said it's a great story and a terrific part, but it will never make any money. They told me, "This would make a lot of sense for you, but no sense for us," ' Halle said.

The actress refused to give up. If the movies didn't want Dorothy Dandridge, maybe TV would, and she was right. The American cable channel HBO finally gave the project the green light. HBO was the perfect home for Dandridge's story, which was too sexually explicit for network, advertiser-sponsored TV, and its subject matter too obscure and risky for a movie studio and the exorbitant costs of releasing and marketing a feature film. HBO also had a reputation as the Tiffany's of TV, best exemplified by its current hits, *Sex and the City* and *The Sopranos*, which the *New Yorker* has called the best television series of all time.

Sweetening the deal, HBO gave Halle final say by also making her executive producer, but there was a catch. To produce an expensive, decades-spanning period film with lavish musical numbers, HBO was offering a budget of only $10 million. However, when Halle is given lemons, she not only makes lemonade, but creates a lemonade-stand empire with franchises throughout the US and abroad.

During the lonely years the project smouldered in development hell, Halle used the time productively to devour every bit of information she could find about the forgotten star and to learn difficult new skills. Fortunately, despite the passage of almost half a century since Dandridge's heyday, many of her peers and collaborators were still around and happy to help a respectful, hard-working young woman who was trying to honour their deceased colleague's career and accomplishments.

'The producing end was like seven years on it,' she said. 'We tried to shop it around for seven years, so that was a long prep time. But playing her, I had to work on singing, I had to learn to tap-dance, all that physical stuff I had to do beforehand. I did a lot of interviewing with Sidney Poitier, Diahann Carroll, people who actually knew her. I spent a lot of time with these people, picking their brains, and sort of trying to get to the essence of who she was. And, if I could find some common thread that they all referred to about her, I could use that.

'Basically, I read every book, every piece of material there was to read about her. I saw tons of pictures. Her manager, who is still alive, let me go through everything that he had of hers, from personal private letters to all of her clothes, her jewelry he had, her family photo album. It was just about finding every piece of information I possibly could before the shoot.'

Everywhere she looked and asked, Halle kept turning up the same thing: lifelong despair. 'I would ask each one of [Dandridge's associates], "If you can tell me one thing that I must capture in order to play her, what would that be?" They all said the same thing: "You have to find a way to be sad on every day, in every scene, in every moment. And always try to hide the sadness. And you'll get the essence of who she was." I thought because they all said that, it had to be true. I thought that was a good place for me to start.'

Halle interviewed Dandridge's co-star in *Carmen Jones*, Harry Belafonte, who encapsulated the tragic actress's life as, 'Right person, right place, wrong time.' That became the advertising campaign slogan (slightly changed to 'Right *woman* . . .') for the HBO production, which debuted on 21 August 1999.

Much has been made of the similarities between Dandridge's life and Halle's, but, while eerie, they are superficial. The most profound difference: Dandridge was a victim; Halle remains a survivor. 'In my own life,' she said, referring to Dandridge's fate, 'I am determined to change the ending. The biggest difference between us is I know I will survive. I can make more things happen for myself. I produced this movie. In her day, actresses weren't having a say' – not to mention receiving executive producer credits.

It is true that both women were born in Cleveland, even in the same hospital. Both were raised by single parents. Both were light-skinned, although, unlike Halle, Dandridge was not biracial despite the fact that her skin was a shade or two lighter than

Halle's. Both stars were beautiful, but, when you compare photos of the two women, you don't have to be a Halle groupie to note that she is even more attractive than her fifties doppelgänger.

Both women repeatedly made poor choices in men who abused them; both had famous husbands. (Dandridge's first husband was the tap dancer Harold Nicholas [Obba Babatundé in the film], half of the Nicholas Brothers tap-dancing team. Both had to fight hard for the few roles available to black women; both made Oscar history. And, in a really spooky *Twilight Zone*-moment, Halle discovered when she tried on one of Dandridge's gowns that both women not only were the same dress size but even had the same tiny waist. (Halle usually has to have her dresses taken in at the waist.) 'Earl [Mills] had an original dress of Dorothy's, and he wanted me to have it for inspiration while we were shooting. And I put in on, and it fit me perfectly. It was very eerie,' she said. 'It felt like validation. I thought, "If the dress fits, wear it." '

Martha Coolidge, who directed *Introducing Dorothy Dandridge*, felt the gown and the role were both a perfect fit for the actress. Coolidge said Halle was a 'dead ringer' for Dandridge. 'The day she put on the Carmen outfit, we all got chills. She also captured her spirit, her talent, and her sensitivity,' Coolidge added.

But her experience with the dress went beyond the bizarre and bordered on the paranormal. 'I was very protective of the gown, and so I kept it in the den, covered in plastic. One day I heard this crackling noise, and I thought it was water boiling on the stove.' The sound, however, seemed to emanate from the den. 'When I looked in, I saw this tiny little baby doll dress floating in front of Dorothy's gown. It freaked me out so much I just ran up to my bedroom and curled up in a ball.'

Then she contacted Geri Branton, Dandridge's closest friend and former sister-in-law (she had been married to Harold Nicholas's brother). 'I was so hysterical I ended up calling Geri. I asked her if she'd ever had anything like that happen to her. She said, "Honey, I talk to Dottie [Dandridge] all the time, and if she is at your house she means you no harm." I thought about it all night and decided that I was supposed to use the dress for inspiration . . .' Temporary inspiration. The apparition or hallucination or whatever it was so unsettled Halle that, when she finished the film, she returned the dress to Earl Mills, even though he had given it to her to keep.

There were other close encounters of the weird kind that made Halle feel some divine or supernatural hand was guiding her to resurrect the spirit of the forgotten star. When she watched TV, the lights in her home would flicker on and off. On other occasions, she would come home and find the patio door wide open. After that, Halle made a point of not only locking the patio door but also turning on the burglar alarm before she went to work on the movie. When she returned home, the door was ajar again.

If Halle was hallucinating these things, she wasn't alone in her dementia. Her housekeeper swore that, whenever Halle left home, she would hear dragging noises coming from Halle's bedroom. 'Every time she heard them, she'd find the chair in front of my vanity pulled out,' Halle told a reporter from *Ebony*, who asked if she felt that Dandridge's ghost had been occupying her chair. 'All I can tell you is [the housekeeper would] push the chair back in, and the next time I'd go out, it would be pulled out again.'

Regardless of their apparent supernatural connection, the two actresses inhabited different times, indeed different universes. Simply put, 1999 was not 1955 (the year Dandridge was nominated for an Oscar for *Carmen Jones*), and, happily for Halle, the parallels between her life and Dandridge's break down upon closer examination.

Although Halle, like Dandridge, came from a broken home where her father left the family early on, Halle at least was raised by a mother she still adores. Dandridge's mother (Loretta Devine) actually left her husband, a minister, to cohabit with a female lover whom Dandridge called 'Auntie' (played by actress LaTanya Richardson). (In an early scene in *Introducing Dorothy Dandridge*, 'Auntie' performs a graphic 'gynaecological examination', shoving her hand up Dandridge's dress and claiming it's to make sure she's still a virgin after a date with a boy. She was.)

Dorothy Jean Dandridge was born on 9 November 1922, in Cleveland's City Hospital five months after her mother, Ruby, left her husband to move in with her female lover.

In *Dorothy Dandridge: A Biography*, the film historian Donald Bogle felt that the actress was practically cursed from birth, and the curse would pursue her throughout a troubled career, relationships and a death that came much too early but that in retrospect seemed almost preordained from the beginning. Bogle wrote:

> The little girl . . . would grow up to be one of her era's most beautiful women and its most famous African-American actress. [She] came into the world at the heart of a heated domestic discord that, in its own quiet, unstated way, would trouble and haunt her. Throughout her life, she would struggle to understand her parents but mainly to piece together the puzzle of her own identity; to discover and define herself first as a daughter, then as a sister, a wife, a mother, an actress, and finally as the most unexpected and elusive of personages, a black film star in a Hollywood that worshipped her, yet at the same time, clearly made no place for her.

Quoting that passage, Christopher John Farley writes in *Introducing Halle Berry*, a 2002 biography of the star, 'The same . . . could have been written about Halle.'

Not really.

Dandridge's mother had been a singer and an actress before morphing into the stage mother from hell who pushed her two daughters into show business early. Dandridge was only four when she began appearing in vaudeville as part of a song-and-dance team, the Wonder Children, with her sister Vivian (Cynda Williams), who seems to have spent most of her life resenting her better-looking sister's superior talent and career.

As a teenager, while Halle was content to run for prom queen and class president for self-validation, Dandridge was singing on the radio and became a regular on the radio-turned-TV series *Beulah*. Her sultry voice and style made her a nightclub favourite as well.

In 1937, Dandridge moved to Hollywood, a fantasy-nightmare universe where the only work women of colour could get in the movies was playing slaves and maids – *fat* slaves and maids.

Above Before her acting career took off, Halle was a successful model, coming second in the Miss USA and third in the Miss World contests.

Above The production notes for the comedy *Strictly Business* describe Halle's character, Natalie, as a 'mind-numbingly beautiful waitress'; the hero, an up-and-coming executive (Joseph C Philips), falls madly in lust with her.

Below With Damon Wayans. Although Halle plays a stripper/prostitute in *The Last Boy Scout*, she refused to take her clothes off for the role.

Above left Halle was the first actress to read for the role of Eddie Murphy's sweet-tempered girlfriend in the romantic comedy *Boomerang*; after her audition, Murphy insisted on casting her on the spot and refused to consider any other actress. Halle told the *Daily Mail* that Murphy seemed bitter and unhappy despite his success.

Above right Although she's biracial herself, for the title role in the TV miniseries *Queen*, in which she plays the daughter of a slave and a white plantation owner, Halle had to have her skin lightened.

Left In *Father Hood*, Patrick Swayze is a small-time crook who abducts his children from an abusive foster home; Halle plays the newspaper reporter who chronicles his flight from the police.

Right In *The Flintstones*, Halle joked that she integrated Bedrock as Fred Flintstone's (John Goodman) sexpot secretary, Sharon Stone.

Below Halle played the second crack addict of her career in *Losing Isaiah*, in which she loses custody of her son (Marc John Jeffries) after dumping him in a trash bin so she can score some drugs.

Right Executive Decision featured Halle as a fearless flight attendant, Jean, who tries to prevent terrorists from blowing up a 747 filled with nerve gas above Washington DC.

Left Based on a true story, *Race the Sun* starred Halle as a science teacher who motivates her failing students by involving them in a science project in which they build and race a solar-powered car across Australia.

Left In *The Rich Man's Wife*, Halle had the title role of a woman married to an abusive alcoholic. When he is killed by a psychotic stranger (Peter Greene) she meets in a bar, she finds herself a prime suspect in her husband's murder.

Right The comedy *B.A.P.S* (Black American Princesses) stars Halle and Natalie Desselle as poor Southern girls who come to Los Angeles with the dream of opening a combination restaurant-beauty salon.

Above In *Bulworth*, Halle was the hit woman hired by a burned-out suicidal US Senator (Warren Beatty) to kill him.

Above Director Martha Coolidge huddles with Halle on the set of *Introducing Dorothy Dandridge*, the story of the first African-American to win a Best Actress Oscar nomination, and who died of a barbiturate overdose at the age of 42. Halle played the title role.

Above In *Introducing Dorothy Dandridge*, Klaus Maria Brandauer played Otto Preminger, Dandridge's mentor and tormentor, who directed her in *Carmen Jones* – the role for which she earned her Best Actress Oscar nomination.

Above Halle looked like a punked out Bride of Frankenstein in the role of Storm, a superhero mutant who can control the weather, in *X-Men*.

Below In *Swordfish*, a renegade government agent (John Travolta, left) and his assistant (Halle) bribe the world's greatest computer hacker (Hugh Jackman, seated) to break into a government bank account containing $9.5 billion.

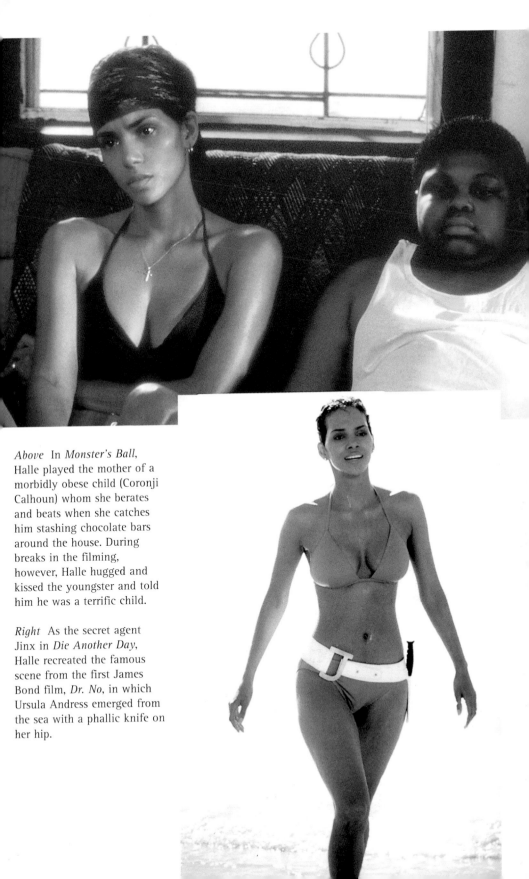

Above In *Monster's Ball*, Halle played the mother of a morbidly obese child (Coronji Calhoun) whom she berates and beats when she catches him stashing chocolate bars around the house. During breaks in the filming, however, Halle hugged and kissed the youngster and told him he was a terrific child.

Right As the secret agent Jinx in *Die Another Day*, Halle recreated the famous scene from the first James Bond film, *Dr. No*, in which Ursula Andress emerged from the sea with a phallic knife on her hip.

Left Halle with first husband, David Justice, then an outfielder for the Atlanta Braves baseball team.

Below Halle's mother, Judith, brought her two daughters up on her own, making sure Halle knew exactly who and what she was; she was pleased when her daughter met Eric Benét, the man Halle called the 'joy of her life' during her Oscar acceptance speech.

It is worth digressing a little here to note that, four years later, Hattie McDaniel would become the first black woman to win an Oscar for playing not only an antebellum mammy, but a character whose actual name was Mammy. And even the hefty McDaniel wasn't porky enough to satisfy the studio's conception of what black women were supposed to look like. MGM made her gain even more weight before they'd let her play Scarlett O'Hara's uppity duenna.

MGM, the studio that bankrolled *Gone With the Wind*, continued to micromanage McDaniel's behaviour, and on 29 February 1940, during the Oscar ceremony at the Coconut Grove in the Los Angeles Ambassador Hotel, the acceptance speech she delivered had been ghostwritten by a studio publicist on the orders of the MGM chief Louis B Mayer, who had sternly admonished McDaniel beforehand not to digress from her canned speech by a single word.

Before moving to Hollywood in 1931, McDaniel had been a prominent vocalist, touring nationally since 1915 with Professor George Morrison's Orchestra. By the time she appeared in *Gone With the Wind* in 1939, McDaniel had worked in almost twenty films, but then, as now, underemployment of minorities in the entertainment industry was so pervasive that the actress sometimes found her life imitating art, and, during lean periods, this on-again-off-again movie star who had become internationally famous playing maids actually worked as a domestic, a cook and a washerwoman. When black activists took McDaniel to task for playing so many servants on film, she said *playing* a maid paid much better than being one. In 1951, McDaniel was still playing maids, but this time she was the first African-American to have the title role in a TV sitcom, *Beulah*, which co-starred Dorothy Dandridge. Even in death, a year later, McDaniel continued to blaze trails of sorts, being the first African-American to be buried in Los Angeles' Rosedale Cemetery.

Now with the advent of Dorothy Dandridge, Hollywood found itself confronted with a slender, wasp-waisted, drop-dead-gorgeous black woman. The movies didn't know what to do with this antithesis of the stereotype, so they cast her in bit parts, beginning with the Marx Brothers classic, *A Day at the Races*, in 1937. She wouldn't get more work until three years later, yet another bit part in the drama *Four Shall Die*.

Dandridge's film career drifted for the next two decades while her hypnotic voice paid the bills with nightclub appearances until she met the man who would arguably be both the best and worst thing that ever happened to her. Part Svengali, part Lothario, he would make her and break her and then remake her – turn her into a major-motion picture actress and destroy her emotionally.

Dandridge's mentor and tormentor was Otto Preminger, a Viennese Jew who had left Europe in the wake of the Nazis, and, like so many of his brilliant co-religionists including Ernst Lubitsch and Fritz Lang, found a safe harbour in Hollywood as a director. He failed to extend the same courtesy or refuge to the woman who became his protégée and lover.

The impossible-to-cast beauty drifted for more than a decade in Hollywood until she hooked up with Preminger, who cast her in an all-black musical based on Bizet's opera, *Carmen*, with the film version relocated to a Florida military base during World War Two. Oscar Hammerstein II wrote the lyrics. (Much to her frustration and despite her ability to pack nightclubs with her singing voice, the studio insisted on having her songs dubbed by the mezzo-soprano Marilyn Horne.)

Contemptuous of Dandridge from the start, Preminger (played by Austria's Klaus Maria Brandauer) didn't feel she had the acting talent to pull off the role, but Dandridge persisted, at one point barging into his office dressed as Carmen. They soon became collaborators off the set as well, with Preminger promising to divorce his wife and marry Dandridge, a promise he never intended to keep and made only to placate her.

Director Martha Coolidge believed Preminger 'really loved her. But she was unwilling to go on being his mistress. There was no place for it to go.' Their relationship was further complicated by the fact, which the movie fails to mention, that Dandridge became pregnant by Preminger and had an abortion.

Preminger, however, was not a complete monster. He negoti-ated a salary for his lover on a par with what white superstars like Ava Gardner were making at the time, but gave her awful advice when he told her to turn down the role of a concubine/slave girl in the film version of *The King and I*, which enraged the studio chief Darryl Zanuck (William Atherton), who blacklisted Dandridge after her refusal. In a weird version of political correctness, Preminger justified his advice by saying Dandridge shouldn't play a slave. The pre-McCarthy-era blacklist Dorothy found herself on was a powerful club wielded against recalcitrant stars by the studios. In the days before stars were free agents, even the biggest names typically signed a contract with a specific studio that bound them for seven years, and the studio also had the option of dropping actors every six months during this period of indentured, albeit well-paid, servitude. Stars were most often let go before their seven years were up owing to waning box-office appeal, but the seven-year clause was also used to keep skittish stars in line. If an actor refused to appear in a movie whose script he or she found lacking, the studio would often put the performer on suspension, and this downtime did not count as part of the seven-year obligation. Famous victims of this blacklist included Katharine Hepburn and Bette Davis. Hepburn put her periods of enforced unemployment in Hollywood to good use and returned to her first love, the Broadway theatre.

After she had made history as the first black person nominated for a Best Actress Oscar (for *Carmen Jones*) and had become the first black woman to appear on the cover of *Life* magazine, Hollywood still didn't know what to do with Dorothy Dandridge. Halle described Dandridge's predicament in an eerily prophetic interview with the film critic Roger Ebert only a few weeks before she herself received an Oscar nomination. 'Part of it is when she got nominated for that Oscar. After that, Hollywood really didn't know what to do with her. She had nowhere to go and that eventually ate her alive. Hopefully, today – well, Angela Bassett got nominated a few years ago, and it didn't eat her alive, so I know it's a new day. There are more opportunities for us.'

A year after losing the Oscar to Grace Kelly, Dandridge starred in *Island in the Sun*, and in a film version of the Gershwin musical *Porgy and Bess* in 1959, also directed by Preminger.

Dandridge's private life was as maddening and frustrating as her professional one. Her marriage to Harold Nicholas produced a severely retarded daughter who had to be institutionalised and made a ward of the state when her mother could no longer afford to pay for private care.

Her second husband, a white nightclub owner named Jack Dennison (DB Sweeney) was rumoured to be physically violent and ran through his wife's fortune in a get-rich-quick real-estate scam in Arizona (which might better have been called a get-*poor*-quick scam). The scene where Dennison knocks Dorothy to the ground and continues to beat her up is almost too painful to watch, must have been even harder to play, and one wonders whether the assault, even though faked, stirred up any flash-backs to the man who beat Halle so badly she was left partially deaf.

While researching her role, Halle met Geri Branton, who insisted that Dandridge's death in 1965 was an accident, because she was about to appear at the legendary Basin Street East nightclub in New York City and had no reason to take her life. Perhaps she was engaging in a bit of projection, but Halle disagreed with Branton about the cause of Dandridge's death. Based on her own experiences, Halle knew that you can have a heavenly career while living in hell. Dandridge's barbiturate overdose may have been accidental rather than suicidal, but Halle believed Dandridge had been committing suicide incrementally for years. 'After playing her life, being on that roller coaster with her, and living through the struggles that I've faced, I believe she was slowly killing herself for a long time,' Halle told *TV Guide* in an interview during which she revealed that she had contemplated suicide herself after her break-up with David Justice. 'I had a really hard time. I've felt that kind of despair. Luckily, I got through it. Now I know I would never take my life. But I know how it feels to feel that much hurt.'

Before filming ended, the expensive project had exhausted its meagre $10 million budget without filming some scenes Halle felt crucial to the story, including Dandridge's iconic walk down the red carpet at the 1955 Academy Awards ceremony.

Halle believed in the project so much, she put her money where her heart was – on the screen. 'Halfway through shooting, we had sort of gone through our budget. And there were some scenes that

I felt really passionate about that were not in there. So I gave up my salary to have those scenes in there. It was like a labor of love,' she said.

HBO, however, was so pleased with the completed product that it returned her salary.

Confronting Dandridge's demons led Halle to confront her own. Despite the story's tragic conclusion, *Introducing Dorothy Dandridge* had a purgative effect on a relationship that had troubled her since childhood. She finally made peace with Jerome Berry. 'I realized I had to stop blaming my father for all the things that were wrong in my relationships,' she said. 'While his absence was part of it, a lot had to do with me and my choices. I would *say* I wanted somebody real in my life, but then I would be attracted to the superficial.'

Introducing Dorothy Dandridge received ecstatic reviews. *Newsweek* magazine called Halle's performance 'an evocation of the beauty and electricity that made Dandridge a legend'. The *Hollywood Reporter* wrote, 'Halle Berry sparkles as Dandridge.' *Daily Variety* perhaps underestimated Halle's physical allure when it said, 'As Dandridge, Berry is sexy and innocent, breathy and every bit as beautiful as the glamorous star. The role is that of a damaged beauty – but not a pitiful one – and Berry hits the mark whether it calls for sultry or sullen.'

Major awards followed the critical praise: five Emmys – including Best Actress in a Miniseries or Movie – a Golden Globe and Screen Actors Guild award in the same category, and (if ever an actress deserved one) an NAACP Image Award for a positive portrayal of a person of colour.

During her acceptance speech at the Golden Globes banquet, she took time to thank the man in her life, the sort of man Dandridge herself could have used in her own life. While Benét beamed as he sat in the audience, Halle said, 'You have given me the biggest gift anybody can give me and that is the freedom to be who I am and for loving me anyway.'

Halle generously felt that Dandridge was also being honoured by all the awards she received for playing her. During her Golden Globes speech, she expressed gratitude that, unlike Dandridge, she was 'the right person, the right time'.

Afterwards, Halle said, 'That was the first time I had ever been nominated for an award like that. And playing her life, there were so many opportunities she was not afforded. A lot of it had to do with the state of racial relations in the country at the time. And the other 50 percent was her own masochistic personality that led to her own downfall, you know? When I was up there [at the Golden Globes podium], I felt very much that I was sort of up there for her. For all the things that didn't come her way, that in that moment I felt that it was really about her, too. Because I was winning for telling her story. I felt very much like it was her moment.'

Perhaps the most gratifying praise – more than any award – came not from a reviewer or a guild but from someone who was more an expert on Dandridge than any professional critic: Dandridge's former sister-in-law and confidante, Geri Branton.

Halle said 'Geri was in the hospital having hip surgery when I first went to meet her. It was really emotional because she said to me, "You were always the one I wanted to play Dorothy, and, now that you're sitting in front of me, I see you're the only one who can play her." When she said that, I just broke down crying.' After seeing the finished film, Branton was even more generous in her praise. 'She absolutely stole the essence of Dottie and she truly understood her,' Branton said. 'I felt like, for two hours, I'd been visiting with Dottie again. She would have been so pleased, so happy.'

But no amount of praise – from critics, friends and peers – could completely remove the fear that haunted both Dandridge and Berry: the eternal quandary of finding employment in a white-dominated industry. Halle said, 'After *Carmen*, Dorothy had a hard time figuring out what to do. She got to play this glamorous leading lady. But then there were no other roles to support who she had become as an actress. After playing Dorothy, I'm kind of in the same place. When I'm looking for another part, I'm coming up so short.'

Halle wasn't being overly pessimistic about her career prospects. Compared with the variegated role she had just played, her next job would demonstrate that, while she may have won a major battle by bringing Dorothy Dandridge's life to the screen, she would still have to keep waging the same war to land a part commensurate with her talent and track record.

But, while Halle was obsessing about finding another movie role with as much as substance as Dorothy Dandridge, she found something much, much more critical to occupy her thoughts and consume her life.

12. THE ACCIDENTAL MOTORIST

It was perhaps the most important event in her life, and Halle Berry doesn't remember any of it. She had just returned from five months in Canada shooting a film and had spent a long night that meandered into the early morning hours catching up with a girlfriend, drinking cola and snacking on crisps.

Her friend lived only two blocks from her home, but, like everyone else in LA, Halle drove there and back. At 2.30 a.m. on 23 February 2000, at the intersection of Sunset Boulevard and Doheny Avenue (which separates Beverly Hills from West Hollywood's Sunset Strip), all Halle can remember is 'vaguely seeing something dark' on her right.

She also doesn't remember how she got there, but the next thing she remembers is being back at home. A short while later, Eric Benét returned from a singing gig. Benét was shocked at what he saw. Halle had a deep gash in her forehead, a gash that cut almost clear to the bone.

Halle was obviously in shock, but her boyfriend knew what to do. He drove her to the accident and emergency department at Cedars-Sinai Medical Center, about five minutes away, where it took twenty stitches to close the wound. (She would later require plastic surgery to hide the gash because, like that of many black people, her skin tends to form keloid, or raised, scars.)

There was another auto-accident victim at Cedars-Sinai at the same time, a 27-year-old realtor and accountant from Santa Monica, California, named Heta Raythata, who was being treated for a broken wrist. Dazed and in pain, Raythata was still enough of a celebrity watcher to look up and think to herself, Wow! That's Halle Berry! I've just seen a real live movie star.

Raythata couldn't know at the time that surprise would be only one of the many emotions she would eventually come to feel about the movie star.

According to a report released by the West Hollywood Sheriff's Department, Halle had been behind the wheel of a white Chevy Blazer, a car rented in Benét's name, when she crashed a red light on Sunset Boulevard and ploughed into a 1996 Pontiac Sunfire driven by Raythata. The realtor's car became a twisted, burning wreck, and she was trapped inside.

Then, according to an eyewitness in a car just behind Raythata, Halle drove off, leaving Raythata entombed in the smouldering hunk of metal. The witness, Marisa Meola, described the scene in an interview with *People* magazine: 'It was a brutal, brutal car accident – that girl could have been dead. To drive away with blatant disregard? I'm extremely outraged.' Meola called an ambulance, which took Raythata to the same hospital where Halle was being treated.

When Raythata finally learned the identity of her mystery hit-and-run woman, she was no longer starstruck. Raythata described her emotions to *People* magazine after the collision: 'I really was very petrified when that smoke was going up in my car and I could not get out. I was totally scared.' Eventually, Raythata's terror would turn into anger when she recounted how her car spun around after being struck. 'She left me in a smoking car wreck. She sped off and made no attempt to get me help. I find everything she has told the press regarding her alleged blackout completely unbelievable. The fact that the DA let her off easy and she is trying to portray herself as a victim is very saddening.'

Actually, Halle was portraying herself only as a victim of amnesia. The normally caring woman couldn't understand how she could have been the culprit in a hit-and-run accident. It just wasn't the sort of thing she would do. Her fifth-grade teacher and guidance counsellor, Yvonne Sims, also found Halle's behaviour inexplicable but she came to her protégée's defence. 'Just trying to figure out what this was all about brought on a lot of very deep soul searching. The idea of leaving someone without any help is so unlike Halle. That's what was so disturbing to her,' Sims said.

Doctors had an explanation for Halle's behaviour after the collision, but it didn't satisfy Raythata, who filed a civil suit against Halle, but it did offer some solace to the actress. 'I've spent two months basically talking to doctors and experts,' Halle told *In Style* magazine in July 2000. 'Football players get banged in the head and then go on to play a whole game because it's *overlearned* behavior. Driving the two blocks to my house, that's overlearned behavior for me.' Neurologists she spoke to told her that others who had suffered head trauma as serious as hers often lose track of days. Halle said, 'I had lost track of 20 minutes. I had also lost track of my self-esteem.'

Medical opinion backed up Halle's contention and proved she wasn't making up excuses to mitigate inexcusable behaviour. Dr Jamshid Ghajar, president of the Brain Trauma Foundation and a neurosurgeon at Presbyterian-Cornell Medical Center and Jamaica Hospital in New York City, confirmed that Halle may have been suffering trauma-induced amnesia when she left Raythata behind. 'It's quite possible she could drive away and not remember it,' he said. 'Concussion and head-injury victims have trouble laying down the memory. They do things in the moment, in a state of shock, and then can't remember.'

To her credit, while in the hospital emergency room, Halle reported what little she could remember of the incident to an off-duty policeman. The following morning, she called the West Hollywood Sheriff's Department to make a formal report. *Us Weekly* claimed the police learned who had hit Raythata by identifying debris from Halle's car left at the site of the accident.

The next day, sheriff's deputies turned up on her doorstep and confiscated her rented vehicle. They did not arrest her, but Halle was terrified by the unfolding nightmare. 'I've never felt so much fear in my entire life. There's something very disarming about when the police show up,' she said.

A spokesperson for the Sheriff's Department inflamed the situation by incorrectly classifying the accident as a 'hit-and-run felony', but, since Halle had reported the accident to the police officer at the hospital, the District Attorney's office decided to charge Halle with a misdemeanour. Even so, she was still terrified. If convicted, she faced a maximum penalty of one year in Los Angeles County Jail and a $10,000 fine.

On 8 March 2000, Raythata also slapped Halle with a civil suit that accused her of gross negligence and infliction of emotional distress. Raythata said that 'injuries to her neck, back and other parts of her body' had left her permanently disabled. In the suit, which was settled on 7 May 2000 for an undisclosed sum, Raythata also alleged that Halle was 'driving and operating the

Blazer at the time of the collision while under the influence of alcohol or other controlled substances'.

Halle released a statement denying she had been intoxicated when the accident occurred:

> To the extent that Halle may have been responsible for anyone else's injuries, she intends to do what she can to make things right. But there is absolutely no evidence indicating that drugs or alcohol played any part in the accident and to insinuate otherwise is both dishonest and reprehensible.

After undergoing the humiliation of being booked and finger-printed at the West Hollywood sheriff's station, on 31 March 2000 Halle was indicted on charges of leaving the scene of an accident.

On 10 May 2000, Halle pleaded no contest in the Beverly Hills division of Los Angeles Superior Court. She was fined $13,500 and ordered to perform two hundred hours of community service. After sentencing, Halle told the judge, 'Your Honour, I would like the court to know that I have taken this matter very seriously from the very beginning. I am pleased that this can be resolved. And I'm very relieved that the true facts of this case have finally come out.' This was an apparent reference to the bogus allegations that she was a repeat offender (though she had been involved in a previous collision, the resulting suit had been dismissed) and drunk driver. The fine was a pittance to someone in Halle's financial bracket, and she didn't find the community-service part of her sentence burdensome, either. 'Community service is part of what I do anyway,' she said. 'Resolving it this way allows me to take some responsibility. Now I can look at myself in the mirror. Thank God no one was killed. There were blessings that night.'

An inveterate optimist, Halle managed to find something good in the nightmare she had endured. After telling the *Washington Post* she planned to do the right thing with Raythata, she said, 'I feel really good about the way [the criminal suit] was resolved. The judge said in open court that rumors [about Halle] of other hit-and-runs were false, as were the drunk-driving and drugs rumors.' The accident and its aftermath, she said, made her 'appreciate all the great things that were happening in my life' – in particular the man who had stayed by her side from hospital room to courtroom, Eric Benét. 'We got to affirm our love and support of one another.'

(Two years later, Halle felt great empathy for another celebrity in jeopardy, Winona Ryder. The celebrity shoplifter, Halle said, 'lives at the corner of my street, so I left her a couple of notes along the way. I just wanted to tell her, "Hang in there. Hold your head up, and it's all going to be OK – no matter how it works out." ')

Her legal ordeal was over, but the public humiliation would play itself out for more than a year, climaxing with Halle as the butt of a joke in front of an audience of literally one billion viewers. She would also become temporarily anorexic and lose fifteen pounds.

Hosting the Oscars in March 2000, Billy Crystal told a joke that, as with many jokes, must have seemed hysterical to everyone but the person at whose expense it was made. Between awards, Crystal cracked, 'I just want you all to know they're gonna make a sequel to *Driving Miss Daisy*. But they're going to make it an action film, and they're going to have Halle Berry drive.'

Half a year later, Halle was still traumatised by the Oscars jibe, which she had seen live on TV. 'I was watching the Oscars, and at that point I was deep in my sickness and not eating and feeling devastated and thinking the whole world is laughing at me. I was sitting there crying, like, "They're making a joke and this is my life and I didn't do it." '

Her *Bulworth* co-star and mentor Warren Beatty helped put Crystal's cruel comment in perspective when Halle called him the next day and lamented, 'Did you hear that terrible thing he said about me last night?' Beatty responded, 'I was there, yeah, I heard it.' Halle waited for words of comfort to follow, but Beatty remained silent. Finally she asked him, 'That was awful, wasn't it?' Beatty said, 'No, Halle, all that means is you're famous. Get over it.' If only Halle had known that, two years hence, her name would also be the buzz of the Oscar ceremony – but this time for glorious rather than ignominious reasons!

Other so-called friends were even more blunt and revealed themselves to be of the fair-weather variety. 'People I thought I was very close to distanced themselves from me,' she said. 'It was very subtle. No one put me down or belittled me. It was the things that people *didn't* say. The support that wasn't offered. They were real happy to stay around when things were great, but when this happened it was like I had the plague.'

But Halle managed to find something relatively positive amid the rejection. 'I got to see who loved me – not Halle Berry in Hollywood, but Halle Maria who grew up in Cleveland. I got to see who liked being around for the parties and accolades and who was really invested in me.'

Halle also feared that the hit-and-run allegations would end her career and her love life. 'I thought the public would abandon me. That I'd lose everything I've worked so hard for. That I would be tainted goods' – especially with the most important person in her life, Eric Benét.

Halle's fears were not ungrounded. She had endured a history of men who abandoned her – first her father, then Wesley Snipes, David Justice. Now, she worried, it was time for Eric to do the same vanishing act.

Her relief was almost palpable when she described what happened against all her expectations. 'As the weeks went by, I thought, "Wow, he's still here!" And not just loving me. Loving me hard. He showed me when I was too weak to stand, he would hold me up. When I was too fragile to think, he'd help me figure it out. When I was too scared to face another day, he'd be my rock.'

When another crisis occurred – and this time not one of her making – Halle would remember the man who had driven her to the ER and stood by her in court and in private. She would remember and forgive and possibly even forget.

But that crisis, which would arise at her greatest moment of triumph, was two years off. And, in the meantime, Halle had a job to do. Lots of jobs. Her worst fears – unemployment, abandonment – never materialised as she found herself starring in the biggest commercial hit of her career.

13. ACTING UP A STORM

Although a police investigation ruled out the possibility that Halle had been driving under the influence when she slammed through the intersection on Sunset Boulevard, another possible cause was never even brought up: exhaustion may have distracted her.

The day before the crash, she had just returned from a gruelling five-month shoot in Canada on the sci-fi film based on the 27-year-old Marvel comic book series, *X-Men*. Halle performed a lot of stunts in the $75 million film à la *The Matrix*, and it may have been nothing more than weariness that propelled her Chevy Blazer through the intersection.

While the cause of the accident will always remain a mystery, almost as mysterious is what prompted her to take a minor role in a movie geared towards a cult audience straight after she had established her credentials as a serious actress and swept all the awards for her last project, *Introducing Dorothy Dandridge*.

No interviewer has ever had the chutzpah to put that question to her, although she has indirectly answered it many times by saying she's just not offered the serious roles that go to white actresses of similar talent and box-office clout.

'I can't get a starring role in a film because there aren't any available [for black women],' she said. 'I look at films like *You've Got Mail* and think, "I could have played that role." But black women don't even get a reading.'

If Halle was lowering herself by appearing in a kids' flick based on a comic book, at least she was in good company. In fact, it may have been the quality of the rest of the cast in addition to the perennial problem of underemployment among black actors that made her feel that, if she was going to slum, she'd slum with the best, including an Oscar winner, an Oscar nominee and two veterans of Britain's Royal Shakespeare Company, who signed on to the story of mutant superheroes and villains who slug it out over the fate of the world.

Owing to a genetic mutation, the title's X-men and -women have evolved into creatures with super powers that include telekinesis, telepathy, shape shifting, control over the weather and all sorts of other talents that terrify the rest of the human race, which treats them like pariahs. A rabid minority even seeks to exterminate them. The good mutants, led by Professor Charles Xavier (Patrick Stewart), hope to reach a peaceful rapprochement with the opposition, which includes a McCarthy-like senator (Bruce Davison) who wants to round up the mutants and put them in camps or worse. The villain, Magneto (Sir Ian McKellen), hatches a plan to turn the entire human race into mutants, thus ending the discrimination and the witch hunt. Unfortunately, in the process of turning them into mutants, Magneto's invention kills the subjects of his mad experiment.

McKellen is a Shakespearean actor, two-time Oscar nominee and a star of the *Lord of the Rings* trilogy, in which he plays Gandalf. Before he became famous as Captain Jean-Luc Picard of the starship *Enterprise* in *Star Trek: The Next Generation*, Patrick Stewart spent nearly three decades with the Royal Shakespeare Company. The supporting cast boasts Anna Paquin, who won a Best Supporting Actress Oscar in 1994 at the age of twelve for *The Piano*, playing a good mutant named Rogue, whose 'super power' is more like a curse. Anyone she touches goes into a coma or worse.

X-Men was directed by Bryan Singer, whose 1995 film, *The Usual Suspects*, won an Oscar for Best Original Screenplay.

With an A-list cast and a stylish director like Singer, it's easier to understand why Halle agreed to play what is really not much more than a bit part as the mutant Storm, who, as her name suggests, can use gale-force winds and lightning to fight the bad mutants. Storm wears an unflattering platinum-coloured wig that looks as if it had been ripped off Veronica Lake's head and a series of smashing black-leather outfits that display her perfect body to perfection, and seem jointly inspired by the trashy lingerie clothing store Frederick's of Hollywood and the Marquis de Sade's tailor.

Halle didn't mention the impressive pedigrees of her co-stars or the director when she explained why she agreed to appear in a bit of fun like *X-Men*. As she has in the past, sometimes the actress almost engages in self-parody when she brings up race to explain her career choices. Playing Dorothy Dandridge involved her in the commendable task of resurrecting a forgotten victim of Hollywood racism. Hurling thunderbolts and beating the hell out of a bad mutant named Toad (Ray Park) would not on the surface seem to make much of a political statement, but that's not how Halle saw the role. For her, *X-Men* was more than a fantasy. It was an allegory about the oppression of minorities.

'The mutants face many of the same obstacles that we do as African-Americans,' she said. 'They're struggling to find equality within a society of non-mutants who fear them out of ignorance. Storm reminds everyone that, if anything is to change, we have to educate people out of their ignorance. That's the substance of who Storm is for me.'

She also implied that her role was somewhat autobiographical. 'I love the theme of the film, which is accepting people for who and what they are. That felt really important to me, especially being a minority in this country. Anyone who has ever felt like an outcast will appreciate the story.' Growing up biracial first in an all-black inner-city neighbourhood and then in an all-white suburb made Halle feel like an outcast.

After her car crash and the media orgy it generated, she could identify with the oppressed supermutants even more. 'When your life gets exploited to the extent my life has been, you feel like a freak.' Her wardrobe helped make Storm a little less cartoonish and the absence of ridiculous superhero costumes such as capes and tights also elevated the film's IQ, she felt.

'I really loved that we weren't wearing silly suits and spandex. [The director] really made them real people. I'm hoping that in the next one they'll even become more real.'

A consummate professional, Halle always arrives on the set of a new film thoroughly prepared, her role obsessively researched. But for *X-Men* she was under director's 'orders' not to do any homework on Storm's illustrative origins. A visitor to the set asked if she had immersed herself in the past 27 years of Marvel's *X-Men* comic books to help flesh out Storm. 'You know, I didn't. Bryan [Singer] didn't want it. [Those] people who didn't grow up with the series, he didn't want us to. He wanted us to read the script and read the back story that he provided us. Because all the characters changed from decade to decade, and they sort of went off in different directions. So Bryan thought it would be really confusing and that it would be easier, and I think, rightfully so, not to go back and read all the comic books.'

Eventually, Halle's perfectionism compelled her to disobey the director and take a peek at Storm's comic-book past. 'I read some [comic books] that pertained to the way he wanted Storm to be played.'

Whether it was a message movie or kids' stuff, X-Men was an unqualified hit soon after it came out in the US on 14 July 2000, followed by an 18 August debut in the UK.

Halle wasn't the only one who may have taken the movie too seriously. The New York Times complained, 'It's disheartening to see the X-Men depicted so earnestly here . . . Clumsy when it should be light on its feet, the movie takes itself even more seriously than the comic book and its fans do, which is a superheroic achievement.' But even the dismissive New York Times critic Elvis Mitchell, who is African-American, couldn't avoid investing the film with a social significance that might have even made Halle blush when the critic felt Professor Xavier and Magneto were stand-ins for the two most important participants of the civil-rights movement: 'Listening to [Stewart and McKellen] trill their vowels at each other is one of the movie's few pleasures, since the parallels to the Rev. Dr Martin Luther King, Jr. (Xavier) and Malcolm X (Magneto) are made wincingly plain.'

While Rolling Stone's Peter Travers felt that the Australian actor Hugh Jackman 'sizzles' as Wolverine, a mutant with self-healing powers and razor-sharp claws of stainless steel, he felt the movie 'sucks' (his term) when it came to the supporting cast, and singled out Halle's role for lacking substance. 'What sucks? Since it's Wolverine's movie, any X-Men or Women who don't hinge directly on his story get short shrift. As Storm, Halle Berry can do neat tricks with the weather, but her role is gone with the wind.'

The San Francisco Examiner's Wesley Morris was apparently a Halle Berry fan and resented her being upstaged by Wolverine and Rogue. 'It's a little disappointing that the film is so hung up with Rogue and Wolverine. We never learn just how powerful Storm is.' Actually, we do. Although she's a minor member of an ensemble cast for most of the film, and what little dialogue she's given is not much more than exposition, she and Toad do enjoy one hand-to-hand duel on top of the Statue of Liberty. Halle, looking like a punked-out Bride of Frankenstein with hair extensions made of lightning, demonstrates that Toad's talented tongue, which can perform even better stunts than the Budweiser frogs, is still no match for a superheroine with Zeus-like prowess. Storm kicks mutant butt.

So did the movie. *X-Men* easily earned back its $75 million budget by grossing $157.2 million in the US and another £14.8 million in the UK with a worldwide total of $300 million.

The message of *X-Men*'s success wasn't lost on studio executives, who, in the words of *Newsweek*, caused a 'superhero stampede' by commissioning four movies based on Marvel comic books to be released in 2003: *Daredevil*, *Hulk*, *The Punisher* and, of course, the superheroes who started the current stampede, *X-Men 2*.

X-Men became Halle's biggest commercial success to that point in her career, and she may have felt that adding a blockbuster to her résumé would make it easier to be considered at least for more serious fare and crack open the door to auditions that she had been previously shut out of.

Or maybe she just liked action flicks, because she didn't use her newfound clout after *X-Men*'s success to make one of many pet projects – including a movie about the sixties radical Angela Davis, which she has often said she hopes one day to star in – or some other film of substance.

Halle Berry, box-office star, was on a roll, and she rolled right into another action film, although the audience for this production was more mature.

But before the workaholic actress began work on what would be her 26th production after little more than a decade in the business, there was some personal business she had been postponing for several years – and now, she decided, it was time to take care of it.

14. GRATUITOUS PRUDERY

Eric Benét had proposed to Halle on 14 August 1999 on a special night in her career, at the premiere of *Introducing Dorothy Dandridge*, in her hometown, Cleveland, and she accepted – but only the engagement. Although they had been a couple for more than two years, Halle was in no rush to take the next step – to the altar.

After the violent end to her marriage to David Justice and a series of abusive lovers, Halle waited almost another two years after her engagement to finalise the deal with Benét. She had enough self-knowledge to realise she had to break a cycle of destructive relationships.

As far back as 1994, she was aware of the problem and vowed not to repeat the patterns of the past – a vow she would not keep. 'I had to hit rock bottom before I stopped it,' she said. 'My nickname used to be Boo-Boo because I'd ask my friends, "Who do these guys think I am, Boo-Boo the Fool?" ' ('Boo-boo' is American slang for a minor mistake or blunder.) As she defined the term, she would remain 'foolish' for quite some time to come.

According to a fellow musician who claimed to know Benét well, the singer had led a monkish life after being traumatised by the death of his ex-girlfriend in a car crash. The friend, Demonte Posey, told *People* magazine in 2000 that Benét had stopped dating until he met Halle – a six-year hiatus from romance. 'He was holding out for the right situation,' Posey insisted.

At the turn of the new year in 2001, Benét and Halle finally decided to get married and set the date for late January. Halle had made the decision with the enthusiastic endorsement of one of Benét's biggest boosters, his future mother-in-law, Judith Berry, who said, 'I love Eric. He's so grounded, so spiritual, so compassionate.'

After the media frenzy surrounding the car accident, Halle was wary of the press. In September 2000, when asked about the future of her relationship with Benét, Halle had stonewalled: 'I am going to be private from now on about my love life.'

And she was. There was no public announcement of the impending nuptials, which took place on a secluded beach in Southern California on 24 January 2001. The few guests in attendance had learned about the wedding when bottles arrived in the mail containing an invitation that indicated where and when to turn up. The 'message in a bottle' presented the upcoming wedding as a *fait accompli* and read, 'To have life we were chosen by love to share eternal love we've chosen each other. Introducing Mr and Mrs Eric Benét Jordan.'

They called their wedding rings 'eternity bands'. Benét wore a vintage white silk suit. Halle's gown, which she described as 'simple, not very weddingish', was designed by Rista Rose. There was a quickie, two-week honeymoon in the Maldive Islands in the Indian Ocean.

The couple waited until the following month before letting the public know of the marriage. On 6 February 2001, during a party for four hundred people hosted by the Black Entertainment Television network on a soundstage in Burbank, California, Halle went on stage to introduce the evening's musical entertainment and mentioned, almost in passing, 'Here is my husband, Eric Benét.'

Halle had had such a good time making *X-Men* that she not only signed on for a sequel, but for her next project chose another action flick, co-starring again with *X-Men*'s wolfish stud, Hugh Jackman. But, if she was hoping to add another commercial hit to her résumé for future clout in getting noncommercial prestige productions off the ground, she blundered in choosing *Swordfish*.

The film's high concept, cast and producer must have made it seem like a sure thing to Halle. (It also didn't hurt, no doubt, that *Swordfish* represented her biggest pay day to date: $2.5 million.) The producer was Joel Silver, the man behind *The Matrix* and the first two *Die Hard* movies. It also boasted the services of a superstar who is also a respected actor, John Travolta. And it was set in the up-to-the-minute world of cyberspace.

Travolta played Gabriel Shears, a renegade government agent who knows the whereabouts of $9.5 billion the US government has salted away to fight terrorism as part of a defunct project code-named Swordfish. Travolta's turncoat character knows where the money is, but he can't get to it because it's buried deep inside a computer, and he needs a hacker to access it. So he sends his assistant, Ginger (Halle), to enlist the services of the greatest hacker of all time, Stanley Jobson (Jackman), recently released from prison and desperate to regain custody of his daughter from his vindictive ex-wife. Ginger offers him $100,000 for the job, which he takes so he can hire a lawyer and be reunited with his child. The urgency of hacker Jobson's financial desperation is underlined by the fact that his wife is now married to the biggest porn producer in Southern California, and Jobson isn't crazy about his daughter's new stepdad. After Jobson accepts Shears's offer, he's given a pre-employment test of sorts. Shears puts a gun to his head and, to test both Jobson's hacker skills and powers of concentration, he makes the hacker break into a Department of Defense computer while a woman fellates him. Talk about on-the-job training!

Halle made one new fan while making *Swordfish*, co-star John Travolta, who, like almost everyone who meets her, can't resist commenting on her looks, but the actor also felt there was a great deal more behind the pretty face and hourglass body. 'She knows that the acting comes first and the looks come second. Looks are the icing on the cake. The cake is your ability to interpret a character.'

Swordfish has state-of-the-art stunts and special effects, including an opening scene in which a hostage is blown to pieces, which required three months of planning and thirteen synchronised cameras shooting the mayhem from various angles. The finale has a bus filled with hostages, suspended in the air by cables attached to a helicopter, until one cable breaks and the bus crashes into a skyscraper. The film also boasts glamorous locations all over the world, from the Cote d'Azure to downtown Beverly Hills, which may explain why the film cost a whopping $80 million to make.

In the opening scene, Travolta delivers an unintentionally ironic line, 'You know the problem with Hollywood? They make horse pucky [shit].' Critics said the same thing about *Swordfish*, which grossed only $69 million in the US after its opening on 4 June 2001, not enough to recoup the cost of making it. (It did an additional £7 million when it was released on 27 July 2001 in the UK.)

But as usual, while panning the film, the critics couldn't resist commenting on Halle's lovely presence in it. Although it compared *Swordfish* to the smell of rotting mackerel and labelled the film a 'dirty fairy tale', the *Los Angeles Times* called Halle's Ginger 'a sexual tornado'. Her nudity was the first thing mentioned in the *San Francisco Chronicle*'s review, which began: 'Despite the presence of Halle Berry's bare breasts . . .' The female film critic for Salon.com also couldn't help but comment on Halle's breasts, but absolved the actress of any complicity in pandering to the public by insisting that her acting ability stopped the nudity from being gratuitous, even though Halle herself had used that term – 'gratuitous' – in an interview with *Cosmopolitan*. But Salon.com's Stephanie Zacharek wrote:

> Berry is proving herself to be increasingly confident and gutsy. In one scene, she flummoxes Stan [Jackman] by flashing him, and the camera, much less of a gentleman than Stan is, lingers on her breasts for much longer than it should. But the look on Berry's face – direct, challenging and unapologetically sexy – keeps the moment from feeling sleazy. Berry plays the scene so that the movie around her is the thing that looks cheap. She struts off with her dignity intact.

Swordfish's only immortality may reside in trivia books, since its subtitle might have been 'Introducing Halle Berry's Breasts'. It marked the first but not the last time Halle would go topless in a film. She had resisted nudity throughout her career until *Swordfish*. Way back in 1991, when she had much less clout than she did in 2001 coming off *X-Men*'s superhuman box-office returns, she refused to strip in *The Last Boy Scout*, even though she played a stripper! After agreeing to appear in the film, but before she signed the contract, she was shocked to discover in the fine print her role required nudity. Although *The Last Boy Scout* would pair her with one of the hottest actors at the time, Bruce Willis, and although she was short of funds, she dropped out of the project, only to be lured back with the promise that a body double would do the stripping for her.

In 1995, she offered one reason for her reluctance to do nudity when she told the newspaper *Newsday* that she didn't feel comfortable with frontal nudity because her breasts were 'really not that special. They're average. I don't know why they want to see them.'

But a year earlier Halle revealed a more compelling reason that had less to do with insecurity about her looks and more to do with being a good wife. Her explanation also suggested a certain Svengali influence her then husband, David Justice, had on her life. Halle told *Ebony* she had promised her husband that there would be no nude scenes. 'That's important to him and I have to respect his feelings because I know there is no way I could watch him do the things I do on film. I couldn't stand to see him kissing somebody else. So, if all I have to do is say, "OK, I won't take off my top," that seems like a small price to pay for all the love and support he gives me.'

Ironically, in contrast to Justice's prudery, it was her next husband's broad-mindedness that freed Halle enough to enable her to flash her breasts for all of three seconds during a sunbathing scene in *Swordfish*. A book covers her chest, then suddenly, for no reason, she lifts the book and reveals that she's topless.

Halle offered conflicting explanations for her change of mind. In an interview with the *New York Times*, she said, 'I told Joel [Silver, the producer] that I didn't want to go topless, and he listened to my reasons and told me to go ahead anyway, and I did.' Had Halle caved in to the demands of a mega-producer with the power to make or break careers, most importantly, hers?

She told *Essence* magazine a different story:

My husband, Eric, was actually the one who told me to stop worrying about pleasing others and to start pleasing myself. I had been concerned about a partially nude scene in the film *Swordfish*. Before that, I had refused to do it. My refusal was strange, because I've been comfortable with my sexuality for a long time. Throughout my home I have sculptures and paintings celebrating the naked body, which I feel represents freedom and grace. So my refusal wasn't based on personal preference, but rather a voice inside my head that said, 'Your people would crucify you for this.' I felt myself carrying the hopes and dreams of my community on my back.

Unlike Justice, Benét told his wife to please herself, not him or any imagined moral majority of black people. 'I remember saying to Eric, 'What will people think?'' she told *Cosmopolitan* in 2002. 'He replied, "You don't have a problem with nudity. Do you really want to be held hostage by what other people think? I thought you were through with that." And he was right.' Halle also offered up politically correct terms like 'self-empowerment', but, before she started to sound too pretentious, she undercut all her sociobabble by poking fun at herself in the *Cosmopolitan* interview. 'It was also like, "I better do it before my tits are on my knees!"'

Halle relied on Benét's career advice about *Swordfish*'s nudity, but, when she tried to return the favour, he ignored her. In September 2001, Benét had a small role (tenth billing) in the film *Glitter*, which starred Mariah Carey as an aspiring singer desperate to make it in the music business. *Interview* magazine asked her if her husband had sought any acting tips:

> You know, he didn't. And I was really disappointed, because I wanted to help him in some way because he's [always been] so strong for me. I include him so much in my decision-making and my career, and when he didn't ask for advice or help, I felt a little crushed. But I realized, after the fact, just like I don't want to sing in front of him, he didn't want to act in front of me. But I told him, 'Next time let me help you decide what movies to do!' He kind of played himself, and I think he would have been able to handle playing something that was not himself, something really different.

(Maybe Benét should have sought his wife's professional help after all. The $22 million *Glitter* grossed only $4.2 million in the US.)

Yet another and more cynical explanation for why Halle went topless was generated by the Hollywood rumour mill, and it was a rumour Halle was quick to spike even if it meant badmouthing one of the most powerful men in Hollywood. The producer Joel Silver claimed he had changed her mind by offering her half a million dollars for three seconds of nudity. 'No way!' Halle said. 'The producer told the press . . . that I got more money for the part – $250,000 for each breast. Totally not true! I would sell these babies for much more money than $500,000. But it made for great publicity.'

When her friend and former co-star Samuel L Jackson claimed in an interview that Halle's nude scene added an extra $20 million to the film's box office, she told the on-line magazine *Cinema Confidential*, 'So when is he going to bare his stuff to make 20 more million dollars . . . if that's what he thinks that does!'

15 SCREEN GODDESSES AND MONSTERS

The script for *Monster's Ball* had been floating around Hollywood since 1995. Even after Robert De Niro and Marlon Brando agreed to star in the film with Sean Penn attached as director, no studio would touch it. (The screenwriters of *Monster's Ball*, Milo Addica and Will Rokos, told the *Washington Post* that studio executives rejected the project because of Brando and co.'s excessive wage demands. The executives also demanded that some of the script's grittier edges get a softer, more commercial makeover, which the writers were unwilling to do.) After that creative trio dropped out, Oliver Stone wanted to direct and got Tommy Lee Jones, an actor with a dozen hit films on his résumé, to star. Still no green light.

Maybe it was because the subject matter was so offputting, so politically incorrect, or, as Eugene Boggs, a black law professor and Screen Actors Guild board member, said, 'The film is a Ku Klux Klan fantasy.'

The film's themes of racism, miscegenation, capital punishment, suicide and child abuse weren't exactly the stuff that blockbusters are made of, either.

Monster's Ball is a difficult film to watch. It features a graphic execution in which the victim's head smokes in the electric chair. (One critic said the sequence was as close as Hollywood has ever come to making a snuff film.) There's also a mother who beats her son for being overweight, plus a bunch of redneck, racist prison guards. And one of the principals commits suicide within the first ten minutes of the film by shooting himself in the chest in his living room while his father and grandfather look on impassively, with the grandfather laconically saying after the suicide, 'He was weak.'

Set in semirural Georgia, *Monster's Ball* is a feel-bad drama about a black waitress whose husband is on death row. Her house is about to be foreclosed on, her car's engine blows up after overheating, and she's in danger of losing her job due to absenteeism caused by her prison visits. Her son is morbidly obese, and she beats him when she discovers his secret cache of

Snickers bars secreted about the house. Without knowing his identity, she meets the white racist prison guard who executed her husband when he stops to pick her up by the side of the road after her son is hit – fatally, it turns out – by a car. The prison guard has his own problems and they resemble the waitress's. His son, also a prison guard, has just committed suicide in despair after his father slapped him around for vomiting while escorting the waitress's husband to the electric chair. The prison guard puts his even more virulently racist father in a nursing home, then invites the waitress, who is about to be evicted, to move in with him, apparently and magically abandoning his lifelong racism. He also buys a petrol station and renames it Leticia in her honour. After a night of heavy drinking and tears, the troubled pair find a bit of solace by making near-X-rated love on the living room couch. The film ends with the prison guard saying, 'I think everything's going to be all right.'

The unpalatable message of *Monster's Ball* seemed for many to be that love, or maybe lust, conquers all, even a lifetime of racism and poverty. The film's tagline summed up the theme: 'A lifetime of change can happen in a single moment.' The theme also eerily reflected the speech Warren Beatty's mad senator in *Bulworth* offered up as a solution to racial divisiveness: 'All we need is a voluntary, free-spirited, open-ended programme of procreative racial deconstruction. Everybody just gotta keep fuckin' everybody till they're all the same colour.'

Is it any wonder that no one in a position of power in Hollywood wanted to touch this script?

Halle did. 'I first received the script from my manager who had gotten the script from [the director's] agent. She passed it onto my manager already knowing that [the director] really wasn't interested in me,' she told *Venice* magazine. 'But she thought I would be right for the role, and if my manager got me to read it, then maybe I would like it and I would fight for it, which is exactly what happened.'

By the time she reached page 30 of the script, Halle was on the phone to her manager, Vincent Cirrincione, asking him to get her a meeting with the new producer–director team attached to the film, Lee Daniels and Marc Forster respectively.

'My character in the movie has a husband on death row, she's losing her house, her car is breaking down and she's beating up on her son. I couldn't stop reading. I called my manager and said, "Say yes, say yes." He said, "I'm glad you love it, but they don't want you." The director thought I was too beautiful or something,' she said.

The film's producer, Lee Daniels, was African-American and an artist's manager with no credits as a producer. Its director Marc Forster was Swiss-German with only two films to his credit, neither of which had been released except at film festivals. Despite the filmmakers' flimsy résumés, the independent production company Lions Gate put up the ludicrously small sum of $3.5 million to make the film, which would be shot in Laplace, Louisiana, near New Orleans, on a TV-movie schedule of only 21 days.

Neither Daniels nor Forster would meet with Halle. As usual, her beauty was her curse. They felt she just wasn't believable as a down-and-out waitress.

But, like his most famous client, Cirrincione was relentless. 'I got aggressive, got Marc's [Forster's] number and kept him talking for 15 or 20 minutes,' Cirrincione said. 'I don't think I'm getting to him, so I tell him it'll get a lot of attention if she's in it because people will think she can't do it.'

Daniels was one of those 'people' and told Cirrincione, 'The only way Halle Berry can come in for this is if she's not Halle Berry.' Daniels later told *Jet* magazine, 'Initially, I didn't want her for the role. She's so beautiful; I couldn't see her as this beaten-down woman at the end of her rope.'

The director raised similar objections. 'Basically, I just wasn't sure about Halle because she's really and truly a glamorous movie star,' Forster said. His concerns were overcome after a face-to-face meeting, which was all that Halle had requested in the first place. Forster said, 'I thought she'd be too glam, but I saw she'd be willing to deglamorize herself. I also saw incredible sadness in her eyes from her past. I thought I'd be able to tap into that.' It's amazing that, without knowing Halle's history of troubled relationships with men, the sensitive director could detect the despair they had caused her.

Cirrincione's persistence finally wore Daniels down, and the producer agreed to see Halle at the Shutters, a luxury oceanfront hotel in Santa Monica, California.

For such a savvy scrapper, Halle chose a self-defeating outfit and makeup for the meeting at which it would be decided whether she could shed her glamour and play a dirt-poor waitress in the Deep South. When she arrived at the Shutters, she looked like what she was, a movie star.

Daniels took one look at this vision of loveliness and got ugly. The first thing the producer said to her was, 'Listen, you're simply not right for this. You're too beautiful for the role.'

Halle couldn't help the way she looked, but, knowingly or not, she began to act like the film's feisty waitress, Leticia, by telling Daniels off. 'Who are you to tell me I'm too beautiful for this role? Who are you to tell me that because I'm too pretty, I can't do this?' Were all poor people ugly, she asked Daniels? 'What makes you think this woman has to look a certain way?'

Halle was so persuasive with Daniels because she had had a lifetime of waging the same battle. 'Frankly, fighting against my looks has become a large part of my career as an actress. I mean, everyone should have such problems, but producers never consider me for anything that isn't glamorous,' she has said.

But Halle doesn't want to seem whiny. Her beauty may seem like a curse that has required an uphill battle throughout her career, but she keeps it in perspective. 'I can think of worse struggles to have, so I'm not complaining,' she said. 'But it has been a struggle, and that's why I fight so hard for roles like this. Even though I do the *X-Men* and the *Swordfish*es, which have a valid place in my career, these kinds of movies [*Monster's Ball*] make me do better because I know that they're not always expected of me.' Or that she can even do them.

In an interview with Roger Ebert, who named *Monster's Ball* best film of the year, Halle said she argued with Daniels that despair and beauty weren't incompatible. 'I remember telling him sad and lonely comes in all different kinds of packages, and most beautiful people are somewhat sad and lonely. They live somewhat of an isolated existence.' Halle's personal life was proof of that. Beauty hadn't spared her spousal abuse, infidelity or a punctured eardrum. And she had won an Emmy playing a woman who was reportedly sad (and beautiful) every day of her life, Dorothy Dandridge.

The meeting with Daniels turned into an audition of sorts, except that Halle improvised all the dialogue.

Her combativeness convinced Daniels after only one meeting. The producer told *People* magazine, 'I said, "Oops. We'd better give this girl the job." '

As director, Marc Forster still didn't want Halle, and she claims she spent two weeks begging him just to see her. 'I was like a fly that would not go away,' she said.

But Forster raised another objection besides glamour. 'Would she be willing to do the lovemaking scene, go to where I wanted to go with it? It's graphic. They are two characters in agony, and they go at it like animals. I was worried, again, that she couldn't do that. But when she proved she was so passionate about the part and willing to do whatever was required, I said, OK,' Forster said.

Unlike Daniels, who needed only a single meeting to change his mind about Halle, Forster required a lot more heavy lifting. 'We had a lot of talks,' she said. 'I expressed my passion. I think I made him realize that my passion matched his own passion for the project. He almost didn't get to direct this film because he was new, and some people didn't believe that he could do it. And so I asked him, "Please don't let me be a victim of the very thing that you yourself are fighting. Because you've never seen me do it, it doesn't mean that I can't." He took a chance.'

Halle did harbour a bit of resentment over the arduous audition process. Playing the difficult role of Leticia, she later told *Daily Variety*, 'paled in comparison to the dog-and-pony show I had to do to get [the filmmakers] to take me seriously.'

Ironically, while Halle was begging for this role, friends and colleagues were telling her it would be career suicide. 'People said, "Are you crazy?" And, with the content of the movie and the nudity, a lot of people said "This could be *it* for you." I said "Well, if it is, then I want to go out doing *it*" – doing what I believe in.'

Monster's Ball arrived at just the right moment in Halle's career and the evolution of her moral values. In 2001, she was willing to beg for a role that she admits a few years earlier she would have rejected out of hand. 'All I'd have to hear was "nude scene" and I'd say, "Don't send me that." I'm sure I passed up wonderful scripts that I never read because I knew they required nudity,' she told the *Los Angeles Times* shortly before the film was released.

Halle's reluctance to appear nude on screen had nothing to do with prudery. Even the atypical intensity of the lovemaking scene hadn't scared her away. The UK's *Sunday Times* said of the sequence, '*Monster's Ball* features the sort of organic bumping and grinding rarely seen in American films.'

Her reluctance reflected something she's been fighting all her life: the desire to please other people at the expense of her own feelings. Or, to put a more positive spin on her no-nudes-is-good-nudes code in the past, she said, 'I worked hard to be what people wanted. I used to be obsessed with wanting their approval, way back to my childhood. Particularly the black community. So many black people would approach me and say, "My daughter aspires to be like you. Stay positive." So I tried to stay that way. I thought that, if I did nudity, I'd let them down and send the wrong message to those girls. But then I realized it's not my job to raise those girls.'

Since there are so few quality roles for women of colour, a myth arose around *Monster's Ball* that every black actress in Hollywood was doing a begging act similar to Halle's. In fact, Halle only somewhat jokingly claimed she could see the 'fingerprints' of all the other women who had clawed at her copy of the script, but according to the screenwriter Milo Addica, the script practically went begging rather than being begged for. 'Most of the actresses we spoke to didn't want to do it,' Addica said.

The film's literally climactic scene with Halle and Billy Bob Thornton as the racist prison guard lasts only three minutes on screen, but it took five hours to shoot and went on into the early-morning hours. 'We shot the sex scene on Day 19 of a 21-day shoot,' said Halle. 'I always say Billy Bob and I dated for three weeks and then we had sex. The sex scene scared me completely, but courage comes in strange ways.'

Shooting the difficult scene was made easier because of the man she had to shoot it with. 'I've wanted to work with Billy Bob ever since *One False Move* [1991],' she said. 'I never quite knew *how* we would, but I knew I wanted to. He is a master of subtlety, and he is by far one of the most interesting people I've ever met. He's very giving, and he's very gentle. In the [sex] scene, we had to have respect for each other, and he completely respected me and never once, in that moment when I felt very vulnerable, did I think that he would take advantage of me or infringe on my privacy.'

On another occasion, she volunteered more praise for her co-star. 'He was great. He was as invested in it as I was. He was as naked, as committed to it, as vulnerable, as free, as I was. I felt like I had a real partner. It wasn't the typical situation where the woman is usually the one who is sort of exploited, you know? We were in this scene together and that felt really good.'

Swordfish's gratuitous nudity turned out to be a blessing after all. It prepared Halle for the much more graphic nudity and sex her character would engage in with Thornton's Hank, the racist prison guard. 'I would never have been able to even think about tackling a role like *Monster's Ball* had I not done *Swordfish* and got through that inhibition that was somewhat holding me back.'

Swordfish's nudity might have been traumatic for another, similarly modest actress, but in retrospect, it was a career-making opportunity for Halle.

When Halle complained to *Swordfish*'s producer Joel Silver that her nude scene in that film was unnecessary, he told her, 'Yeah, I know, but I want it anyway.' Halle made only one demand after she landed the role in *Monster's Ball*. She had come a long way from the actress who less than a year earlier had caved in to a powerful producer like Silver simply because 'he wanted it', when she told Forster, 'I would only do it if Billy Bob agreed to be as naked as I was.'

In contrast, the producer of *Monster's Ball* would be much more simpatico and considerate of Halle's feelings – and even Thornton's, although men typically don't have the same squeamishness about nudity as women do. Daniels made both stars a rare promise. He gave them the final cut of the nude scene. They could sit in on the editing process and, if they didn't like a particular shot, it would be excised. Even more unusual, Daniels made a $3.5 million gamble and promised that, if Halle or Thornton *really* hated the entire sex scene, the film would not be released. (In another interview, Forster claimed *he* made that offer.)

Forster or Daniels or whoever made the promise had a calming and liberating effect on Halle when it came time to shoot the pivotal sequence. 'I knew that I had that power [to cut any offending shot], so it freed me to go wherever. I knew if it didn't look right or if it went too far, that later I could go, "Gee, what have I done?" and we could erase it,' she said.

The power of veto was power to her elbow. 'That's the only way I think we both felt free enough to just go there,' she said. 'Because we knew that if we went too far, and woke up the next morning and saw it, we could say, "Uh-oh. What were we thinking? Axe it all out." That gave us the freedom. We had that power. But we ended up leaving it all in. We didn't cut anything.'

Perhaps the most amazing factoid about the famous lovemaking scene – which was reported in only one place, Britain's *Sunday Times* – was that the entire sequence was improvised. 'All spontaneous. Nothing was rehearsed,' Halle told the paper. 'We agreed to be as naked as each other and – for lack of a better word – just go for it. The ground rules were, anybody who didn't need to be in that room wasn't allowed to be in there. And that there would no actual sex going on. Actually, that's my *only* ground rule.'

There are two other graphic sex scenes in *Monster's Ball*, but Halle didn't have to appear in either of them. Both scenes at first seem gratuitous and involve Thornton's character and his son (the Australian heartthrob Heath Ledger) in hiring the same prostitute for sex. Both men mount the woman in the exact same way, from behind, while she supports the weight of her body on her elbows resting on a desk. Only later do you realise the scenes weren't gratuitous at all. When Leticia and Hank begin to make love, he also tries to mount her from behind, then quickly changes his mind, and they assume the missionary position. The film contrasts commercial sex with the prostitute with the face-to-face lovemaking between Halle's and Thornton's characters. Or, as Roger Ebert wrote in his review, 'Their intimate scenes are ordinary and simple, a contrast to Hank's cold, mercenary arrangement with a local hooker.'

While the black law professor Eugene Boggs felt that the romance between the racist guard and a black woman was a Ku Klux Klan wet dream, at least one person, also of colour, believed Halle's beauty lent credibility to the film's theme that love conquers all, even a lifetime of bigotry.

Samuel L Jackson, her *Jungle Fever* and *Losing Isaiah* co-star, did a Q&A with Halle for *Interview* magazine and brought up the 'beauty' word. Jackson told her, '*Monster's Ball* might have been different if it was another actress who was not as attractive as Leticia. Because in my mind, it's easy for Billy Bob Thornton to want to have a relationship with you.'

Halle deflected the compliment with a surprising admission: 'Do you think so? Because there have been some men I've wanted to date that've wanted nothing to do with me!' Jackson laughed and offered a possible explanation for the past rejections. 'They were just scared of you.'

Leticia is a tormented character, and Halle became so enmeshed with her that she virtually stayed in character when she went home at night during the shoot. 'When we worked on it, I really didn't leave her,' she said. 'We shot in only 21 days and we worked such long days that at the end of the day all I had time to do was go home, sleep, get up, and do it again. And I was in Louisiana, without my family. So for those 21 days, for all practical purposes, I *was* Leticia. It was a good way to work on this character. I didn't have to worry about my family and going home and switching gears because I was on location by myself.'

Halle and Thornton loved the finished lovemaking scene and didn't ask for a single change. The American ratings board, however, did, threatening the film with that box-office poison, an NC-17 rating (no one under eighteen admitted), if approximately one minute wasn't cut. The objectionable sequence: 'Too much thrusting,' the ratings board said. The excised minute was restored for the European release.

The ratings board decision surprised Halle because she didn't think the scene had any prurient element – just the opposite. 'With *Monster's Ball*, it's not even about sex, that scene; it's so unsexy and it's not about sexual titillation,' said Halle. 'It's about two people getting what they need – and that's the air to breathe.

It's not a sexual thrill or sexual pleasure. Without that scene you don't understand why these people will be together; you understand after it why you want them to be together, why you root for them. And without that I don't think you would be able to make that big leap you have to make with their characters.' That 'big leap' is the belief that a white racist and a black woman can find peace in each other's arms.

Even though she didn't believe the scene was primarily about sex, she admitted she had a moment of panic before filming began. 'It scared me completely. I look at it now and think, "Who is that girl up there?" ' The glamorous Halle Berry had performed a feat worthy of great actor-chameleons such as Meryl Streep and Robert De Niro: she had disappeared into the role.

To create the sense of a 'real' event happening in real time, Forster decided to shoot the scene as one long continuous take, without stopping every few minutes to rearrange the camera for a different angle and lighting adjustments. That made a difficult scene even more difficult because it was so exhausting. Other than his decision to shoot the scene whole, Forster pretty much told his two actors to do their own thing. Halle said, 'We didn't choreograph it. We didn't worry about what we looked like, if my boob was sagging or our butts were showing. Between the two of us, we had two pasties on, and that's it. It was all about being in the moment.' Pasties are self-adhesive strips of paper, often attached with Velcro (ouch!) to cover parts of the body to avoid that fatal NC-17 rating.

Halle was happy with the scene, but she worried about her husband's reaction and arranged a very private screening of the film for just the two of them. Benét walked out of the room right after the sex scene ended even though the film had about five more minutes to go. Halle was concerned. Had he left in disgust? Was Benét turning out to be a sexist prude just like her previous husband, who didn't want his wife nude for the whole world to see?

But Benét returned after a short break and watched the rest of the film, then turned to his wife and said, 'You know, it was worth it, and I'm so proud of you. I don't know if America's gonna get it. I don't know what will happen with it, but I'm proud of you that you took that risk and that you really went there.'

Maybe *Swordfish* had genuinely desensitised Halle to the issue of nudity because she found another scene in the film much harder to play even though she remains fully clothed in it.

The night before her husband's execution and after learning she will be evicted from her home for failure to pay the mortgage, Halle's Leticia takes out her rage on her obese son, Tyrell, calling him a 'fat little piggy' and beating him after finding candy bars he's stashed away under a couch cushion and other places. The youngster, Coronji Calhoun, had never appeared in a film before and was not a professional actor.

'That was harder than the butt-naked love scene because he had real issues with obesity,' she told *People* magazine in 2002. Between takes and slaps, Halle mothered the newcomer. The magazine interview continues:

That was tough, let me tell you. Coronji is only 9 or 10 and really is dealing with an overweight issue. It really required heart-to-heart talks with him, and kissing him and hugging him every minute before and right after we shot the scene. I was telling him, 'This is a movie. Everything I do or say is not real. I really think you're wonderful.' And he said, 'Well, whatever you're going to do, Halle Berry, it won't be worse than what the kids at school do to me.'

He told me a lot of other things that made me connect with him. I was really worried we could damage him in some way.

When *Venice* magazine asked her the hardest scene to play in *Monster's Ball*, she again cited the scene with her on-screen son and fretted about her effect on his emotional health:

I think the scene where I sort of had to abuse my son [was the most difficult]. That was really hard because he was a real little boy. Ten years old and struggling with issues of obesity, you know? He wasn't an actor, never acted before. And I thought, 'Wow, I could really damage him psychologically.' I thought I could. I was afraid I would.

She took the neophyte under her wing and became his mentor and acting coach:

> I just talked to him a lot about the process of acting. Explained things to him, methods that different people used, you know? I tried to give him a crash course in all the acting I knew. And then tried to hug him and kiss him a lot – before the takes and after the takes. When I'd see him in the morning, I'd try to be as nurturing and as loving as I could all the time. We had a really good connection so that when we did work, he felt more like it was work and not me [abusing him].

Her concern about the youth continued even after the project wrapped and the cast and crew dispersed. 'I didn't want to say [to him], "OK, thank you very much. See you." I felt I needed to keep in touch with him, and I've stayed in his life.'

(One wonders whether, while pummelling the unfortunate youngster, Halle had any post-traumatic stress flashbacks to similar scenes from her own childhood. She hinted at that possibility when she told *Daily Variety*, 'Making the movie was very cathartic because I got to purge myself of all kinds of different emotions I had brewing inside of me.' Her memory of past abuse undoubtedly coloured and prompted her compassionate behaviour towards Coronji Calhoun between takes.)

The overweight youngster wasn't the only person Halle comforted while shooting *Monster's Ball*. To research her role as the wife of an executed murderer, Halle visited death row at the Louisiana State Penitentiary in Angola. Producer Lee Daniels recalled, 'She held their hands. She cried.'

Halle's asking price before *Monster's Ball* had ballooned to $2.5 million, but she agreed to appear in the very-low-budget *Monster's Ball* for only $100,000. After expenses, she estimated she cleared only $5,000. She brought the same generosity to the set with her, staying at Best Western motels with the rest of the cast, and doing her own makeup, although she doesn't seem to be wearing any in the film (and she still looks stunning). Sean 'Puffy' Combs, who plays her doomed husband, also abandoned any superstar perks

SCREEN GODDESSES AND MONSTERS

the rap and clothing mogul might have been expected to demand, and visitors at one film location were shocked to see the rapper moving furniture on the set.

Monster's Ball was released in a handful of American cinemas the day after Christmas 2001 to make the cut-off date for Academy Awards consideration with a nationwide release after the New Year. (It came out in the UK on 7 June 2002.)

Not surprisingly, since he named it best picture of the year, Roger Ebert led the chorus of near-universal praise for *Monster's Ball*, concluding his review with his feelings about the conclusion of the film. 'As for myself, as Leticia rejoined Hank in the last shot of the movie, I was thinking about her as deeply and urgently as about any movie character I can remember.' Although he recognised the graphic sex scene as embodying the movie's theme that love can trump a lifetime of racism, Ebert criticised the director's handling of the scene, which he felt verged on voyeurism. 'The film's only flaw is the way Marc Forster allows his camera to linger on Berry's half-clothed beauty.' No one else complained about that. Ebert was also the only critic or commentator who explained the film's obscure title, which is the Old English term for a condemned man's last night on earth – in this case Combs's death-row inmate.)

The *Washington Post*'s Desson Howe had only praise for the rookie director and his film:

> As directed by Swiss native Marc Forster (who made the almost unknown *Everything Put Together*), the movie holds you in thrall from first frame to last. Hatred is hatred unslaked. So is racism, ugliness, love, lust and sorrow. When Leticia beats her teenage [sic] child, or makes desperate, drunken love on her sofa, there's something liberating about her directness. It feels real.

Halle must have felt it was worth every penny she gave up of her usual asking fee when she read the *Post*'s assessment of her performance: '. . . Berry, whose acting skills have rarely enjoyed the showcasing they deserve, certainly makes her stamp here.'

A rare nay vote was cast by the *Village Voice*'s Michael Atkinson, who began his review with the dismissive 'as headlong wallows in hatred and degradation go, Marc Forster's *Monster's Ball* self-consciously outgrunges the year in American film, but the upshot is curiously unconvincing.' (The critic also refers to Halle's waitress as a 'shell-shocked floozy' even though her character confesses that she hasn't been with a man since her husband went to prison.)

Monster's Ball easily made back its $3.5 million budget by earning $31.3 million in the US and an additional £2.2 million in the UK.

The low-budget film nobody wanted to make became an award magnet, accumulating nominations and awards on its inevitable trip to the show of shows, the Academy Awards. *The Times* (London) said the effect on Halle's career recalled the old joke that Sharon Stone was the first actress to gain respect by taking her clothes off.

Along the way to the big night in March 2002, Halle picked up the Best Actress award (a Silver Bear) at the Berlin International Film Festival, the same honour from the National Board of Review and the most portentous preview of Oscar glory to come, the Screen Actors Guild Award, voted by the Guild's 98,000 members. There were fears that *Monster's Ball* would be overlooked by the Oscars because not enough people had seen the film, but many members of the Screen Actors Guild (SAG) are also Academy members and voters, and enough Guild members had obviously seen *Monster's Ball* to give Halle top honours. (The Guild – and Halle – also made history that night: she became the first black to win its Best Actress award.)

In her acceptance speech at the Shrine Auditorium near downtown Los Angeles, she said, 'So many good things have come my way because of this project. My life is indelibly different because of that work, that journey, this award. It has paid off, big time.'

But the really 'big time' was yet to come.

16. HALLE'S COMET

When the Academy of Motion Picture Arts and Sciences announced the Best Actress nominees on 12 February 2002, Halle found herself competing with Nicole Kidman for *Moulin Rouge*, Sissy Spacek for *In the Bedroom*, Renée Zellweger for *Bridget Jones's Diary* and Judi Dench for *Iris*.

Even after winning the SAG award, the Oscar nomination took Halle by surprise. She was certain that the little film would be overlooked. She said, 'I never thought that people would be nominated for Academy Awards. [The screenwriters were the only other Oscar nominees.] That was never in my thinking. I knew that it was a jewel of a movie. I knew that it was special when I read it. That's why I was willing to fight so hard for it. But I thought, "I don't know if people are ready to deal with some of these issues." But as an actor I knew that the roles were just brilliant characters. Really colorful and full. I just didn't think anybody would be nominated for an Oscar, especially me.'

Las Vegas bookmakers shared her scepticism and weren't placing their bets on Halle, who was – to make an un-PC pun – truly the dark-horse candidate in the category. Bally's-Paris Hotel-Casino picked Kidman as the winner at 2–1 odds. She had just been cruelly and abruptly dumped by her husband Tom Cruise after suffering a miscarriage, and many Oscar handicappers felt she would get the sympathy vote. Caesar's Palace gave Spacek 5–2 odds. The actress's career had been in free fall for years after she had won the 1980 Oscar for *Coal Miner's Daughter*, and Academy voters have always been suckers for *Rocky*-like comeback stories, although arguably even fewer people had seen the micro-budgeted ($1.7 million) *In the Bedroom* than had seen *Monster's Ball*. Bally's-Paris considered Halle a distant long shot at 6–1 odds, the same odds it gave Judi Dench, but you didn't have to be a gambling genius to predict the improbability that Halle would take home the big one. In its 73 controversial years, the Academy of Motion Picture Arts and Sciences had never given its Best Actress award to an African-American, and only two black women had won Best Supporting Actress honours – Hattie McDaniel for 1939's *Gone With the Wind* and Whoopi Goldberg half a century later for *Ghost*. Only the Canadian website CTVNEWS.com felt Halle and Spacek were 'evenly matched for strong performances in understated, low-budget films', but the site nevertheless gave Spacek a slight edge over Halle, adding, '. . . you can pretty much count out pseudo-Brit Renée Zellweger and real-Brit Judi Dench.'

It seemed a much safer bet that Halle would join the list of also-rans in the Best Actress category, a list that began with her alter ego Dorothy Dandridge, followed by Diana Ross for *Lady Sings the Blues* (1972), Cicely Tyson for *Sounder* the same year, Diahann Carroll for *Claudine* (1974), Whoopi Goldberg for *The Color Purple* (1985) and Angela Bassett for *What's Love Got to Do With It* (1993). At Oscar time, black actresses were always, if they were lucky, bridesmaids, never brides. Just about the only thing Halle had going in her favour was that Oscar loves it when an actor or actress plays against type, only one example of which is the glamour magnet Grace Kelly's 1955 win for playing a mousy frump in *The Country Girl*. And, in *Monster's Ball*, a woman so beautiful Revlon chose her as its spokesmodel spends most of the film wearing a waitress's uniform, no visible makeup and a hairdo popular in the 1950s when it was called a 'pixie cut'.

Monster's Ball's producer Lee Daniels worried about Halle's state of mind as she read all the Vegas statistics predicting she would lose on Oscar night. When he called and asked how she felt, she said, 'Traumatised.'

Almost as if to will her into winning despite his own misgivings, Daniels talked up Halle's chances in public whenever he got the chance. (It also didn't hurt the film's box office to keep it in the cinemagoing public's mind.) After appearing on CNN and touting Halle's prospects, he confessed to Halle's biographer, Christopher John Farley, that he was engaging more in wishful thinking than accurate prognosticating. 'In my heart of hearts I knew it was total b.s. I didn't think she was really going to win. History speaks for itself,' Daniels said.

The producer did believe Denzel Washington, who was nominated for best actor for his role as a corrupt cop in *Training*

Day, had a shot at winning, but mostly as a 'consolation prize' for all the other 'bruthas' and 'sistuhs' who had been sidelined by the Academy Awards in the past. Washington, who had won a Best Supporting Actor Oscar for *Glory* in 1990, might pick up a second statuette this time, Daniels suspected, 'just so they could say they did the right thing by black folks. But I didn't think she was going to win.'

(In contrast to Daniels's positive outlook, years earlier, Otto Preminger with typical cruelty told Dorothy Dandridge a snowball had a better chance in hell than she had of winning the Oscar in 1955. When Dandridge asked for an explanation, he said laconically, 'The time is not ripe.')

Four days before the Oscars, *Daily Variety* asked Halle how winning an Academy Award would affect her career. 'I really don't have a pulse on how it will change things. I just hope that maybe next time I won't have to fight so hard to get an audition.'

Even at this late date, she still hadn't picked out a gown to wear to the gala, although she was playing fashion director for her mother. 'It's more about what my mother's going to wear. She's going with me and she's never been to one of these things. I just want her to feel really good and wonderful.'

The 74th annual Academy Awards ceremony was held at its new home, the Kodak Theatre, at the legendary corner of Hollywood Boulevard and Vine Street, on 24 March 2002.

Halle usually favours the conservative *haute couture* of Valentino, but for this special night she chose a gown designed by the relatively unknown Elie Saab. A burgundy-coloured skirt with a mini-train that looked like wings was topped by a see-through net blouse that had floral embroidery strategically covering parts of the body they just won't show on TV. But when she first saw the gown, Halle felt it still revealed too much and had Saab add more embroidery to cover some hot spots. It was hard enough for Halle to do nudity on film in the relative privacy of a closed set. She didn't plan to expose choice parts of her anatomy in front of the Oscar ceremony's estimated audience of a billion viewers.

'When I first saw [the Saab gown] months before, I thought, "I don't have anywhere *that* special to go." So when I was nominated for the Oscar, that's when I said, "Get that Elie Saab dress. If this isn't a big enough event, I don't know what is," ' she said in December 2002.

The *New York Post* later praised Halle's modesty. 'Let J.Lo [Jennifer Lopez] wear the R-rated numbers. Halle's content to be seen in PG-13 gowns. On most women – including most of her fellow Oscar-goers – the dress wouldn't have worked,' the *Post*'s Libby Callaway wrote two days after the gala. Nicole Kidman, by comparison, was criticised for wearing a pinkish, almost white frilly number that seemed to match the colour of her skin, and perhaps the gown's washed-out look reflected her emotional state post-Cruise.

Although Halle eschews drugs and liquor, she needed a bottle of champagne to avert a minor disaster as she got ready for the big night. Only two hours before show time, she discovered that an orange diamond ring worth $3.5 million lent to her by the Beverly Hills jeweller Harry Winston was too big for her finger. Dawn Moore, a Winston employee, made the trek from Beverly Hills to Hollywood in only thirty minutes during rush hour to make sure Halle didn't lose the precious bauble. 'You can bet we wanted to make sure it didn't fall off,' said Moore, who tried tape and string to make the ring tighter – but nothing worked. Then Moore noticed a bottle of Veuve Clicquot in one of Halle's gift baskets and inspiration struck. Moore ripped the foil off the cork and wrapped it around the ring's platinum band. 'It fit her perfectly and off she went,' Moore said. Halle ended up wearing aluminium foil to the Oscars!

After the ceremony, Winston executives may have been having second thoughts about the tradition of lending valuable gems to the famous to promote their brand name. That same evening, MC Whoopi Goldberg temporarily lost a $6 million eighty-carat yellow diamond attached to her necklace. According to the *New York Post*, a frantic Goldberg was on her hands and knees backstage searching the floor for the missing stone. One of several security guards assigned by Winston to guard all its celebrity mannequins that night told Goldberg that the diamond had probably fallen into her cleavage. Goldberg dismissed that theory, but, when the beefy guard volunteered to go on a fishing expedition inside her gown, Goldberg decided to check for herself and found the gem right where the guard had predicted.

As Halle walked down the red carpet clutching her husband's arm like a lifesaver, she must have had a weird feeling of *déjà vu*. She had already played this scene before, as Dorothy Dandridge arriving at the 1955 Oscar ceremony. This time, she no doubt hoped, the ending would be different, just as her life had never become the tragic mess into which Dandridge's had degenerated.

Halle wasn't the only person of colour being honoured that night. In addition to Denzel Washington, Will Smith had been nominated in the same category for a brilliantly reviewed performance as the One and Only Muhammad Ali in *Ali* (directed by Anthony Mann). That night, Sidney Poitier, the first and – until later in the evening – only black to win a best actor Oscar (for *Lilies of the Field* in 1964), was set to receive something called the Brass Ring award for lifetime achievement. Cynics felt the Halle–Denzel–Will–Sidney quartet of honorees was Oscar's too-little-too-late way of apologising for mostly ignoring African-Americans in the past.

Poitier wasn't one of the cynics, however, and his acceptance speech focused on gratitude for how far Hollywood had come rather than antagonism about how far it had yet to go in its portrayal and employment of black people.

Halle had the honour of handing Poitier the Brass Ring statuette while he waited for the standing audience to stop cheering so he could deliver a speech that would soon have the audience on its feet again. Poitier said, 'I arrived in Hollywood at the age of twenty-two in a time different than today's, a time in which the odds against my standing here tonight fifty-three years later would not have fallen in my favour. Back then, no route had been established for where I was hoping to go, no pathway left in evidence for me to trace, no custom for me to follow.

'Yet here I am this evening at the end of a journey that in 1949 would have been considered almost impossible, and in fact might never have been set in motion were there not an untold number of courageous, unselfish choices made by a handful of visionary American filmmakers, directors, writers, and producers; each with a strong sense of citizenship [and] responsibility to the times in which they lived; each unafraid to permit their art to reflect their views and values, ethical and moral, and moreover, acknowledge them as their own. They knew the odds that stood against them and their efforts were overwhelming and likely could have proven too high to overcome.'

Poitier continued, 'Still, those filmmakers persevered, speaking through their art to the best in all of us. And I've benefited from their effort. The industry benefited from their effort. America benefited from their effort. And in ways large and small the world has also benefited from their effort. I accept this award in memory of all the African-American actors and actresses who went before me in the difficult years, on whose shoulders I was privileged to stand to see where I might go.'

Poitier's upbeat speech ironically had an unsettling effect on Halle as she waited for her category to be announced. Lee Daniels saw the consternation on her face and left his seat to talk with her during a commercial break and find out what was wrong – in particular, why her knees were visibly shaking. Poitier's speech had magnified the significance of Halle's nomination and placed the burden of history on her slender shoulders, she felt. She told Daniels, 'This is bigger than me. This is not about you, Lee, and this is not about me. We can't lose this.'

Daniels was about to give Halle a shot of optimism when he noticed that her fellow nominee Sissy Spacek was only a few feet away. So he whispered his encouragement instead and said, 'Halle, we're gonna take this motherfucker home tonight.' Halle laughed, but her knees didn't stop quivering. 'We need to win this for our people,' she told Daniels, who later confessed that the courage and hopefulness with which he tried to infuse Halle didn't reflect his genuine feelings. He was certain, even then, that Halle was going to lose.

Finally, it came time to hand out the Best Actress award. The presenter was Russell Crowe, who had won the Best Actor Oscar the previous year for *Gladiator*. It's an Oscar tradition that the year's previous winner in the Best Actor category announces the current year's Best Actress winner. And, as part of the same tradition, the previous year's Best Actress winner, Julia Roberts, who won for *Erin Brockovich*, would announce this year's Best Actor.

Crowe ran through the usual ritual: the reading of the names of the five nominated actresses, a pregnant pause while he ripped open the envelope, then, 'And the winner is . . .' (Another pause for dramatic effect – actors just can't resist an opportunity to be theatrical.)

And the winner was the woman whom the Vegas bookies had predicted had worse prospects than a blizzard in Hades. As soon as Crowe announced Halle's name, the TV cameras all zoomed in on her. She displayed the usual reaction of an Oscar winner, a combination of paralysis, shock, incredulity and euphoria. You can almost read a just-announced winner's mind, which seems to be thinking, I'm hallucinating all this. Did they really call my name or did I just imagine that? Many past Oscar winners have described an odd sense of disassociation, of becoming separated from their bodies, even like an accident victim floating above a car wreck while his or her body is still in the car.

Somehow, dazed and purblind from tears, Halle managed to make it to the podium. She screamed and cried for what seemed like an eternity. Her reaction reminded some detractors of the behaviour of a typical weeping beauty-pageant winner, which Halle had been, at the moment her name is called out as the new Miss America or whatever. Halle continued to cry and cry until it became almost embarrassing to watch. Even her husband began to feel uncomfortable. Benét later told *Us Weekly*, 'It looked like she was about to completely lose it and just get horizontal' – i.e. faint. And still his wife continued to weep. No acceptance speech. Just tears. Britain's *Sunday Times* felt she came close to equalling Sally Field's 'you really like me!' acceptance speech and said, 'Berry . . . treated a global audience to one of the greatest displays of public lachrymosity in modern times.' The reporter noted something no one else saw when he also claimed that Halle had 'stringing mucus' dripping from her nose and volunteered a 'tip for lady nominees: pack a hanky'.

Benét was seated in the front row and took action before Halle's tears turned into a tsunami. He stood up and clapped his hands together even harder than before. 'I just wanted to be a beacon of love. And Halle, like she always does, pulled it together,' he said.

She did indeed – with a little help from the presenter, Russell Crowe. He had stood in Halle's place the year before, and he had a good idea of the flood of emotions that engulfed Halle's mind at the moment. In a classic case of peer counselling, the Oscar winner whispered in Halle's ear, 'Breathe, mate. Just breathe. It's going to be OK.'

Her tearful paralysis eventually subsided, and, like the consummate professional she is, Halle Maria Berry delivered an acceptance speech that was amazing for its depth and inclusiveness, for its sense that more than just another actress was being honoured, that history was being made that night. And it was.

To calm herself down, she began by invoking the deity and the ghosts of Oscars past. 'Oh, my God! Oh, my God! I'm sorry. This moment is so much bigger than me. This moment is for Dorothy Dandridge, Lena Horne, Diahann Carroll. It's for the women who stand beside me, Jada Pinkett, Angela Bassett, Vivica Fox. And it's for every nameless, faceless woman of colour that now has a chance because this door tonight has opened. Thank you. I'm so honoured. I'm so honoured. And I thank the Academy for choosing me to be the vessel through which [God's] blessing might flow.'

Then it came time for the ritual thank-yous, which often run to embarrassing lengths, but there was a sense that black people had been waiting 74 years for this moment, and Halle should be given all the time she needed after such a long wait. It's interesting to note that the first person she thanked was not her husband or her mother, but the man whose intercession had led her to the podium that night, her surrogate father and *consigliere* since the beginning of her acting career. It was time to thank the man who kept the dismissive producer of *Monster's Ball* on the phone for fifteen minutes when he kept saying no to auditioning Halle.

'I want to thank my manager, Vincent Cirrincione. He's been with me for twelve long years, and you fought every fight and you loved me when I've been up, but more importantly you've loved me when I've been down. You have been a manager, a friend, and the only father I've ever known. Really. And I love you very much.'

At her greatest moment of triumph, it amazes one that Halle's thoughts, however tangentially, touched on the man who had abandoned the family almost thirty years earlier, her biological father, Jerome Berry. And there was just a *soupçon* of enmity in describing (inaccurately) Cirrincione as the 'only father' she had ever known, since she had in fact known her real father for a total of five years during the two stormy periods he was on the premises.

Then it was time to acknowledge the woman who had instilled in her the self-confidence that led to this moment. 'I want to thank my mom, who has given me the strength to fight every single day, to be who I want to be and to give me the courage to dream, that this dream might be happening and possible for me. I love you, Mom, so much.'

Halle must have had conflicting emotions about the next item on her thank-you list, her husband. The public didn't know it yet, but at this happiest time in her professional life her personal life, in particular her marital relationship, was in crisis. But that bit of messy laundry wouldn't be aired until months later. Now it was time to focus on the positive aspects of their troubled relationship.

'Thank you, my husband, who is just a joy of my life; and [his daughter] India, thank you for giving me peace because only with the peace that you've brought me have I been allowed to go to places that I never even knew I could go. Thank you. I love you and India with all my heart.'

Then there were the professional thank-yous. Halle hadn't reached the top of her profession without being savvy enough to know that it's good strategy to stroke the people who have helped you in the past, and, more important, those who may help you in the future.

She thanked Lions Gate, the independent production company that had given the go-ahead to *Monster's Ball* after all the major and minor studios had rejected the script. She thanked two executives at Lions Gate, including the head of publicity, who had managed to get enough Academy voters to see a film not many other people had seen, and Lions Gate's president. 'Thank you, Mike Paseornek, Tom Ortenberg, for making sure everybody knew about this little tiny movie. Thank you for believing in me. Our director, Marc Forster. You're a genius. You're a genius. This moviemaking experience was magical for me because of you. You believed in me, you trusted me, and you gently guided me to very scary places.'

Now was not the time or place to say, 'I told you so' and remind Forster that he originally refused even to meet her. The same might have been said about the next object of her gratitude. 'I want to thank Lee Daniels, our producer. Thank you for giving me this chance, for believing that I could do it. And now tonight I have this. Thank you.'

Her professional obligations weren't through yet, and she got to the part of her acceptance speech that most winners reach, where even huge fans are thinking, 'Get the hook!' and wish the orchestra would drown out the winner as he or she thanks people the public has never heard of or cares about. But they were important to Halle's career, and they had to be acknowledged. 'I want to thank my agents [at] CAA. Josh Lieberman especially. I have to thank my agents. Kevin Huvane, thank you. Thank you for never kicking me out and sending me somewhere else . . . Who else? I have so many people that I know I need to thank. My lawyers! Neil Meyer, thank you. OK, wait a minute. I got to take . . . seventy-four years here! I got to take this time!'

It was really get-the-hook time when she began to thank the same person twice. 'I got to thank my lawyer, Neil Meyer, for making this deal. I need to thank lastly and not leastly Spike Lee for putting me in my very first film and believing in me. Oprah Winfrey for being the best role model any girl can have.'

(Winfrey happened to be in town, at the A-list party of the year, thrown by *Vanity Fair* magazine, at Morton's restaurant. *Us Weekly* reported that, when Halle thanked Winfrey from the podium, the talk-show host leaped to her feet and for once in her life was speechless. Another guest at Morton's told *Us*, 'Oprah just stood up from the dinner table and stayed there, beaming and weeping, for the whole speech. Everybody was screaming and crying through the whole thing.')

Then, Halle bizarrely expressed gratitude for the producer who had made her so uncomfortable by insisting on the nude scene in *Swordfish*. 'Joel Silver, thank you.' Heck! You never know. He might be producing a blockbuster for her someday, although after this evening's honour she'd have the clout to keep her top on.

In a nice symmetry of sorts, she even thanked the man who had put her Oscar humiliation into perspective two years earlier – after Billy Crystal poked fun at her hit-and-run nightmare. 'And thank you to Warren Beatty. Thank you so much for being my mentor and believing in me. Thank you! Thank you! Thank you!'

Missing from Halle's otherwise encyclopedic list of people to thank was her *Monster's Ball* co-star, Billy Bob Thornton. It almost certainly was an unintended omission, caused perhaps by the excitement of the moment, and not due to ill will, since she had praised her co-star in previous interviews, in particular expressing gratitude for his gentle and respectful treatment of her during their difficult lovemaking scene. She quickly made amends. The next day, she posted a thank-you note to Thornton on her fan club's website.

Halle later explained why she had forgotten to thank Thornton and also Peter Boyle, who played Thornton's racist father. She was winging it! Her speech was totally ad-libbed. For once, she had ignored her long-time role model and mentor's advice to write down an acceptance speech in advance. 'My dear friend Oprah Winfrey said, "If I were you, I'd write a speech," ' she told the *Sunday Times* in June 2002. 'I said, "Oprah, come on, I'm gonna feel like such an idiot with a speech in my purse and then not having to use it." I left out Billy Bob. How *could* I? I left out Peter Boyle. I left out the writers, who were also nominated. I should have written something. Though I've thanked them since.'

When she finished her acceptance speech, Halle retreated backstage, where two entire rooms were filled with reporters and photographers waiting to beam to the rest of the world the kaleidoscope of emotions and gratitude Halle felt on the happiest night of her life.

To her credit and in contrast to narcissistic exclamations of the past of the 'you really like me' variety, Halle put the award and her achievement in perspective. She set it in a historical context that was much bigger and more important than that one beautiful woman had become the first African-American to win top honours at the Oscars.

'I never thought this would be possible in my lifetime,' she said in the press room backstage. 'I hope we will start to be judged on our merits and our work. This moment, it's not really just about me. It's about so many people that went before me. It's about people who are fighting alongside me and now it will be indelibly easier. It's not about me, but about so many other women of colour.

'Tonight means that every woman of colour should be hopeful, because it can happen. And I hope that's what tonight brings. Will tonight change the industry? I don't know. But if it changes the minds of those people who felt defeated, if now they feel hopeful, eventually those inspired hearts will make a change. I believe that.

'I had to fight for this,' she said with understatement, 'and now this is so worth it. I've got my mother here, my husband, my manager, and we are just going to party until noon tomorrow.'

Despite the screaming and beauty-queen weeping that comprised her initial reaction to the award, upon reflection, and after some long, deep breaths, Halle was ready to put her victory in context when a reporter asked her if she at last felt validated by the Oscar. She has a long memory, and she remembered to be grateful for everything that had preceded this career-capping night. 'Well, it's a different kind of validation. But I've felt validated along the way. For one, I've felt validated that as a woman of colour I've been able to make a living for the last twelve years just on acting, no side gigs. That in itself is validating to me because so many SAG [Screen Actors Guild] actors just don't work, and don't make a living at acting. But this is another level of validating. This is the icing, the candles on the cake, the cherry on the sundae. It feels incredible,' she said.

Not everyone thought history had been made that night, even though the evening's Best Actor winner was also a person of colour, Denzel Washington. The next day, a powerful talent agent, Rob Kim, implied that change in Hollywood occurs at a glacial pace, and no one should expect a Golden Age of black employment to begin, although the time would be golden for two particular black people.

Kim, of the United Talent Agency, told the *Los Angeles Times*, 'The wins that we saw on Oscar night are arguably well deserved – they gave some great performances. I don't know that it necessarily matters that much. Does [Halle's] win mean more roles for African-American women? I don't think so. I think more people will want to hire Denzel and more people will want to hire Halle Berry.'

Spike Lee also doubted that the evening represented a sea change in the movie industry's underemployment of minorities.

'Hollywood would simply pat itself on the back and revert to type,' he told Britain's *Sunday Times*, which pointed out a significant statistic the American press never brought up: 'Between 1990 and 2000, 9 per cent of all nominees in the leading Oscar categories were non-white – statistics not much out of step with the ethnic make-up of the USA.' (Actually, blacks make up 12.7 per cent of the American population, but 9 per cent is a healthy start.) The *Sunday Times* also scolded BAFTA, the British equivalent of the Oscars, for not giving its top award to a black person since Sidney Poitier won an award in 1959.

But history was made that night, and Halle's win had international repercussions and attracted the attention of other blacks who didn't think the evening's honours were significant only for the honorees. Even a Nobel laureate took note. At four in the morning while Halle and her husband celebrated at a party in Beverly Hills hosted by Elton John, Halle was called to the phone.

It was Nelson Mandela calling . . .

Another incident that reportedly took place at Elton John's Oscar party never happened, according to Halle. The *New York Post*'s scabrous but reputable 'Page Six' gossip column reported a few days after the Oscar ceremony that Halle had run into the Revlon chief Ron Perelman at Elton John's party and demanded a rise now that the company's 'spokesmodel' was a history-making Oscar winner. According to the *Post*, when Perelman congratulated her on her Oscar win, she replied, 'Of course, now you'll have to pay me more.' The *Post* claimed Perelman 'stalked off'. The next day, again according to the *Post*, Perelman told company lawyers to hold Halle to her contract, which had a year to run, at the same fee while at the same time capitalising on the higher profile the Oscar had created for Revlon's spokesmodel. The *Post* also claimed Revlon paid Halle less than her immediate predecessor, Cindy Crawford. An unidentified 'insider' told the *Post* that Halle 'was underpaid anyway'. Another insider said, 'No way is Ron going to give her more money.'

Halle's publicist, Karen Samfilippo, told the *Post* that her client had 'no comment' about the paper's allegations. A week later, Halle broke her silence and denied the incident had taken place in an interview with another *Post* columnist, Liz Smith. 'People honestly seem to believe that I ran into Ron at Elton John's Oscar party and insisted Revlon give me a raise! It's not true,' Smith quoted her as saying. Smith got a hold of Perelman, who also spiked the rumour. 'First of all,' he said, 'I love Halle Berry. She's been a wonderful personality for Revlon. Second, I never was at the Elton John party. Third, it simply never happened! Halle is terrific. She's sensational. She won the Oscar, it was groundbreaking, and she deserves it.'

(Six years after she signed with the company, Halle was still Revlon's frontwoman, and the company launched a multimillion-dollar ad campaign to promote a new line of products called the 007 Collection, tied in to the release of *Die Another Day*, the James Bond film Halle co-starred in. The *New York Times* said the ad campaign represented a huge gamble for Revlon because the company was $1.7 billion in debt. But the *New York Times* didn't tell the whole story. The new line of cosmetics actually consisted of two collections, one named after 007. But, by 2002, Halle had become such a valuable commodity that the other line from Revlon was called the Jinx Collection, named after the character she played in the Bond film.)

Revlon also got publicity from Halle's Oscar win when her makeup artist, Laura Mohberg, explained why, despite the Niagara of tears shed during Halle's acceptance speech, her mascara and eyeliner hadn't run. Halle wore waterproof and water-resilient products by Revlon. *Us Weekly* gave Revlon what amounted to a free ad when it reported that Halle wore Revlon's ColorStay Makeup in Caramel for foundation, Creme Shadow in Skinlights as eyeshadow and ColorStay Extra Thick Lashes in Black waterproof mascara. No wonder Ron Perelman spoke so highly of Halle.

Halle's history-making Oscars triumph invited the inevitable backlash, which came from some expected as well as unexpected quarters.

Four days after the ceremony, cyberpunks hacked into her official website, and defaced her photo by drawing a moustache and beard on it. The juvenile prank had an ugly and ominous element, however. The hacker left his alleged email address on the site, which contained the letters 'KKK'. The site's webmaster temporarily shut down hallewood.com and removed Halle's whiskers and the racist initials, then beefed up security before putting the site back online.

Halle was unfazed by the incident. A spokesman for the actress said, 'It sounds very juvenile and childlike. It's like what we used to do as children with Magic Markers.' Her spokesman didn't address the more serious issue of the racist email address. The tabloids, without offering any proof, suggested the hacking was the work of disgruntled Nicole Kidman fans, who were disappointed that their favourite hadn't won the Best Actress Oscar for *Moulin Rouge*. That hypothesis didn't explain the KKK signature, either.

The night before the Academy Awards, Halle had attended a party in her honour thrown by Lions Gate, Revlon and Vincent Cirrincione at Mirabelle, a restaurant on the Sunset Strip in West Hollywood. The guest list included two long-time mentors, former co-star Samuel L Jackson and Oprah Winfrey, Louis Gossett, Jr, and a woman whose presence at a party celebrating Halle's Oscar prospects would later turn out to be profoundly ironic – Angela Bassett.

After the Oscar ceremony, at Elton John's party, Halle revealed the advice Winfrey had given her at the Mirabelle party. 'Last night, Oprah said to me, "If you're so lucky and they call your name, keep both feet under you and speak. And *speak*." And I kept thinking, "Speak! Pull it together and speak." I didn't want to disappoint her and everybody. That's what was on my mind. I left out a few people, but nobody's perfect. Oscar's nice and warm. I'm gonna sleep with two men tonight. It's my only chance to sleep with another man!' Winfrey also told the actress, 'My heart is beating for you.' Halle's levity about being unfaithful to her husband 'with another man' would also turn out to be deeply ironic in the light of following events.

Much, much more troubling to Halle than some bratty, albeit racist, teenagers' cyberprank had to be the reaction of a colleague she had thanked during her acceptance speech.

In the 1 July 2002, issue of *Newsweek* magazine, Angela Bassett claimed she had turned down Halle's role in *Monster's Ball* because she felt it demeaned black women. 'It's about character, darling. I wasn't going to be a prostitute on film. I couldn't do that because it's such a stereotype about black women and sexuality. It's about putting something out there you can be proud of 10 years later. I mean Meryl Streep won Oscars without all that.' (Ironically, only a few months earlier, Halle had admiringly noted that, unlike Dorothy Dandridge, Bassett did not let an Oscar nomination 'eat her alive', but now it seemed that Halle's Oscar win might be gnawing at Bassett.)

Bassett insisted she wasn't criticising Halle personally and claimed she cried when Halle's name was announced at the Oscar ceremony. Could they have been tears of frustration? Bassett, however, said, 'I can't and don't begrudge Halle her success. It wasn't the role for me, but I told her she'd win and I told her to go get what was hers. Of course, I want one, too. I would love to have an Oscar. But it has to be for something I can sleep with at night.'

Regardless of the legitimacy of her criticism, Bassett's credibility was undercut by two people closely associated with *Monster's Ball*. Tom Ortenberg, president of Lions Gate, which released the film, told the *Los Angeles Times* after the *Newsweek* interview had run, 'Nobody was ever offered the role of Leticia except Halle Berry. Anyone who says anything to the contrary is misspeaking.'

Lee Daniels, the producer of *Monster's Ball*, said that he had expressed an interest in meeting Bassett, but had never offered her the role, and the meeting never took place. Daniels told Christopher John Farley, 'To me, it sounds like Angela Bassett's got sour grapes or something, you know what I mean? Get your own Oscar, baby.'

Halle's defenders were quick to point out that Bassett's career had been in a downturn since her 1993 Oscar nomination, that she had appeared in such forgettable fluff as *Critters 4* and hadn't had a starring role in five years.

Vivica Fox, one of the colleagues Halle thanked in her acceptance speech and described as a peer 'standing beside me', came to Halle's defence and said on *Access Hollywood*, the TV infotainment show, that *Monster's Ball* had given Halle a chance 'to shine'. To Bassett, she said, 'Don't be trippin' on Halle! Halle got it down! OK, don't hate! Congratulate Halle!'

Bassett's denunciation may have been a case of sour grapes, but her criticism didn't make much sense. Halle's character in *Monster's Ball* is a waitress, not a hooker, and her white leading man is shown to be just as sexual an 'animal' as his black lover. Not only is Leticia not a prostitute, she reveals in the film that she's been celibate since her husband went to prison.

In the wake of the furore caused by her *Newsweek* interview, Bassett tried to mend fences by saying through a spokesperson, 'Angela supports Halle 1,000%, and her comments were about her [Angela's] choices and her preferences, and not Halle's.'

Although Bassett's was the minority opinion, it was an opinion shared by other minorities. The producer-director Roy Campanella II, who is in development on a TV movie about the black singer and actress Lena Horne, felt *Monster's Ball* 'associates a level of animalistic sexuality to black women in a manner that could easily be seen as demeaning. I believe Angela has a valid point.'

Halle's defenders thought she was also the victim of a sexist double standard. Denzel Washington won the Best Actor Oscar for his portrayal of a vicious cop who murders a friend, double-crosses his partner, fathers an illegitimate child and brutalises almost everyone he comes in contact with. David E Fossett, a TV executive, told the *Los Angeles Times*, 'Denzel's role was demeaning too, to African-Americans and cops. But men have it easier. We can get away with a lot. And Denzel, he has such a reputation of being like Sidney Poitier.' However, Fossett neglected to mention that, when Poitier played a cop in *In the Heat of the Night*, his rectitude contrasted with Rod Steiger's racist cop.

The black entertainment executive Lee Bailey also felt Halle was a victim of sexism and that people of colour should unite behind her, not stab her in the back. 'There's definitely a double standard,' he said. 'It involves sexuality. Women can't engage in that without being whores . . . Halle is in a class by herself. She is an outrageously beautiful woman who is getting over. People are jealous of that . . . [she] is still getting flak from black folks. It's overwhelmed her historical achievement. The role is still a source of irritation. And it's wrong. There's a lot of hatin' going on.'

Lions Gate's Ortenberg welcomed the debate ignited by Bassett, but felt her criticism had more to do with the lack of good roles for black women than stereotyping them. Controversy about Halle's performance underlined the fact that it was multidimensional, warts and all. Unfortunately, people objected to the warts. 'She played a character with faults. Her character is very real, and her choices hit close to home. It provokes a level of discomfort. Halle is to be applauded [for] the fact that she made this role so much her own that she can provoke that kind of passion,' Ortenberg said.

In contrast to his adulatory biography of Halle, Christopher John Farley took the actress to task in an essay he wrote for *Time* magazine, where he works as a senior editor. Farley wasn't crazy about Denzel Washington's win, either:

> Berry plays a woman who falls in love with a recovering white racist. After Berry learns that her new love also happens to be the man who executed her husband, she puts up some token resistance, then meekly sticks with him. Even Lifetime TV-movie heroines fight back harder when they find out the men in their lives aren't who they purported to be.

Lifetime is the American cable channel with a predominantly female audience. Farley's piece continues:

> Washington portrays a murderous, on-the-take narcotics detective . . . Like most filmgoers, I'd rather not see African-American actors play only plaster saints. Yet if Hollywood responds to Berry's and Washington's victories by serving up more leading roles that revel in the negative, then the result could be more distorting and destructive than if African-American actors were not recognized at all.

Farley made no objections to Halle's role in his biography, and his criticism reflects the different world he inhabits, compared to Halle's down and out waitress, and also ignores an important plot point in the film. Leticia makes it clear in the film that she doesn't love her husband and tells him she visits him on death row only for the sake of their son. So she shouldn't be expected to feel any real enmity against the prison guard (Thornton), who's just doing his job by pulling the switch. Leticia is broke, carless and about to be homeless. Is it any wonder that she accepts kindness, not to mention a car and a roof over her head, from this racist guard, especially since he never displays his racism in her presence and she could easily be unaware of it? Harvard grads such as Farley don't have to worry about homelessness, and when their cars break down they can afford to take them to a mechanic, an option not available to Leticia's minimum-wage slave.

Halle refused to be sucked into a controversy that pitted one black woman against another in an industry that often mistreats or ignores them. She was a class act when she said through her publicist, Karen Samfilippo, 'Those are Angela's remarks. She should address them . . . There is nothing I need to add to that.'

Another reason for Halle's sang-froid about Bassett's criticism may have been due to the fact that at this time she had much more important things to worry about than whether getting stark-naked with a white man on film demeaned her race or made her a whore.

While she was publicly joking about sleeping with two men, Benét and the Oscar statuette, her husband's attitude towards fidelity would turn out to be no laughing matter for the actress.

17. STAND BY YOUR MAN

In 1993, Halle made a prediction that so far has not come true. Then 29, she told *TV Guide*, 'My 30s will be about stopping the cycle, understanding who I am and not repeating the same mistakes. I tell you, my track record with men is zippo.'

As it turned out, she would not improve her track record with Eric Benét. The *Star* broke the story in April 2002, but this time the outrageous tale was not just another tabloid fantasy, as the mainstream press eventually got up to speed and confirmed many of the details about Benét's affair with a 33-year-old model, Julia Ripley. It helped that the tabloids had photographic proof – pictures of Benét and Riley leaving the apartment he still kept in his hometown of Milwaukee, Wisconsin. (Britain's *Times* said poor Halle had a 'propensity for tabloid-friendly crises'.)

Riley and Benét had been together since 1995, and the relationship continued, according to her, after Benét married Halle in 2001. Even the wedding ceremony, according to Australia's *Woman's Day*, couldn't keep thoughts of Riley out of Benét's mind. According to Riley, Benét phoned her a few hours before the ceremony and whispered into the phone, 'I love you.'

'He told me he had to be quiet and discreet because everybody was downstairs, including Halle, and they were getting ready for the big day,' *Woman's Day* quoted Riley as saying. The only problem with this story is that Halle and Benét were married on a secluded beach in Southern California, so there was no 'upstairs' from which he could make his surreptitious phone call. During the same phone call, Riley told the reputable *New York Post*, Benét informed her that he had wired her the money she had requested.

The tabloids broke the story in early April 2002, only weeks after the Oscar win made Halle an international cynosure and celebrity. Riley told *Women's Day*, 'Just days before Halle stood up and collected her Oscar award in front of the whole world, her husband was in bed with me! She may be a top Hollywood star, but she doesn't know how to keep her man.'

While the story remained only tabloid fodder and didn't leak into the legitimate press, both Halle and her husband ignored it. In May 2002, Benét's attorney Bobby Rosenblum said, 'Eric completely denies this. He has had no extramarital encounters since he wed Halle.'

Few people take the tabloids – which employ some of America's finest writers of fiction – seriously. Indeed, few people admit even to reading them. But finally, in December 2002, Halle and her husband broke their silence and talked to the mainstream press. Halle was circumspect about the details. Her husband was more forthcoming.

Benét told the UK's *Daily Mail* in the 6 December 2002 issue, 'The truth is, we are going through a personal crisis. I have made some terrible mistakes, but I love my wife. I am so in love with Halle and we are committed to each other, our marriage and our love. We are united and trying to make our way through this.'

Halle said in the same article, 'I just love Eric and marriage is about sticking together through the tough times. We are doing exactly that, and I feel good about it.'

Riley's claim that Benét phoned her hours before his wedding was unlikely since the nuptials took place on the beach, but Halle perhaps unwittingly lent credence to another claim by Riley that she and Benét made love in Milwaukee a few days before the actress's Oscar triumph, when Halle told the reputable *Essence* magazine, 'During the period of my most significant public success, my private life faced a staggering crisis. All romantic relationships suffer crises; no woman can claim otherwise.'

Although Riley gave lurid details of her alleged lovemaking with Benét in various tabloid interviews, she did not reveal what Halle implied in her interview with *Essence*. Halle knew about the affair 'during the period of my most significant public success'. Oscar time.

With that knowledge, one wonders what was really going through her mind during her acceptance speech at the Academy Awards when she said, 'Thank you, my husband, who is just a joy of my life . . . I love you . . . with all my heart.' And when Halle seemed unable to speak at the podium and Benét stood up to calm her down, and in his words functioned as a 'beacon of love', was it a public show of support that contrasted with their personal crisis?

After her hit-and-run accident, Halle feared everyone would desert her, including her husband, but he stayed and supported her through her public ordeal and humiliation. Maybe she felt she owed him. In fact, in January 2001, before she knew of the affair, Halle mentioned the debt she felt towards her husband, although, in the light of later events, the quote is sadly ironic now. 'I finally got it right,' she told the 18 January 2001, issue of *USA Weekend*, shortly after their marriage. 'I've chosen the right person for me. And he's very supportive. Whatever I wanna do, he's cool with. And when we hit hard times, which we have – I had my accident – he stood right there by my side and supported me, believed in me.'

There may have been another reason Halle decided to stand by her man – her man's daughter. *Her* daughter. She had adopted his daughter, India, after India had said to Halle, 'You're the mom I always dreamed of. Could you make me your real daughter?'

India came into Halle's life when India was seven. Halle felt that Eric had done a terrific job raising India as a single parent, but she also felt India was at an age when 'girls start to need a mother'. Her adopted daughter has filled all her maternal instincts, Halle has said, and, if she ever has a biological daughter, that child 'won't mean any more to me than [India] does'.

Halle is a hands-on mother. She once skipped the movie premiere of *Ali* to stay home and coach India in memorising her lines for a forthcoming school play and put together a thrift-store costume.

Halle has gained as much from her adopted daughter as India has received from the woman she calls 'mommy'. On her website, Halle describes the curative effect her daughter has had on her life – and interior décor. Children haven't yet been taught how to behave like adults and, as such, see things very simply and say what they want without considering whether they should or shouldn't. Because of this, Halle has learned from India that she can say what she is thinking. She's also experienced joy and laughter. Her home used to be filled with sculptures and pristine, but now it's a 'wreck' but she likes it. She says, 'I used to come home for solitude and quiet. Now I come home for love.'

Halle may have decided to try to make the marriage work so India wouldn't lose her second 'mother' after having lost her birth mother in a car accident. Or maybe she was just living up to her old self-description of being a 'jerk magnet'. In a documentary that aired on the Lifetime channel in 1998, she recalled the 'magnet-ude' of her problem with a hearty but shocking belly laugh: 'If there was a loser in a town, I'd find him and date him and fall in love . . . and be devastated when it didn't work out, maybe get beat up in the process.' In an interview with *The Times* (London) in November 2002, she added that some of these boyfriends 'would steal my jewellery, secretly be married or just plain treat me bad. I would find him.'

During her interview with *Essence*, Halle declined to confirm rumours that Benét had checked into the Meadows, a rehab clinic in Wickenburg, Arizona, that specialises in treatment for sex addiction. She did confirm that the two had begun psychotherapy together. And the august London *Times* not only confirmed tabloid reports of Benét's treatment for sex addiction at the Meadows, but said Benét had committed adultery '10 times with some of her friends'. Notice the plural. Even the delusional tabloids only claimed Benét was unfaithful with one woman, Julia Riley. *The Times* also offered a motive for his philandering, other than the obvious one, sex. The paper claimed his failed singing career and his wife's phenomenal movie career created a man who 'couldn't cope', although it did note that there were tears running down his cheek during Halle's Oscar acceptance speech. Crocodile tears or tears of remorse? Only the fiction authors at the tabloids know for sure.

The *Globe* tabloid quoted an unnamed source's claim that Halle had given her husband an ultimatum – treatment or divorce. And she attacked her marital problems with the same steely resolve she had brought to her career. According to an interview in *Essence*, Halle made her husband sign a contract promising to commit to long-term marriage counselling. She also made him agree to continue therapy even after the current storm had passed. 'I think a little prevention is worth a lot of cure. I am proud Eric has joined me in doing the hard work to save our family.'

It *would* be hard work – and long. The magazine *Relate* has said that the trend in the UK is to agree to a dozen or so counselling sessions, but the custom among typically overachieving American celebrities is to meet with a therapist three or four times a week for an entire year. And, as with many other celebrity perks, therapists to the stars are on call 24 hours a day.

Unusual as it seemed that the couple would turn therapy into a contractual agreement, their deal was actually another new trendy Hollywood phenomenon, a status symbol like employing a personal trainer or personal shopper. Before Halle and Benét went public with their arrangement, the American actress Reese Witherspoon revealed that she and her husband, the actor Ryan Phillippe, had signed a similar contract – on the day they were married! 'A little prevention' indeed. Witherspoon shared Halle's preventive prescription and said, 'We agreed that sometimes we would need help and arrange this so that the good times might help us prevent some bad times.'

Halle's co-star in *Monster's Ball*, Billy Bob Thornton, was asked by his wife, the actress Angelina Jolie, to sign a therapy pre-nuptial, but he rejected the suggestion as 'intrusive and pointless'. Jolie might have been right. The couple later split.

Riley in the *Woman's Day* interview claimed she and Benét had been in a relationship for seven years. In December 2002, a reporter from *Access Hollywood* cornered Halle and Benét at the premiere of *Evelyn*, which starred her *Die Another Day* co-star, Pierce Brosnan. Benét told *Access Hollywood* that Riley's claim about the length of their relationship was 'completely not true', but while his wife stood there, no doubt wishing the ground would swallow her up, he did not deny the existence of the affair and admitted their relationship was going through a 'personal crisis' and that he made 'terrible mistakes' in the marriage.

But nothing fatal, apparently. *Us Weekly* reported that, the day after the embarrassing ambush interview by *Access Hollywood*, Halle and Benét were photographed having breakfast at Joan's restaurant in Hollywood. Halle said, 'We're sticking together.'

By June, however, industry observers made a point of noticing that Halle rarely appeared in public with her husband and failed to thank him in her acceptance speech that month when she received an award from *Essence* for *Monster's Ball*. Rumours of divorce became so prevalent that Halle's publicist felt compelled to issue a public denial. 'If you'll notice, Halle didn't name anyone [in her acceptance speech],' publicist Karen Samfilippo said. 'She said she already did that at the Oscars. Eric has a career as well, you know. He's been working in the studio.'

Halle further scotched rumours of divorce or separation when she told *TV Guide* in November 2002, 'I love him and we are very much together. Everybody goes through some crisis. But when you're a celebrity, it becomes bigger than it actually is. Eric and I are committed to going through the tough times together.'

Proof of their renewed commitment came in December 2002, when WENN, the entertainment-news wire service, reported that the couple planned to renew their marriage vows in a very private ceremony at a posh hotel in Hawaii on New Year's Day 2003. WENN claimed the renewal ceremony was a 'desperate attempt' by Halle to save her marriage and that she had contemplated leaving him after she learned of his alleged affair with Julia Riley. A close friend of the couple told WENN, '[Eric] suggested renewing their vows and making a proper go of things. He is desperate not to lose Halle and she, in turn, will do everything to save the marriage.'

Concrete proof of their commitment came with the news towards the end of 2002 that the couple were building what *Vogue* described as their 'dream house' in Beverly Hills, near the home in the Hollywood Hills that Halle had lived in for the past eight years, before and after she had met Benét. Halle hopes to 'furnish' their new dream home with more children. In early 2003, she said, 'It has been a great year, and now I want to get pregnant. But I know that if that doesn't happen, I will still be fulfilled.' After all, she already has India in her life.

In an interview with *Vogue* in December 2002, Halle implied, however, that Benét was still on probation of sorts. The interviewer played armchair psychoanalyst and wondered whether her attraction to abusive men represented a re-enactment of her relationship with her father. Victimised as a child, was she allowing herself to be victimised all over again? But Halle refused to accept victim status and offered her relationship with Benét, despite his roving eye, as proof. 'But I'm *not* a victim, because I *chose* those situations. I think the only situation I feel like I've been victimized by is by my relationship with my father, and I didn't choose him.'

But she did accept a Freudian interpretation of her romantic mismatches, which Britain's *Sunday Times* attributed to the 'impact of her alcoholic and abusive father [who] seemed to have left her with a penchant for ne'er-do-well male companions'.

Halle didn't disagree with that explanation. 'Therapists have said that to me,' she said. 'I've tried to dissect it. I do believe that's why I've chosen these men. It's to help me heal that part of myself that was so damaged by my father. And each time out – even though on paper it looks horrific – little by little it is helping to heal that wound.'

And she offered Benét as proof that she was making progress in the healing process, although she refused to describe herself as completely healed. 'Eric's a very kind, sensitive, gentle soul. Very unlike, in that regard, any man I've ever been with. He's also a really good father, which is what initially attracted me to him, seeing that he was a great dad to a little girl. It touched a really special chord in me.'

Her *Vogue* interrogator wanted to know if she felt she had finally broken the pattern of choosing the wrong mate. Halle was not yet ready to let Benét off the hook and said, 'I don't know if I've broken the pattern. Too early to tell. So I'm not even gonna put that out in the world and make a fool out of myself. But unlike a lot of the other guys, with Eric, I know that I really like him.'

Then she mentioned another tie that binds her to Benét despite his peccadilloes. 'And if we divorce in five years, I know we'll be friends because of India. She's mine now, and that's never going to change.' Benét's immutability was another issue, and this jury of one was still out on the defendant and the verdict on him.

As for Julia Riley's various claims, among others, that Benét liked to be tied up during sex and that Halle didn't make love to him as often as he wanted, Benét told the UK's *Daily Mail*, 'It is sad how some people will stoop just to get a cheque.' One wonders whether Benét's crack about chequebook journalism reminded Halle that her own father had allegedly sold his story to a tabloid for a six-pack of beer.

In 2002, when the story of Benét's philandering made international news, Halle's description of the perfect mate, which she related to *Ebony* magazine in 1999, must by then have seemed bitterly ironic:

> There was a time after the divorce [from David Justice] when I was really bitter. I convinced myself I didn't want to get married again and that was OK because I didn't need to rush into another relationship. Now that I'm stronger and wiser, I know what I need in a relationship. I know what it looks like, what it feels like. I know what I want in a man.

The interviewer asked for specifics, and Halle Berry's response indicated that Benét's behaviour had not fulfilled that need when she described her ideal mate:

> Someone who values the institution of marriage and all that means. It's one thing to be out with the cameras flashing and the fans waving, but I need someone who I can share the quiet moments with. Someone who can be happy sitting on the sofa with me, just looking at the sunset and have that be enough.

According to Julia Riley, at least, that was not enough for Eric Benét.

But, at the Golden Globe Awards in Beverly Hills on 19 January 2003, Benét appeared very devoted to his wife to the point that he carried the train of her gown, a pastel-blue number with spaghetti straps that prompted the TV news programme *Entertainment Tonight* to put Halle on its 'Best Dressed' list for the evening.

18. BILLION-DOLLAR BABE

Halle had the blessing of a gruelling work schedule to keep her mind off marital problems, although the work she chose after *Monster's Ball* raised some eyebrows among pundits who thought she should continue to tackle serious issues in serious films.

Halle didn't have much time to savour her Oscar victory or fret about an errant husband. Only three days after the Academy Awards ceremony, she found herself rising like a naiad, or more accurately like Ursula Andress in 1962's *Dr No*, from the sea off Cadiz in southern Spain, clad in an orange bikini with a phallic knife on her hip – the same outfit and weapon Andress had worn in the first James Bond film.

Halle was co-starring in the twentieth Bond outing, *Die Another Day*, opposite Pierce Brosnan as the British secret agent with a licence to kill and have as much sex as he can possibly squeeze into a two-hour-plus movie.

Halle had become, amazingly, a Bond girl, a designation she accepted without shame or angst about feminist issues of political correctness. In fact, she revelled in her new screen identity. She taunted a reporter from Britain's *Sunday Times*, 'I'm a Bond girl. Go ahead and say it. Say it! Classic Bond babe! And it's great!'

In the latest 007 lallapaloosa, which cost $142 million to make, she plays Jinx, an undercover agent for the US's National Security Agency, a real-life spy organisation more secretive than the CIA. Jinx belongs to a sexy sorority of previous Bond babes with suggestive names like Plenty O'Toole, Pussy Galore and Octopussy. When he did a Q&A with Halle for *Interview* magazine, her former co-star Samuel L Jackson poked fun at those sexist names and asked Halle if her Bond character would be named Cinnamon Buns. Halle joked that she would try to get the producers to change Jinx's name to Jackson's suggestion.

Premiere magazine described her as the first Bond girl to report to the set toting an Oscar. It left unanswered the embarrassing question, 'What is a serious actress doing in a film whose heroines and villainesses had *double-entendre* names for female genitalia?'

The Times (London) pointed out that it took another Bond babe, Kim Basinger in *Never Say Never Again*, fifteen years to escape the '007 curse' and win a Best Supporting Actress Oscar in 1998 for *Hollywood Confidential.*

Halle made no apologies for her decision and answered the question without even being asked. 'It's a dream come true to be in a Bond movie.' First of all, she signed on to the project before she had the clout and prestige of being an Oscar winner or even a nominee. Second, she liked the fact that for a change she was wooed for the part, and it hadn't required her usual MO of practically crashing the offices of studio executives and casting directors to be considered for roles everyone thought she was all wrong for. It didn't hurt that she was offered her biggest pay day to date, $4 million, although Hollywood's double standard in the compensation department was in full operation as Brosnan took home $20 million for his fourth outing as 007.

Oscar hadn't turned Halle into a film snob. In fact, post-Oscar, Brosnan didn't notice any change in his co-star. 'When she won, it was a joyous occasion. But when she came back, it was business as usual. She came back the same woman she was when she left,' Brosnan said.

Halle embraced the lowbrow genre of popcorn pix or what she inventively labelled 'mall movies'. 'Hopefully, I'll have opportunities and choices I didn't have before, but I certainly don't want to think, now that I have an Oscar, I can only do certain things,' she told the *Sunday Times* in June 2002. 'I still want to take risks and do little great movies, and then do big "mall movies", because there's a need for that in my career too. It's got to be balanced.'

A reporter on the set of *Die Another Day* asked if she was worried that *Monster's Ball* was bracketed by two pieces of fluff on her résumé, *X-Men* and *X-Men 2*. 'Not really,' Halle said in the December 2002 issue of *Vogue*. 'You have to get in the game in a serious way, and the game is, partly, being in movies that make a lot of money.'

The issue of race and, ironically, artistic freedom also coloured her decision to don Jinx's orange bikini among other ravishing outfits, including an evening gown not much bigger than, well, a bikini. Although she knew the bikini scene was *un hommage* to *Dr*

No's similar introduction of Ursula Andress, she wasn't thrilled about doing it. 'When I read that, I thought, "They've got to be kidding me." I really wasn't sure if I wanted to do that, but . . . I hope it has a modern spin on it,' she said to *Premiere*. On another occasion, however, Halle seemed to embrace her Bond-girl roots and said, 'I saw the first movie, *Dr No*, and I remember thinking, Wow, how sexy and groovy and cool the women are.'

Although she had reservations about her wardrobe, a part of Halle welcomed being presented as a sex object, more important-ly, a *black* sex object. 'For so many years black women have been desexualized,' she said. 'If you weren't blonde with blue eyes, then you weren't sexy in America. I think it's starting to change. For a long time I battled trying to feel sexy because I didn't think I was.' You can almost hear the high school prom queen falsely accused of stuffing the ballot box because she wasn't pretty enough to win legitimately echoing in Halle's estimation of what being black and a Bond girl meant to her.

If Halle still felt insecure about her looks after all these years, she had only to look at the June 2002 issue of the lads magazine, *FHM*, whose readers voted her the third most beautiful star, after the No. 1 tennis babe Anna Kournikova and the bubblegum pop star Britney Spears. And, if she required more assurances about her attractiveness, she could find comfort in the fact that for four years in a row she had made *People* magazine's '50 Most Beautiful People' list, and in 2003 a poll of American plastic surgeons voted her eyes and cheeks the best of any movie star's.

Appearing in a blockbuster would also, ironically, give her the power to get funding for uncommercial, risky fare. Brosnan has used his clout from the Bond series to appear in small films such as *Evelyn* and *The Tailor of Panama*. If *Die Another Day* 'helps more people around the world know who I am, then the next time I put out a *Monster's Ball*, more people will come to see it. Then I get to make more *Monster's Balls*,' Halle said.

Also, it had always galled her when white producers and executives told her that 'black doesn't travel' – i.e. black movie stars aren't big overseas. Bond films typically do two-thirds of their business abroad. 'It may seem frivolous,' she said, 'but it's all part of the plan to become a global name. We've been told that "black doesn't travel", and we're trying to change that. When you're known around the world, then people will give you $10 million for a movie and know they'll make it back, plus you then have the freedom to make little movies domestically that you love for the work' – rather than the paycheque.

It was also fun to be bad, if only on film. Halle has said that, while her older sister became rebellious in reaction to their father's abuse, she overcompensated by always trying to be the good girl, prom queen, student council president and honour society member, etc. When we first meet Jinx, she appears to be a femme fatale and Bond's enemy. 'It would be great to play a bad girl. I've never done that on film before. We can't be bad in [real] life. You get in trouble and go to jail. So it would be a thrill to do things in a surreal world, with lots of fighting and bad-ass stuff. I don't do that in life.'

There was a good deal of fighting in the film, and Halle had to learn a new and dangerous skill. Jinx is a professional knife thrower and Halle turned into a holy terror on the set. 'I stepped up my workouts and learned to work with knives. I almost took a few eyeballs out in the practices,' she said.

Halle may also be the first Bond girl to bed Bond twice in the course of a single film, although her contract stipulated absolutely *no* nudity. For a serious film like *Monster's Ball*, Halle would be willing, albeit reluctantly, to bare all, but, for a film franchise whose ritualised sex and violence one critic called 'kabuki popcorn', she was keeping her clothes on. When asked about rumours that she would appear nude in *Die Another Day*, she said, 'That is absolutely not me; I have a clause that is, actually, quite to the contrary! I will not be nude anytime soon. Who knows how these rumors get started? Just like the one about how I got paid extra to be nude in *Swordfish*; God knows where these things come from.'

Although Halle refused to strip for James Bond, she didn't rule out nudity in future films. Nudity in a popcorn movie like *Die Another Day* would end up being just one of the many stunts in the movie – a publicity stunt. But serious fare was a different matter, and, after the positive experience of the love scene in *Monster's Ball*, Halle was keeping an open mind about opening her blouse. 'If I have a strong belief that it's what the character would do, then I'd use my body in any way that would best serve that character. I live my life for me,' she said.

Ironically, it was her nude scene in *Swordfish* that caught the eye of *Die Another Day*'s director, the New Zealander Lee Tamahori, who said Jinx was originally conceived of as 'the classic Latin spitfire', but, when he couldn't find a Latina fiery enough, he recalled Halle. More specifically, he recalled the scene in *Swordfish* where she flashes her breasts for about three seconds. Tamahori said, 'The Bond movies run around the world being exotic. They cast Russian women who kill with their thighs. They had [cast] Asian with Michelle Yeoh [in 1997's *Tomorrow Never Dies*.] It was time to head off into some other ethnicity. Almost like a lottery, I think.' And Halle was the $4 million winner. 'I had seen *Swordfish*, and it just kind of blew me away, what she was capable of doing. I realized that she could crack this action-genre thing wide open,' said Tamahori.

Besides being the only Bond girl to have sex with 007 twice, she's also the first one to be shown actually having sex with him, although strategically positioned sheets and low lighting ensure that Halle's no-nudity clause was enforced. Tamahori said, 'In lovemaking, Bond's PG requirements have traditionally meant you can only show postcoital sex. You know, clothes strewn around the room, the camera slowly pans over to the bed. But we thought, "Why couldn't Bond have the best lay of his life?" So we shot a very hot love scene. Whether it survives the censor's cut – or the producers' – we'll see.'

It did. Before they shot the scene, Tamahori made it clear that this was a match between equals – inside the bedroom and out. 'I said to Halle, "No matter what you think, this character has got to be as kick-ass as Bond." If you look carefully at the [first] love scene, she actually takes him to bed and leaves him in the morning. And she's on top and she's got a knife in her hand during the lovemaking scene. Pierce and Halle love that,' Tamahori said.

Halle uses the knife to slice open a fig, which she shares with Brosnan during the first love scene. In a movie full of potentially lethal stunts, the simple act of eating a fig, which Halle said she improvised, almost killed her – literally – and Brosnan found himself playing a real-life hero, saving the heroine's life. Halle recalled, 'Pierce and I were doing this love scene. I was trying to be way too sexy for my own good. I pull out this knife, trying to give the scene an air of danger, and start cutting a fig. I ate a slice.' At this point Brosnan cracked an ad-libbed joke.

Brosnan picks up the story from there. 'She started laughing, and then she gagged. And suddenly there was no sound coming out. She was on the bed, gagging and waving her arms, and I was banging her on the back. I was about to put my arms around her and start doing the Heimlich [manoeuvre], but the both of us were kind of naked. And then she somehow expelled the fruit, which was a good thing because I had never given anyone the Heimlich before. And I was certainly in no position to give it to Halle at that moment.' (The Heimlich manoeuvre involves applying pressure to the abdomen in order to expel the object that is being choked on.)

Halle said the crew didn't offer assistance and just stared at her and Brosnan.

Press reports of another accident on the set were exaggerated and claimed that shrapnel from an exploding grenade had blinded the actress during one stunt, leading headline writers to pun such groaners as, FOR YOUR EYE ONLY and SWOLLENEYE. Halle said it was just a speck of dust that scratched her cornea, but the film's insurance carrier insisted on a trip to the hospital, where she was given some eye drops and immediately returned to the set.

But after winning the Oscar Halle had become such a public cynosure that her alleged blinding made international news, and the producers of Die Another Day felt compelled to put out a press statement assuring everyone that their most precious asset was just fine:

> Ms Berry experienced some discomfort when a gust of wind blew some dust into her eye during filming of an action sequence. Contrary to media speculation, it was not as a result of debris from a smoke grenade. As a precautionary measure, the production sought medical attention for what was a slight inflammation. We are happy to report that Ms

Berry suffered no lasting ill effects and returned to work immediately.

Brosnan didn't escape the dangerous shoot unscathed, either. He neglected to warm up before shooting a scene that required him to run, and he injured his knee, putting him out of commission for two weeks. Once recovered, the actor, who at fifty is fourteen years Halle's senior, seemed to be in better shape than his co-star. One scene required the pair to run alongside a moving plane. Brosnan left her behind – if not in the dust at least on the tarmac. 'The minute I took off running, I saw smoke coming out of Pierce's feet. My legs just couldn't go fast enough. I had to go home a failure,' Halle said.

If their two bedroom scenes work, and they do, part of their effectiveness may have been due to some genuine bonding the two stars experienced while making the film. 'Working with Pierce is wonderful,' Halle said. 'He wears Bond like an old shoe, and wears it well. He's so sure of himself within the character. That dynamic is really comforting. He's always there with a lot of support.' Brosnan became a charter member of this mutual admiration society and said, 'She's an incredible dramatic actress, but she can also play an action hero with the best of them. It was a great treat to be able to work with her, and we had a great time doing so. Working with Halle is definitely on top of the list.'

Brosnan saw something else in Halle, which others have also commented on: a subtle but profound sadness – the results, no doubt, of such a stormy life. 'Halle's got great soul and humility, and she knows what suffering is. She knows what it is to have to fight and to be on the outside. I don't think she's had an easy life,' he said.

Die Another Day also has the distinction of being the first Bond film to cause if not an international incident at least an international temper tantrum. The bad guys in this outing are megalomaniacal North Korean military officers (Rick Yune and Will Yun Lee) who plan to dominate the world with an orbiting death ray (more kabuki popcorn). Although another Korean officer is portrayed as a good guy who seeks a rapprochement with the West, the official North Korean newspaper, *Rodong Sinmun*, condemned the film for its negative portrayal of the Stalinist state. The newspaper said, 'The army and people of [North Korea] with burning hatred for the Yankees are in full readiness to fight a death-defying battle.' And something called the 'Secretariat of the Committee for the Peaceful Reunification of the Fatherland', a government agency in the North Korean capital of Pyongyang, called the film 'a dirty and cursed burlesque aimed to slander and insult the Korean nation . . . a premeditated act of mocking' that shows the United States is 'the headquarters that spreads abnormality, degeneration, violence and *fin de siècle* corrupt sex culture'.

Although feminists would insist that any character with the epithet 'girl' attached to it doesn't promote feminism, Halle considered Jinx liberated and liberating, which didn't stop her from referring to the character as a 'girl'. 'I found her to be my kind of Bond girl – smart, tough, physical, mysterious and independent.' Halle felt Jinx was the equal and equivalent of 007. 'She does what he does – knives, swords, guns, gymnastics. She's able to challenge all of the men in the movie, but she's also sexy. I think a woman who can be all of those things is the deadliest weapon there is.'

Maybe her Oscar and the fact that *Die Another Day* would end up being the top-grossing Bond film of all time had something to do with it as well, but the producers valued Halle's participation in the film so much that they not only asked her to sign on for a sequel, an offer never made to a Bond babe before, but have stated they are considering a spin-off based on Jinx – without 007. MGM, which released *Die Another Day*, also recognised the value of having an Oscar winner on board, and the ad campaign prominently featured Halle alongside Brosnan.

While this book was being written, *Die Another Day*'s screen-writers, Neal Purvis and Robert Wade, were developing a treatment that they hoped would lead to an entire Jinx franchise and one as lucrative as forty years of Bond have been for MGM. Much as she liked going global and proving that black *does* travel, Halle was taking a wait-and-see attitude towards becoming too closely linked to one film role, a phenomenon that might be called Roger Moore Syndrome. (Moore's acting career never recovered from decades of Bondage, and for years Sean Connery didn't escape typecasting after he left the series.) Halle said, 'If she could stay the character I've come to know and love, and would evolve even further . . . then I'm absolutely interested.'

The long-time Bond producer Michael Wilson hoped to keep Halle's interest in the franchise and welcomed her input on Jinx's further evolution. 'For somebody to win an Academy Award for a dramatic piece and then to do this with the same enthusiasm, and not feel it is a step down, is wonderful. And if she has a back story for Jinx all worked out, well, I'd like to hear about it,' Wilson said.

When *Die Another Day* debuted in the US on 22 November 2002, the critics typically panned it. *Daily Variety* went so far as to call the film a 'betrayal of the Bond franchise' because its computer-generated effects went beyond hi-tech and entered 'quasi-sci-fi territory'. Halle also earned a rare negative review when *Variety* complained, 'After the promising beginning, unfortunately, most of what Berry is called up to do is pretty generic action stuff.' The *New York Times* said Tamahori was not a 'natural action director. Many of the big chases and gunfights are incoherently cut together, and some of the special effects have a tacky, off-the-rack look that would be more suitable in a *Spy Kids* movie.' The *New York Times* barely mentioned Halle's presence other than to comment on the sports bra and tank top she wears in a fight with the film's villainess (Rosamund Pike). While acknowledging the obvious – Halle's ethereal beauty – the *Los Angeles Times* felt Jinx was just another Bond babe, not the liberated co-equal of 007 that had attracted Halle to the part:

> Berry brings about as much conviction as you might expect to a role that, essentially, is the bodacious equivalent of a hit of Viagra. First seen rising up from the Caribbean waters [actually the Atlantic Ocean] as Ursula Andress did in *Dr No* . . . the Academy Award-winner has been brought in to jump-start Bond's engine and as a consequence she never fully transcends the standard Bond girl limitations. It isn't only that Berry lacks the ferocious determination, it's that the Bond movie she's signed on to lacks it as well.

The *San Francisco Chronicle* made it clear that it felt Halle was slumming here after *Monster's Ball*: 'Berry deflects the indignity of Bond-girl status as if by resolving to be cheerful.' But the *Village Voice* put such nit-picking in context when it said, 'Dissing a Bond movie is quite like calling a dog stupid.'

Fortunately for MGM, which desperately needed a hit on its quarterly report, *Die Another Day*, like all previous 007 outings, was critic-proof. In its first three days of release in the US, the film, whose budget was $142 million, grossed $47.2 million, the biggest opening in the franchise's history. Within ten days, it had passed the $100 million mark. After its release on 3 January 2003, in the UK, it did an additional £33.7 million. Worldwide receipts were predicted to reach $425 million, and that was before the film was released on video and DVD in the summer of 2003. (Video/DVD rentals and sales typically account for two-thirds of a film's total receipts, so the final tally will surpass a billion dollars.)

Although its critic panned the film, the *Los Angeles Times'* business reporter felt he knew who was responsible for making *Die Another Day* the top Bond film of all time: 'The movie probably benefited from the casting of Oscar winner Halle Berry, who as the CIA [sic] seductress Jinx introduces a new breed of Bond girl.'

At the film's Los Angeles premiere, Halle was again surprised by a reporter from *Access Hollywood*, whom she asked, 'Who would have thought of me as a Bond girl?' When the reporter replied that she seemed like a natural in the role, Halle visibly bristled and said, 'Well, *I* never would have thought it.'

Toy manufacturer Mattel brought out a new $75 pair of Ken and Barbie dolls in conjunction with the film's release. *Access Hollywood* had obligingly brought along two of the dolls to show Halle. One resembled Pierce Brosnan and sported 007's trademark tuxedo and black tie. The female doll was, like Barbie herself, a blonde Caucasian.

Halle probably shrugged off the negative reviews of *Die Another Day* because the film's commercial success made a wish she expressed way back in 1993 come true. 'I want to be in a mega box-office hit, and get all the money and success Michelle Pfeiffer did,' she said.

And she did. After *Die Another Day*'s release, Halle's asking price doubled to $8 million per film.

19. WEATHERING ANOTHER STORM

Just as she didn't turn up her nose at playing a Bond girl after winning an Oscar, Halle embraced her popcorn past in action films when it came time to reprise her role as Storm in *X-Men 2*.

'I'm looking forward to our putting on the suits again,' she said. Halle neglected to mention another reason she was appearing in consecutive fluff. She was contractually obligated to. As a condition of starring in the first *X-Men*, all the cast members were obliged to sign a contract agreeing to appear in at least one sequel. The contractual obligation resulted in some weird phenomena. Rebecca Romijn-Stamos, who played the blue fleshed shape shifter Mystique in the original *X-Men*, was gutted like a fish by Wolverine's stainless-steel fingernails and died. Somehow, and the studio wasn't saying how, Mystique has a miraculous resurrection and appears in the sequel, as does Bruce Davison's politician, who also died in the original.

The $100 million production began filming in Canada in late 2002 with the cast and crew forced to endure freezing locations in Calgary, Vancouver, Toronto and Victoria, British Columbia.

In the sequel to the 2000 hit, the United States government is still harassing those maligned mutants. Their main persecutor this time around, a US Army colonel, William Stryker (Brian Cox), is pressing hard for passage of a bill called the Mutant Registration Act, which was introduced after an attack by one of the bad mutants outraged public opinion and prompted further oppression of these highly evolved creatures.

Magneto (Ian McKellen), the leader of the evil mutants, was last seen entombed in a plastic prison where his superhuman ability to control metal objects renders him powerless. In the sequel, Magneto escapes from his polyurethane pen and forms an unlikely alliance with the leader of the good mutants, Professor Xavier (Patrick Stewart). They team up to fight Colonel Stryker, who is planning an assault on Xavier's finishing school for promising young mutants. Stryker may also be the madman who surgically implanted the steel claws that make Wolverine (Hugh Jackman) such a sharpie. At the end of the first instalment, Wolverine left the relative safety of Professor Xavier's school and hit the road to find out who grafted the painful prostheses on to his skeleton, and in the sequel he continues the search for his roots and tormentor.

The sequel has at least one new character from the original Marvel comic books, a mutant named Nightcrawler, played by the Scottish actor Alan Cumming, best known as the decadent MC in the Broadway revival of *Cabaret* and as Boris Grishenko in *GoldenEye*. Nightcrawler's appearance was so secret that Cumming was required to wear a hood when he travelled from his trailer to the set to avoid the prying lenses of the paparazzi who trailed the production wherever it went with more fervour than Colonel Stryker's witch-hunt. (Cumming's hood turned out to be a waste of time because somehow *Newsweek* managed to catch the actor in full mutant drag, and his appearance was something of a disappointment because he looks just like the Wolfman from the thirties and forties films. To achieve that look, the unfortunate actor had to spend ten hours in the makeup chair every day of the shoot. When pressed to reveal *anything* about the plot of the sequel, Cumming joked, 'You do get to see my nipples once. But it's just a glimpse.' And no doubt Nightcrawler's 'nudity' is integral to the part. Cumming neglected to say whether he had been paid $250,000 – Halle's mythical fee per breast in *Swordfish* – to bare his pecs. Another reason Cumming didn't reveal anything substantial about the plot may have been that he didn't know much. To prevent leaks, the entire cast was kept in the dark about much of the storyline. Famke Janssen, who reprises her role as the beautiful mutant Dr Jean Grey, said, 'Even I don't know how the movie ends.'

Nightcrawler wasn't the only addition to the cast of characters, but its director Bryan Singer refused to identify them. 'We want to keep those characters a surprise. But there will be some really interesting new characters, both young and old,' he said in 2001.

Because of the Marvel comic books' 27-year history and the success of the original, *X-Men 2* had a huge following, which the press unkindly described as geeks, determined to find out anything they could about the sequel, and, hard as the studio tried to plug leaks, titbits escaped the maw of 20th Century-Fox. A bread-and-butter report in the *Hollywood Reporter* about Cinesite, one of several special-effects houses that worked on the film, revealed that there would be a 'generator sequence', mansion scenes and a dogfight. The *Reporter* also revealed the return of Mystique without saying how she is brought back to life after her evisceration by Wolverine. Ruth Scovill, the president and CEO of Cinesite, said, '*X-Men 2* is an imaginative and entertaining story with extraordinary visuals. We are perfectly positioned to create the effects and illusions that Bryan Singer envisions for his film.'

The director didn't get the same enthusiastic co-operation from other quarters. The production was reportedly beset by problems both personal and elemental. The weather wasn't cooperating during the Canadian shoot, and, for a while, neither was the cast.

X-Men 2 originally planned to film the climactic battle between the mutants and the villains in Vancouver, but the scene required snow, and there wasn't enough snowfall in Vancouver, so the cast and crew relocated to the more frigid terrain of Kananaskis, near Calgary, Alberta, but that site also failed to produce enough of the white stuff. The production ended up taking a cue from ski resorts and rented snow-making machines. 'We have had to create tons of snow,' Singer said.

Singer was having other problems as well, according to the wire service WENN.

The reputable WENN claimed that Halle told Singer that he could 'kiss my black ass' after Singer allegedly tried to get the film's popular executive producer, Tom DeSanto, fired.

Besides being out of character for the famously considerate and courteous actress, the story contradicts earlier accounts that she and Singer enjoyed their collaboration, which, she told *Venice* magazine in 2002 shortly before the first instalment was released, 'was good'. She went on: 'Directing [the first *X-Men*], there was so much pressure. The fans were just like, you know . . .' She paused to laugh. 'Oh my God. I was so glad I wasn't him. And I thought he did a really great job dealing with all of it. Every day he'd be on the Internet, wanting to know what they said next. He did a really good job. He took those comic book characters and made them real.' That doesn't sound like the sentiments of someone who would tell a collaborator to kiss her arse and inject race into the insult as well. Halle takes racial issues too seriously to vulgarise skin colour.

The WENN story ran that Singer's driver on the set allegedly gave the director a painkiller that made it impossible for him to finish the day's filming. Singer, in an interview in *Newsweek*, confirmed that a crew member had given him a painkiller for a hip injury but said that it in no way meant that he was unable to work that day. However, his friend Tom DeSanto admonished the crew member and was in turn 'fired' by Singer. Though the production was shut down for a day, irritating the cast, including Halle, the problem was soon resolved.

Halle did walk off the set, but not in a huff. She briefly left the *X-Men* production in Vancouver and returned to Los Angeles to receive an award from the Make-A-Wish Foundation, which makes fantasies come true for seriously ill children. The event, held on 26 October 2002 at the St Regis Hotel & Spa in LA's Century City, raised $200,000, and honoured Halle for helping teenager Kimberly English, an aplastic-anaemia patient, achieve her dream of becoming a fashion model. Wearing a strapless Armani gown, Halle said in her acceptance speech, 'I've never forgotten the joy of granting a wish.' Kimberly English also attended the gala and said, 'It made me feel good that something wonderful came out of my being sick.'

A month later, Halle attended an even more glamorous event – and found herself rubbing shoulders with another perennial tiara wearer. The London premiere of *Die Another Day* at the Royal Albert Hall was attended by the former Bonds Roger Moore, Timothy Dalton and George Lazenby, along with his current incarnation, Brosnan, and his leading lady, who attended with her husband. The Queen and Prince Phillip also attended the charity premiere, which benefited the Cinema and Television Benevolent Fund. After Halle had shaken the Queen's hand, the monarch turned to Brosnan and said, 'So you're the modern James Bond, are you? I've met the other three downstairs.'

While Halle was in London, she blasted the British for being racist, according to WENN. She allegedly claimed that the Brits looked down on her because she's biracial and also because her mother is originally from Liverpool – which didn't seem to hurt the Beatles and many other bands who contributed to the famous Mersey Sound. The US film industry also got a drubbing from the star, who said she still suffers discrimination in Hollywood because of her race. '[Racism] permeates every industry. I'd tell people in the UK my family are from Liverpool, and they'd be like, "Oh, dear," ' WENN quoted her as saying in November 2002. The same month, she told *The Times* (London) that, despite the Oscar and the positive reviews, she still felt embattled but had come to accept it. 'I'm pretty much used to the fight. That's pretty much what my career has been about.'

Halle returned from the Make a Wish Foundation gala to a chaotic set. Besides a mutinous cast, there were other mishaps on location, including a potentially lethal accident that involved Halle. Despite his superhuman powers, Patrick Stewart's Professor Xavier is a wheelchair-bound paraplegic, and one scene, whose details escaped the studio 'censors', called for Halle and Alan Cumming's Nightcrawler to carry the disabled professor up a steep snow-covered mountain slope in Vancouver. Stewart recalled the scene: 'I had one arm over Halle's shoulder and one arm over Alan's. They started trudging up this mountain slope, dragging my legs through the snow. Suddenly Halle screams, "I'm going, I'm going!" And she slides down, pulling me down with her. Alan comes next, and suddenly the three of us were flat on our faces in the snow. We broke up laughing, because it was so ironic. Superheroes? We can't even keep upright in the snow!'

Whether or not *X-Men 2* breaks box office records as her previous film, *Die Another Day*, did, it may already belong in the record books as having taken the controversial practice of product placement to stratospheric levels. For the uninitiated, product placement is the displaying of manufacturers' products on screen as props – for a fee. It's the cinematic equivalent of a very subtle, soft-sell TV commercial. Product placement probably began in 1982, when M&M refused to let Steven Spielberg use their multicoloured sweets in *E.T.: The Extra-Terrestrial*. So the director ended up using Reese's Peanuts as a pivotal part of the plot, and, after that blockbuster's release, sales of Reese's products sky-rocketed. Since then, product placement has become big business, as manufacturers vie to turn their products into 'movie stars'.

Before *X-Men 2* even began filming, 20th Century-Fox had managed to line up $70 million in fees for product placement and promotional tie-ins with Mazda, Dr Pepper, Baskin-Robbins, Kraft and the Radio Shack, a hi-tech gadget retailer. Fox's head of publicity, Jeffrey Godsick, crowed, 'It's the strongest and largest campaign we've ever had at the studio.' Mazda paid an undisclosed fee to have its latest model, the RX-8, 'star' in one scene. As part of the deal, Mazda agreed to display *X-Men 2* movie posters in its dealerships around the world, among other promotional efforts. Dr Pepper planned to emblazon a *billion* cartons of the soft drink with X-Men characters. In the weirdest promotion on record, the ice-cream giant Baskin-Robbins, famous for its 32 flavours, agreed to create additional flavours based on the film's superheroes. One doesn't even want to contemplate what the Nightcrawler ice cream will taste like, although it's a good bet Mystique's flavour will be something 'blue'. Radio Shack, like Mazda, planned to put movie posters in all seven thousand of its stores, and it was also scheduled to create a new hi-tech product based on the movie, but the company, unsurprisingly, refused to disclose any details about the new gadget. A Radio Shack gizmo with Storm's power to control the weather would have been helpful when Canada refused to cooperate and provide sufficient snowfall. Kraft, the food manufacturer, was set to put the mutants on packages of Oreos, Ritz Bitz, Chips Ahoy!, Cheese Nips, Tang and Kool-Aid.

The film was scheduled to be released in the UK and the US on 1 and 2 May 2003, to get a jump on what would be a summer of 'monstrous' competition from other 'no one over 18 allowed' flicks like *The Hulk*, *Terminator 3* and *The Matrix Reloaded*.

EPILOGUE: THRIVE ANOTHER DAY

Halle Berry didn't need to worry about starring in crass acts like mutant movies or being in Bondage to a series of Jinx spin-offs because by 2003 her name was attached to so many class acts as well.

But, most importantly for the actress, for the first time in her fourteen-year career, she was enjoying full employment in an industry where unemployment is the norm for most of its participants and even more so for minorities.

Halle sounded relieved when she described how her Oscar win had influenced her newfound opportunities. 'I'm getting called up [to star in films.] That's new for me and exciting. The biggest change, at least career-wise [post-Oscar], is that I've never before had five projects in development all at once. I've got jobs now, like, in advance. Before when a movie was finishing, I'd be calling my manager: "Oh my God, we've got to get another job!" And now I've got two years of work planned out, and it's great.'

And it wasn't just the quantity but the new and improved quality of the projects offered after her Oscar victory. 'One of the greatest results [of winning the Oscar] is the fact I'm getting some really great parts,' she told the *Daily Variety* columnist Army Archerd, who asked if she was also getting 'great money'. Halle sidestepped that enquiry and said, 'I feel more opportunities are starting to happen. And I'm just reveling in it.'

After years of famine, Halle was ready to feast. And she chose a lavish and variegated buffet to get her teeth into. She was actually being conservative when she claimed that she had five upcoming films. Many more projects had been attached to her name, however tenuously or even accurately. Whenever an actor or actress is hot, wannabe producers and even legitimate ones will often leak items to the press claiming that the star *du jour* 'is considering' or 'is in talks' about a movie they hope to produce. Just one egregious example of how a hot actor can be 'attached' to the most unlikely project concerns the star Sylvester Stallone. During his glory days and multiple screen incarnations as Rambo and Rocky, the Hollywood trade papers announced that Stallone would play the title role in Martin Scorsese's *The Last Temptation of Christ*. (One almost expects to pick up the trades one day and read that Denzel Washington is 'in talks' to star in an all-black version of *Oedipus Rex*, tentatively titled, *Yo Mama*.)

Although nothing quite that preposterous has been associated with Halle's upcoming film schedule, some of her alleged future films seem unlikely at best, including reports that she would star in a big-screen version of the sixties sitcom *I Dream of Jeannie* as the belly dancer who lives in a bottle and calls her boyfriend 'master'. A fatuous item appeared in Marilyn Beck's syndicated column three weeks after Halle's Oscar win, when the entire entertainment industry lay at the actress's feet, claiming that Will Smith and Halle wanted to co-star in a feature film version of *I Dream of Jeannie* with Smith in the astronaut role created by Larry Hagman in the original TV series, but that Sony had rejected both actors.

In November 2002 Lewis Gilbert, who directed the 1983 romantic comedy *Educating Rita*, which starred Michael Caine and Julie Walters, claimed that he had lined up both Halle and Denzel Washington to reprise the Pygmalion-like tale of a professor and the cockney woman he 'educates' with an all-black cast. No other news outlet besides WENN reported this alleged match-up between that year's top Oscar winners. He told WENN:

> My view [it quotes Gilbert saying] was that you couldn't make a new film as good as the original unless you did something very different to it. That's why I find the idea of making it with a black cast so appealing. Making it a black film will take it sufficiently away from the original to make it fresh, but not too far away. There are so many good black actors in America. You only have to think of the two black actors who took the best actor awards at this year's Oscars.

After finishing principal photography on the exhausting *X-Men 2* in the Canadian tundra, Halle knew what she would *not* be doing next. 'It won't be being a superhero, I can tell you that much,' she said, laughing with a reporter from *Venice* magazine. 'I want to go do another *Monster's Ball*, another little character. I'm seeking that out right now.'

Although Halle believed she had five films in development, *Entertainment Weekly* claimed she had eight projects on her plate, although the magazine may have been counting various film-makers' fantasies as real-life projects. At the top of the list of most likely to be filmed next, according to the *Hollywood Reporter*, is *Gothika*, a psychological thriller with supernatural overtones. Halle will play a psychologist who wakes up one day and without knowing why discovers that she's become a patient in the mental hospital where she works – or worked. It's an institution for the criminally insane, and Halle's psychologist is accused of murder. Her shrink turns sleuth as she tries to figure out how she got into this dangerous mess. Penelope Cruz plays another patient in the hospital. Joel Silver is set to produce. This time, it's a safe bet the producer won't demand Halle 'flash her goodies', as she described her nude scene in Silver's *Swordfish*.

All the years Halle has spent in therapy with and without her husband may turn out to have been invaluable research because in *Need*, she is set to play another psychologist who learns that her husband is having an affair with one of her suicidal patients (Marisa Tomei) and decides to get revenge – by terrorising the patient. The trade papers describe *Need* as '*Fatal Attraction*-esque'. Luis Mandoki, who made pop star Jennifer Lopez a bona fide movie star with *Angel Eyes*, will direct. *Daily Variety*, which claimed *Need* had been in 'development hell' for a long time until Halle became attached to the project, reported that a deal for Halle to star in *Need* is 'imminent', while *Entertainment Weekly* insisted it was definitely going into production in autumn 2003.

Halle apparently had a terrific working relationship with *Die Another Day*'s director Lee Tamahori, because she has signed on to work with him again in *The Guide*, another supernatural-flavoured drama based on Thomas Perry's bestselling novel, *Shadow Woman*. Halle will play Jane Whitfield, a Native American shaman who uses ancestral magic plus state-of-the-art computer science to help people in trouble to escape their past and assume new identities. When the shaman gets married, she retires from her practice for a while but returns to work when a previous client finds herself stalked by a psychotic killer. *Entertainment Weekly* speculated that this could be another lucrative film franchise for Halle because there are three more novels about the shaman which could also be adapted.

Brown-Eyed Girl is one of those 'small pictures' that Halle now has the clout to get off the ground, thanks to her having starred in monster blockbusters like *Die Another Day* and a pair of *X-Men*. Directed by Martha Coolidge, who also directed *Introducing Dorothy Dandridge*, *Brown-Eyed Girl* is a character study about the romantic life of an average woman. It will be a stretch for Halle to play 'average'. Although she has had the title of executive producer on several projects, a title that is often more honorific and a sign of clout, on *Brown-Eyed Girl* Halle will be the hands-on producer, working closely with the writer Gary Williams to shape her character.

An unlikely screen project for Halle is her alleged plan to reprise Pam Grier's title role in what the *Sunday Times* called the 'ultimate blaxploitation flick' – 1974's *Foxy Brown*, about a woman seeking revenge against the gangsters who murdered her boy-friend. In the 1970s, both whites and blacks criticised 'blaxploita-tion' films as being just that – exploitative of blacks as they stereotyped life in a 'hood that seemed to exist only on a Hollywood backlot. After all her years of fighting an industry that has not treated people of colour well, it seems unlikely that Halle would resurrect a genre that remains a historical embarrassment.

However, Halle's manager Vincent Cirrincione insists she is committed to the project, which like *Brown-Eyed Girl*, will be produced by MGM. '*Foxy Brown* was one of those things she's always talked about doing,' Cirrincione told *Variety* in May 2002. 'And a few years ago, she saw [the script of] *Brown-Eyed Girl*, liked it, but it didn't work out. It was just total coincidence that they all ended up at MGM. Some things are meant to be.' Cirrincione also said that Halle's excellent working relationship with MGM, the home of *Die Another Day*, made deals for both projects happen quickly.

Financially strapped MGM, rumoured to be up for sale, hopes to turn the character of Foxy Brown into a lucrative franchise to beef up its faltering balance sheet. As for the original's politically incorrect depiction of blacks, MGM's president of production, Alex Gartner, promised a feminist-friendly Foxy, saying, 'We're going to take some license in updating the character. We're going to take all the positive aspects of Foxy as a powerful, empowered woman, and we're going to create a larger-than-life vehicle for Halle.'

To date, Halle is said to be 'in talks' to star in another remake of the 1949 classic, *The Set-Up*, about a prizefighter who refuses to take a dive. The A-list director Sidney Lumet (*Dog Day Afternoon, The Pawnbroker*) is definitely attached to the project, as are Benjamin Bratt (the former Mr Julia Roberts and one of the stars of *Law & Order*) and *The Sopranos'* James Gandolfini as the incorruptible boxer and his corrupt manager, respectively. Berry would play the boxer's romantic interest. Despite the talent already on board, *Entertainment Weekly* predicted that it would be highly unlikely Halle would take a supporting role as a girlfriend. Apparently the magazine hasn't seen her five minutes on screen in *X-Men*.

In the 'for your consideration' Oscar category is a *Monster's Ball*-type feel-bad movie that Halle will definitely star in called *October Squall*. Its creepy storyline is even less palatable than *Monster's Ball* romance between a black woman and a white racist. In *October Squall*, Halle will play a rape victim who becomes pregnant and decides to keep the baby. As the child reaches his teens, he begins to display the same antisocial behaviour as his rapist father. The grim drama is based on a true story. The film's director, Lyndon Chubbuck, said Halle loved his film *The War Bride* and suggested a future collaboration. 'She called to say she wanted to do a movie with me, and I pitched this one,' said Chubbuck, who conceded that he had been having trouble bankrolling the film until Halle signed on. 'With all the money that has been offered to us because of Halle, I'm 100 percent confident I'll be shooting this next year,' Chubbuck said in late 2002. The director's confidence was well placed. The project has been green-lighted and was due to begin shooting in 2003.

Based on the novel by Trisha Thomas and described as a '*Bridget Jones's Diary* meets *Waiting to Exhale*', *Nappily Ever After* is a romantic comedy about a black woman's road to self-discovery and how she reaches it by changing her hairdo. The heroine, Venus Johnston (Halle), decides she's tired of all the hassle that comes with 'processing', i.e. straightening, her frizzy – a.k.a. 'nappy' – hair and cuts most of it off. Her new Afro has a liberating effect on her that prompts her to dump her commitment-phobic boyfriend. Venus is amazed to discover how differently people respond to her new look, in particular, her ex-boyfriend, who takes up with another woman who wears the heroine's old style of processed hair. The film's hair-raising plot is vaguely autobiographical. In November 2002, Halle's husband decided his dreadlocks involved too much upkeep and decided to get rid of them. Instead of going to a professional, Benét asked Halle to lop them off. She did, but the sentimental actress decided to preserve the shorn hair for posterity – in a Ziploc bag. One critic questioned whether Halle could do light comedy and wrote, 'B.A.P.S. doesn't give us a lot of hope.' The critic must not have caught Halle's hysterical Mae-West-meets-Marilyn turn in *The Flintstones*. Halle and her manager, Vincent Cirrincione, will also produce.

And then there's the one that got away – *Gigli* – but not because the filmmakers didn't want Halle to star in it. *Gigli* is about a dim hit man (Ben Affleck) who is ordered to kidnap the mentally retarded brother of a powerful district attorney from the private care facility where the brother has been institutionalised in order to blackmail the DA into cooperating with the hit man's boss. Berry would have played a hit woman, but the role ended up going to Affleck's real-life fiancée, Jennifer Lopez, after scheduling conflicts with *X-Men 2* forced Halle to drop out of the potentially embarrassing screwball comedy about mental retardation, to be directed by *Beverly Hills Cop*'s Martin Brest. Although she doesn't have quite as classy or commercial a film résumé as Halle's, Lopez will reportedly earn $12 million for *Gigli*. That's $4 million more than Halle's current asking price.

Halle liked the power that executive-producing *Introducing Dorothy Dandridge* gave her, even though that 'power' included giving up her salary to recreate Dorothy's walk down the red carpet at the 1955 Oscar ceremony. She dons that hat again and teams up once more with *Dandridge*'s producer HBO in the feature film *Lackawanna Blues*, based on the Obie award-winning autobio-graphical play by Ruben Santiago-Hudson. The play concerns Santiago-Hudson's childhood in a boarding house in Lackawanna, New York, in the 1950s and 1960s. It is run by a lovable woman he called Nanny after his drug-addicted mother abandoned him. Halle will work behind the camera as executive producer and won't star in the film.

In the summer of 2003, while *X-Men 2* was playing in cinemas around the world, Halle was shooting *Their Eyes Were Watching God*, a TV movie produced as part of the 'Oprah Winfrey Presents' film series that originally paired Halle with Winfrey in *The Wedding*. Based on the 1937 classic novel by Zora Neale Hurston, *Eyes* stars Halle as a liberated woman whose behaviour puts in her conflict with the conservative inhabitants of a town in the Deep South. The TV movie will air on the American network ABC during the 2003–4 season.

It says a lot about Halle's loyalty and the depth of her friendship with Winfrey that the Oscar-winning actress took a huge pay cut and deigned to return to the less prestigious medium of television in order to work with her long-time mentor and confidante.

No one, not even detractors such as fellow blacks who have condemned her for playing a prostitute in a Ku Klux Klan fantasy, has ever accused Halle of not being a loyal friend and lover, a profoundly decent human being whose loyalty encompasses an errant husband in rehab and a troubled co-star with a dangerous weight condition long after their professional association has ended.

In the summer of 2003, Halle could look on her professional and personal past with some regret but much more satisfaction. She had survived childhood abuse, teenage taunts and a troubled tabloid-friendly adulthood.

'No matter what gets thrown my way, I can deal with it. I'm strong enough to deal,' she insists. And, although at times she seems to be setting herself up for disappointment with statements like, 'I'm very hopeful that there will be a day when I'm happy *all* the time', the optimism of the highest-paid black woman in the film industry and the only one to win a Best Actress Oscar may not be so cockeyed or unrealistic after all.

AUTHOR'S NOTE ON ACADEMY AWARD DATES

'Dating' Oscar can be tricky and confusing. The actual Academy Award ceremony takes place during the calendar year following the year of the nominated films' release, but the winners are often referred to as having won the Oscar for the year the films came out, rather than the year in which the Oscars were actually presented to the winners. So, for example, although Halle Berry received the Best Actress Oscar for *Monster's Ball* at the 24 March 2002, ceremony, some reference works list her as having won the 2001 Oscar, the year of *Monster's Ball*'s release.

For the sake of consistency, when this text refers to the Oscar itself, the year that the honoured film was released – along with the actors, writers, etc. – is used. But when the text refers to the actual event, the year it took place is listed. Similarly, Dorothy Dandridge in the text is described as having received a 1954 Best Actress Oscar nomination for *Carmen Jones*, but she attended the Academy Awards as a nominee in 1955, and Hattie McDaniel won the Best Supporting Actress award for *Gone With the Wind* in 1940, not the famous year associated with the film's release, 1939.

FILMOGRAPHY

JUNGLE FEVER (1991)
A Universal Pictures release of a Forty Acres & a Mule Filmworks presentation

CREDITS
Producers, Spike Lee, John Kilik, Monty Ross; director, Spike Lee; screenplay, Spike Lee; cinematographer, Ernest Dickerson; editor, Sam Pollard; music, Stevie Wonder, Terence Blanchard; production designer, Wynn Thomas; set decorator, Ted Glass; costumes, Ruth E Carter; production managers, Preston L Holmes, Brent Owens; rating, R; running time, 132 minutes; released in the US 7 June 1991.

CAST
Wesley Snipes (Flipper Purify), Annabella Sciorra (Angie Tucci), Spike Lee (Cyrus), Samuel L Jackson (Gator Purify), Halle Berry (Vivian), Ossie Davis (the Good Reverend Doctor Purify), Ruby Dee (Lucina Purify), Anthony Quinn (Lou Carbone), Lonette McKee (Drew), John Turturro (Paulie Carbone), Veronica Webb (Vera).

AWARDS
Cannes Film Festival (1991) won: Best Supporting Actor, Samuel L Jackson; nominated: Golden Palm. ASCAP Film and Television Music Awards (1992) won: Most Performed Song from Motion Pictures, 'Gotta Have You', Stevie Wonder. New York Film Critics Circle Awards (1991) won: Best Supporting Actor, Samuel L Jackson. Political Film Society, USA (1992) nominated: PFS Award Human Rights.

STRICTLY BUSINESS (1991)
A Warner Bros release of an Island World presentation

CREDITS
Executive producer, Mark Burg; producers, Pam Gibson, Andre Harrell; director, Kevin Hooks; screenplay, Nelson George, Pam Gibson; cinematographer, Zoltan Davis; editor, Richard Nord; music, Michel Colombier, Jo Jo Hailey K-Ci Hailey; production designer, Ruth Ammon; costumes, Beulah Jones-Black; sound, Lise Richardson; rating, PG-13; running time, 83 minutes; released in the US 8 November 1991.

CAST
Tommy Davidson (Bobby Johnson), Joseph C Phillips (Waymon Tinsdale III), Anne Marie Johnson (Deidre), Sam Jackson (Monroe), Halle Berry (Natalie), David Marshall Grant (David), Jon Cypher (Drake), Kim Coles (Millicent).

THE LAST BOY SCOUT (1991)
A Warner Bros release of a Geffen Pictures and Silvers Pictures presentation

CREDITS
Executive producers, Shane Black, Barry Josephson; producers, Michael Levy, Joel Silver; director, Tony Scott; screenplay, Shane Black; story, Shane Black & Greg Hicks; cinematographer, Ward Russell; editors, Stuart Baird, Mark Goldblatt, Mark Helfrich; music, Michael Kamen; production designer, Brian Morris; art director, Christian Wagener; set decorators, John Anderson, Thomas Roysden; costumes, Marilyn Vance-Straker; production manager, Steve Perry; rating, R; running time, 105 minutes; released in the US 13 December 1991.

CAST
Bruce Willis (Joe Cornelius Hallenbeck), Damon Wayans (Jimmy Dix), Chelsea Field (Sarah Hallenbeck), Noble Willingham (Sheldon 'Shelly' Marcone), Taylor Negron (Milo), Halle Berry (Cory), Bruce McGill (Mike Matthews).

AWARDS
MTV Movie Awards (1992) nominated: Best Action Sequence; Best On-Screen Duo: Daman Wayans, Bruce Willis.

BOOMERANG (1992)

A Paramount Pictures release of an Eddie Murphy Productions presentation

CREDITS

Executive producer, Mark Lipsky; producers, Brian Grazer, Warrington Hudlin; director, Reginald Hudlin; screenplay, Barry W Blaustein & David Sheffield; story, Eddie Murphy; cinematographer, Woody Omens; editor, Earl Watson; music, Johnny Gill, Marcus Miller; production designer, Jane Musky; costumes, Francine Jamison-Tanchuck; rating, R; running time, 118 minutes; released in the US 1 July 1992; UK 30 October 1992.

CAST

Eddie Murphy (Marcus Graham), Robin Givens (Jacqueline Broyer), Halle Berry (Angela Lewis), David Alan Grier (Gerard Jackson), Martin Lawrence (Tyler), Grace Jones (Strangé).

AWARDS

MTV Movie Awards (1993) nominated: Best Comedic Performance, Eddie Murphy; nominated: Best Breakthrough Performance: Halle Berry; nominated: Most Desirable Female, Halle Berry; nominated: Best Song, 'End of the Road' (Boyz II Men).

CB4 (1993)

A Universal Pictures release of a Universal Pictures presentation

CREDITS

Executive producers, Sean Daniel, Brian Grazer; producer, Nelson George; director, Tamra Davis; screenplay, Chris Rock & Nelson George and Robert LoCash; story, Chris Rock & Nelson George; cinematographer, Karl Walter Lindenlaub; editor, Earl Watson; music, John Barnes; production designer, Nelson Coates; art director, Martin Charles; set decorator, Susan Benjamin; costumes, Bernie White; production manager, David Witz; rating, R; running time: 89 minutes; released in the US 12 March 1993.

CAST
Chris Rock (Albert), Allen Payne (Euripides), Deezer D (Otis), Chris Elliott (A. White), Phil Hartman (Virgil Robinson), Theresa Randle (Eve), Ice-T (Himself) Halle Berry (Herself), Ice Cube (Himself).

FATHER HOOD (1993)
A Buena Pictures release of a Hollywood Pictures presentation

CREDITS
Executive producers, Jeffrey Chernov, Richard H Prince; producers, Gillian Gorfil, Nicholas Pileggi, Anant Singh; director, Darrell James Roodt; screenplay, Scott Spencer; cinematographer, Mark Vicente; editor, David Heitner; music, Patrick O'Hearn; production designer, David Barkham; art director, Dins WW Danielsen; set decorator, Suzette Sheets; costumes, Donfeld; production manager, Richard H Prince; rating, PG-13; running time, 95 minutes; released in the US 27 August 1993.

CAST
Patrick Swayze (Jack Charles), Halle Berry (Kathleen Mercer), Sabrina Lloyd (Kelly Charles), Brian Bonsall (Eddie Charles), Diane Ladd (Rita), Michael Ironside (Jerry).

THE PROGRAM (1993)
A Buena Vista Pictures release of a Touchstone Pictures presentation

CREDITS
Producer, not credited; director, David S Ward; screenplay, David S Ward and Aaron Latham; cinematographer, Victor Hammer; editor, Paul Seydor; music, Michel Colombier; production designer, Albert Brenner; art director, Carol Woods; set decorator, Kathe Klopp; rating, R; running time, 112 minutes; released in the US 24 September 1993.

CAST
James Caan (Coach Winters), Halle Berry (Autumn Haley), Omar

Epps (Darnell Jefferson), Craig Sheffer (Joe Kane), Kristy Swanson (Camille), Abraham Benrubi (Bud-Lite Kaminski).

THE FLINTSTONES (1994)
A Universal Pictures release of an Amblin Entertainment presentation

CREDITS
Executive producers, Joseph Barbera, William Hannah, Kathleen Kennedy, David Kirschner, Gerald R Molen, Steven Spielrock; producer, Bruce Cohen; director, Brian Levant; screenplay, Tom S Parker & Jim Jennewein and Steven E de Souza; cinematographer, Dean Cundey; editor, Kent Beyda; music, David Newman; production designer, William Sandell; art director, Christopher Burian-Mohr, Nancy Patton, William James Teegarden; set decorator, Mary Brandenburg; costumes, Rosanna Norton; production managers, Paul Deason, William Plant; rating, PG; running time, 91 minutes, released in the US 27 May 1994; UK 22 July 1994.

CAST
John Goodman (Fred Flintstone), Elizabeth Perkins (Wilma Flintstone), Rick Moranis (Barney Rubble), Rosie O'Donnell (Betty Rubble), Kyle MacLachlan (Cliff Vandercave), Halle Berry (Sharon Stone), Elizabeth Taylor (Pearl Slaghoople).

AWARDS
MTV Movie Awards (1995) nominated: Most Desirable Female, Halle Berry. Razzie Awards (1995) won: Worst Supporting Actress, Rosie O'Donnell; won: Worst Screenplay; nominated: Worst Remake or Sequel; nominated: Worst Supporting Actress, Elizabeth Taylor.

LOSING ISAIAH (1995)
A Paramount Pictures release and presentation

CREDITS
Producers, Naomi Foner, Howard W Koch, Jr; director, Stephen Gyllenhaal; screenplay, Naomi Foner; cinematographer, Andrzej

Bartkowiak; editor, Harvey Rosenstock; music, Mark Isham; production designer, Jeannine Claudia Oppewall; art director, William Arnold; set decorator, Jay Hart; costumes, Mary Malin; production manager, Ronald G Smith; rating, R; running time, 111 minutes; released in the US 17 March 1995; UK June 1996 (video only).

CAST
Jessica Lange (Margaret Lewin), Halle Berry (Khaila Richards), David Strathairn (Charles Lewin), Cuba Gooding Jr (Eddie Hughes), Samuel L Jackson (Kadar Lewis), Marc John Jefferies (Isaiah).

AWARDS
Image Awards (1996) nominated: Outstanding Lead Actress in a Motion Picture, Halle Berry.

EXECUTIVE DECISION (1996)
A Warner Bros. release of a Silvers Pictures presentation

CREDITS
Executive producer, Steve Perry; producers, Joel Silver, Jim Thomas, John Thomas; director, Stuart Baird; screenplay, Jim Thomas & John Thomas; cinematographer, Alex Thomson; editors, Stuart Baird, Derek G Brechin, Dallas Puett, Kevin Stitt, Frank J Urioste; music, Jerry Goldsmith; production designer, Terence Marsh, set decorator, Marvin March; art director, William Cruse; costumes, Louise Frogley; production manager, Paul Moen; rating, R; running time, 134 minutes; released in the US 15 March 1996; UK 10 May 1996.

CAST
Kurt Russell (Dr David Grant), Steven Seagal (Lt Col. Austin Travis), Halle Berry (Jean), John Leguizamo (Rat), Oliver Platt (Dennis Cahill), Joe Morton (Cappy).

AWARDS
Blockbuster Entertainment Awards (1997) won: Favourite Actress, Halle Berry; won: Favourite Actor, Kurt Russell. NCLR Bravo

Awards (1996) nominated: Outstanding Actor, John Leguizamo. Razzie Awards (1997) nominated: Worst Supporting Actor, Steven Seagal.

RACE THE SUN (1996)
A TriStar Pictures release and presentation

CREDITS
Producers, Richard Heus, Barry Morrow; director, Charles T Kanganis; screenplay, Barry Morrow; cinematographer, David Burr; editor, Wendy Greene Bricmont; music, Graeme Revell; production designer, Owen Paterson; production manager, Emile Chautard; rating, PG; running time, 82 minutes; released in the US 22 March 1996.

CAST
Halle Berry (Miss Sandra Beecher), Casey Affleck (Daniel Webster), Eliza Dushku (Cindy Johnson), Kevin Tighe (Jack Fryman), Steve Zahn (Hans Kooiman), J Moki Cho (Gilbert Tutu).

GIRL 6 (1996)
A Fox Searchlight Pictures release of a 40 Acres & a Mule Filmworks presentation

CREDITS
Executive producer, John Kilik; producer, Spike Lee; director, Spike Lee; screenplay, Suzan-Lori Parks; cinematographer, Malik Hassan Sayeed; editor, Sam Pollard; music, Prince, Georges Bizet; production designer, Ina Mayhew; set decorator, Paul R Weathered; costumes, Sandra Hernandez; production manager, Caryn E Campbell; rating, R; running time, 108 minutes; released in the US 26 March 1996; UK 7 June 1996.

CAST
Theresa Randle (Girl 6), Isaiah Washington (Shoplifter), Spike Lee (Jimmy), Jenifer Lewis (Boss #1, Lil), Halle Berry (Herself), Quentin Tarantino (QT), Madonna (Boss #3), Debi Mazar (Girl #39); Naomi Campbell (Girl #75), Peter Berg (Caller #1, Bob).

AWARDS
Independent Spirit Awards (1997) nominated: Best First Screenplay, Suzan-Lori Parks.

THE RICH MAN'S WIFE (1996)
A Buena Vista Pictures release of a Caravan Pictures presentation

CREDITS
Executive producer, Jennifer Ogden; producers, Roger Birnbaum, Julie Bergman Sender; director, Amy Holden Jones; screenplay, Amy Holden Jones; cinematographer, Haskell Wexler; editors, Wendy Greene Bricmont, Glenn Garland; music, John Frizzell, James Newton Howard; production designer, Jeannine Oppewall; rating, R; running time, 94 minutes; released in the US 13 September 1996; UK May 1997 (video only).

CAST
Halle Berry (Josie Potenza), Peter Greene (Cole Wilson), Clive Owen (Jake Golden), Frankie Faison (Detective Ron Lewis), Charles Hallahan (Detective Dan Fredricks), Allan Rich (Bill Adolphe).

B.A.P.S (1997)
A New Line Cinema release of an Island Pictures presentation

CREDITS
Executive producers, Michael De Luca, Jay Stern; producers Mark Burg, Loretha C Jones; director, Robert Townsend; screenplay, Troy Beyer; cinematographer, Bill Dill; editor, Patrick Kennedy; music, Stanley Clarke; production designer, Keith Brian Burns; set decorator, Casey Hallenbeck; costumes, Ruth Carter; production managers, Carla Fry, Tom Herod Jr; rating, PG-13; running time, 91 minutes; released in the US 28 March 1997; UK 1 August 1997.

CAST
Halle Berry (Nisi), Martin Landau (Mr Blakemore), Ian Richardson (Manley), Natalie Desselle (Mickey), Troy Beyer (Tracy), Luigi Amodeo (Antonio).

AWARDS
Acapulco Black Film Festival (1998) nominated: Best Actress, Halle Berry.

BULWORTH (1998)
A 20th Century-Fox release and presentation

CREDITS
Executive producer, Lauren Shuler Donner; producers, Warren Beatty, Pieter Jan Brugge; director, Warren Beatty; screenplay, Warren Beatty & Jeremy Pikser; cinematographer, Vittorio Storaro; editor, Robert C Jones, Billy Weber; music, Ice Cube, Chuck D, Dr Dre, Flavor Flav, Method Man, Ennio Morricone, John Philip Sousa; production designer, Dean Tavoularis; set decorator, Rick Simpson; costumes, Milena Canonero; production managers, Jamie D Boscardin, John Rusk; rating, R; running time, 108 minutes; released in the US 15 May 1998; UK 22 January 1999.

CAST
Warren Beatty (Senator Jay Billington Bulworth), Halle Berry (Nina), Don Cheadle (LD), Nora Dunn (Missy Berliner), Oliver Platt (Dennis Murphy), Jackie Gayle (Macavoy), Paul Sorvino (Graham Crockett), Michele Morgan (Cheryl).

AWARDS
Academy Awards (1999) nominated: Best Original Screenplay. Chicago Film Critics Association Awards (1999) nominated: Best Screenplay. Golden Globes (1999) nominated: Best Motion Picture – Comedy/Musical; nominated: Best Actor in Motion Picture – Comedy/Musical, Warren Beatty; nominated, Best Screenplay. Golden Satellite Awards (1999) nominated, Best Actor – Comedy/Musical (Warren Beatty). Grammy Awards (1999) nominated, Best Instrumental Composition for a Motion Picture or Television, Ennio Morricone. Image Awards (1999) nominated, Best Actress, Halle Berry; nominated, Best Supporting Actor, Don Cheadle. Los Angeles Film Critics Association Awards (1998) won: Best Screenplay. Motion Picture Sound Editors (1999) nominated, Best

Sound Editing – Dialogue; nominated, Best Sound Editing – Music. Venice Film Festival (1999) nominated: Best Actor, Warren Beatty. Writers Guild of America (1999) nominated: Best Original Screenplay.

WHY DO FOOLS FALL IN LOVE (1998)
A Warner Bros release of a Rhino Films presentation

CREDITS
Executive producers, Gregory Nava, Mark Allan, Harold Bronson; producers, Paul Hall, Stephen Nemeth; director, Gregory Nava; screenplay, Tina Andrews; cinematographer, Ed Lachman; editor, Nancy Richardson; music, Stephen James Taylor, Diane Warren; production designer, Cary White; art director, John Chichester; set decorator, Jackie Carr; costumes, Elisabetta Beraldo; production manager, Mark Allan; rating, R; running time, 116 minutes; released in the US 28 August 1998.

CAST
Halle Berry (Zola Taylor), Vivica A Fox (Elizabeth Waters), Lela Rochon (Emira Eagle), Larenz Tate (Frankie Lymon), Paul Mazursky (Morris Levy), Pamela Reed (Judge Lambrey), Alexis Cruz (Herman Santiago).

AWARDS
ALMA Awards (1999) won: Outstanding Latino Director of a Feature Film, Gregory Nava; nominated: Outstanding Supporting Actor in a Feature Film, Alexis Cruz; nominated Outstanding Actor in a Feature Film in a Crossover Role, Miguel A Núñez Jr. Acapulco Black Film Festival (1999) won: Best Actor, Larenz Tate; nominated: Best Soundtrack; nominated, Best Screenplay.

X-MEN (2000)
A 20th Century-Fox release and presentation

CREDITS
Executive producers, Avi Arad, Tom DeSanto, Richard Donner, Stan Lee; producers, Lauren Shuler Donner, Ralph Winter; director, Bryan Singer; screenplay, David Hayter; cinemato-

grapher, Newton Thomas Sigel; editors, Steven Rosenblum, Kevin Stitt, John Wright; music, James Seymour Brett, Michael Kamen, Michael Price, Jeremy Sweet; production designer, John Myhre; set decorator, James Edward Ferrell Jr; costumes, Louise Mingenbach; production managers, Whitney Brown, Ross Fanger, Dara Weintraub; rating, PG-13; running time, 104 minutes; released in the US 14 July 2000; UK 18 August 2000.

CAST
Hugh Jackman (Wolverine), Patrick Stewart (Professor Charles Xavier), Ian McKellen (Magneto), Famke Janssen (Dr Jean Grey), James Marsden (Cyclops), Halle Berry (Storm), Anna Paquin (Rogue), Rebecca Romijn-Stamos (Mystique), Bruce Davison (Senator Robert Kelly), Tyler Mane (Sabretooth).

AWARDS
Academy of Science Fiction, Fantasy & Horror Films (2001) won: Best Science Fiction Film; won: Best Director, Bryan Singer; won: Best Writing, David Hayter; won: Best Actor, Hugh Jackman; won: Best Costume, Louise Mingenbach; won: Best Supporting Actress, Rebecca Romijn-Stamos; nominated, Best Special Effects; nominated, Best Performance by a Younger Actor, Anna Paquin; nominated, Best Makeup, Gordon J Smith, Ann Brodie; nominated, Best Supporting Actor, Patrick Stewart. Blockbuster Entertainment Awards (2001) won: Favourite Supporting Actor – science fiction, James Marsden; won: Favourite Supporting Actress – Science Fiction, Rebecca Romijn-Stamos; nominated: Favourite Supporting Actress – Science Fiction, Famke Janssen; nominated: Favourite Villain, Ian McKellen; nominated, Favourite Actress, Anna Paquin; nominated, Favourite Male – Newcomer, Hugh Jackman; nominated, Favourite Actor – science fiction, Patrick Stewart.

SWORDFISH (2001)
A Warner Bros release of a Silver Pictures presentation

CREDITS
Executive producer, Jim Van Wyck; producers, Jonathan D Krane, Joel Silver; director, Dominic Sena; screenplay, Skip Woods;

cinematographer, Paul Cameron; editor, Stephen Rivkin; music, Afrika Bambaataa, Paul Oakenfold, Christopher Young; production designer, Jeff Mann; set decorator, Jay Hart; costumes, Ha Nguyen; production manager, Ronald G Smith; rating, R; running time, 99 minutes; released in the US 8 June 2001; UK 27 July 2001.

CAST
John Travolta (Gabriel Shear), Hugh Jackman (Stanley Jobson), Halle Berry (Ginger), Don Cheadle (Agent AD Roberts), Sam Shepard (Senator Reisman), Vinnie Jones (Marco).

AWARDS
Image Awards (2002) won: Outstanding Actress in a Motion Picture, Halle Berry. Razzie Awards (2002) nominated: Worst Actor, John Travolta; World Stunt Awards (2002) nominated: Best Stunt Co-ordinator, Dan Bradley.

MONSTER'S BALL (2001)
A Lions Gate Films release of a Lee Daniels Entertainment presentation

CREDITS
Executive producers, Michael Burns, Michael Paseornek, Mark Urman; producer, Lee Daniels; director, Marc Forster; screenplay, Milo Addica & Will Rokos; cinematographer, Roberto Schaefer; editor, Matt Chessé; music, Asche and Spencer; production designer, Monroe Kelly; set decorator, Leonard R Spears; costumes, Frank Fleming; production manager, Rob Ortiz; rating, R; running time, 111 minutes; released in the US 26 December 2001; UK 7 June 2002.

CAST
Billy Bob Thornton (Hank Grotowski), Halle Berry (Leticia Musgrove), Heath Ledger (Sonny Grotowski), Peter Boyle (Buck Grotowski), Sean Combs (Lawrence Musgrove), Coronji Calhoun (Tyrell Musgrove).

AWARDS
AFI Awards (2002) nominated: Best Actor – Female – Movies, Halle Berry; nominated: Movie of the Year. Academy Awards (2002) won: Best Actress, Halle Berry; nominated, Best Original Screenplay, Milo Addica, Will Rokos. BAFTA Awards (2003) nominated: Best Actress in a Leading Role, Halle Berry. Berlin International Film Festival (2002) won: Best Actress, Halle Berry; nominated, Best Director, Marc Forster. Chicago Film Critics Association (2002) nominated: Best Actress, Halle Berry. Florida Film Critics Circle Awards (2002) won: Best Actor, Billy Bob Thornton. Golden Globes (2002) nominated: Best Performance by an Actress in a Motion Picture – Drama, Halle Berry. Golden Satellite Awards (2002) won: Best Original Screenplay, Milo Addica, Will Rokos; nominated: Best Performance by an Actress in a Motion Picture – Drama, Halle Berry; nominated: Best Performance by an Actor in a Motion Picture – Drama, Billy Bob Thornton. Independent Spirit Awards (2002) nominated: Best Screenplay, Milo Addica, Will Rokos. MTV Movie Awards (2002) nominated: Best Female Performance, Halle Berry. National Board of Review (2001) won: Best Actress, Halle Berry; won: Best Actor, Billy Bob Thornton. Screen Actors Guild Awards (2002) won: Outstanding Performance by a Female Actor in a Leading Role, Halle Berry. Writers Guild of America (2002) nominated: best original screenplay, Milo Addica, Will Rokos.

DIE ANOTHER DAY (2002)
A Metro-Goldwyn-Mayer release of a Danjaq presentation

CREDITS
Executive producer, Anthony Waye; producers, Barbara Broccoli, Michael G Wilson; director, Lee Tamahori; screenplay, Neal Purvis & Robert Wade; cinematographer, David Tattersall; editors, Andrew MacRitchie, Christian Wagner; music, Mirwais Ahmadzai, David Arnold, Madonna, Monty Norman; production designer, Peter Lamont; set decorators, Ute Bergk, Simon Wakefield; costumes, Lindy Hemming; production managers, Chris Brock, Philip Kohler, Janine Modder, Iris Rose; rating, PG-13; running time, 132 minutes; released in the US 22 November 2002; UK 18 November 2002.

CAST
Pierce Brosnan (James Bond), Halle Berry (Jinx), Toby Stephens (Gustav Graves), Rosamund Pike (Miranda Frost), Rick Yune (Zao), Judi Dench (M), John Cleese (Q), Michael Madsen (Damian Falco), Will Yun Lee (Colonel Moon), Kenneth Tsang (General Moon).

AWARDS
Empire Awards, UK (2003) won: Best Newcomer, Rosamund Pike. Golden Globes (2003) nominated: Best Original Song – Motion Picture, 'Die Another Day,' Madonna, Mirwais Ahmadzai. Golden Satellite Awards (2003) nominated: Best Original Song. Hollywood Makeup Artist and Hair Stylist Guild Awards (2003) nominated: Colin Jamison. Image Awards (2003) nominated: Outstanding Supporting Actress in a Motion Picture, Halle Berry. Motion Picture Sound Editors (2003) nominated: Best Sound Editing in Foreign Features. Razzie Awards (2003) nominated: Worst Supporting Actress, Madonna; nominated: Worst Original Song. Visual Effects Society Awards (2003) nominated: Best Special Effects in a Motion Picture, Chris Corbould; nominated: Best Models and Miniatures in a Motion Picture, John Richardson.

X-MEN 2 (2003)
A 20th Century-Fox release of a Donner/Schuler-Donner Productions and Marvel Entertainment presentation

CREDITS
Executive producers, Avi Arad, Tom DeSanto, Kevin Feige, Stan Lee; producers, Lauren Shuler Donner, Ralph Winter; director, Bryan Singer; screenplay, John Byrne, Chris Claremont, Michael Dougherty, Daniel P Harris, David Hayter, Jack Kirby, Stan Lee, Zak Penn, Bryan Singer, Len Wein; cinematographer, Newton Thomas Sigel; editor, John Ottman; music, John Ottman; production designer, Guy Dyas; set decorator, Elizabeth Wilcox; art directors, Geoff Hubbard, Helen Jarvis; costumes, Louise Mingenbach; production managers, Stewart Bethune, Ross Fanger; rating, N/A; running time, N/A; released in the US 2 May 2003; UK 1 May 2003.

CAST

Patrick Stewart (Professor Charles Xavier), Hugh Jackman (Wolverine), Ian McKellen (Magneto), Halle Berry (Storm), Famke Janssen (Dr Jean Grey), James Marsden (Cyclops), Rebecca Romijn-Stamos (Mystique), Anna Paquin (Rogue), Alan Cumming (Nightcrawler), Bruce Davison (Senator Robert Kelly), Brian Cox (General William Stryker), Kelly Hu (Yuriko Oyama), Shawn Ashmore (Iceman), Aaron Stanford (Pyro), Katie Stuart (Shadowcat), Kea Wong (Jubilee), Daniel Cudmore (Colossus), Shauna Kain (Siryn), Bryce Hodgson (Artie), Cotter Smith (US President McKenna).

TELEVISION

LIVING DOLLS (1989)
Warner Bros Television

CREDITS
Writer, Ken Patton; music, Jonathan Wolff; costumes, Betsey Potter; sound, Roy Pahlman; first telecast, 26 September 1989; last telecast, 30 December 1989; ABC-TV, 8.30 p.m.

CAST
Michael Learned (Trish Carlin), Leah Remini (Charlie Briscoe), Deborah Tucker (Caroline Weldon), Alison Elliott (Martha Lambert), Halle Berry (Emily Franklin), David Moscow (Rick Carlin).

KNOTS LANDING (1991–2)

CREDITS
Executive producers, Michael Filerman, David Jacobs; producers, Mary Catherine Harold, Lynn Marie Latham, Bernard Lechowick, John Romano; first telecast, 20 December 1979; last telecast, 13 May 1993; CBS-TV.

CAST
William Devane (Gregory Sumner), Donna Mills (Abby Sumner), Lisa Hartman (Ciji Dunne), Michele Lee (Karen MacKenzie), Ted Shackelford (Garrison Ewing), Michelle Phillips (Anne Sumner), Joan Van Ark (Valerie Waleska), Nicollette Sheridan (Paige Matheson), Larry Riley (Frank Williams), Halle Berry (Debbie Porter).

QUEEN (SIX-HOUR MINISERIES, 1993)

CREDITS
Executive producers, David L Wolper, Bernard Sofronski; producer, Mark Wolper; director, John Erman; teleplay, David

Stevens; book, Alex Haley; editors, James Galloway, Paul LaMastra; set decorator, Joseph Litsch; costumes, Helen Butler-Barbon; aired 14–18 February 1993; CBS-TV.

CAST
Halle Berry (Queen), Timothy Daly (Colonel James Jackson, Jr), Ann-Margret (Sally Jackson), Ossie Davis (Parson Dick), Danny Glover (Alec Haley), Patricia Clarkson (Lizzie), Lonette McKee (Alice), George Grizzard (Mr Cherry), Jasmine Guy (Easter).

AWARDS
Emmy Awards (1993) won: Outstanding Hairstyling for a Miniseries or Special, Linda De Andrea; nominated: Outstanding Miniseries; nominated: Outstanding Sound Mixing, Robert J Anderson, Jr, John Asman, George R Groves, Jr, David E Fluhr; nominated, Outstanding Supporting Actress in a Miniseries or Special, Ann-Margret; nominated: Outstanding Costume Design for a Miniseries or Special, Helen P Butler; nominated: Outstanding Editing for a Miniseries or Special, Paul LaMastra, James Galloway; nominated: Outstanding Makeup for a Miniseries or Special, Steve LaPorte, Richard Blair, Thomas Floutz, Angela Levin, Rose Librizzi. Golden Globes (1994) nominated: Best Performance by an Actress in a Supporting Role, Ann-Margret. Image Awards (1995) won: Outstanding Television Movie or Miniseries; won: Outstanding Lead Actress in a Television Movie or Miniseries, Halle Berry; won: Outstanding Lead Actor in a Television Movie or Miniseries, Danny Glover.

SOLOMON & SHEBA (TV MOVIE, 1995)

CREDITS
Producers, Dino De Laurentiis, Martha Schumacher; director; Robert M Young, teleplay, Ronni Kern; cinematographer, Giuseppe Maccari; editor, Arthur Coburn; music, David Kitay; production designer, Pier Luigi Basile; costumes, Gabriella Pescucci; debuted in the US 26 February 1995; Showtime Networks Inc.

CAST

Jimmy Smits (King Solomon), Halle Berry (Nikhaule/Queen Sheba); Kenneth Colley (Nathan), Ottaviano Dell'Acqua (Hanani), Nickolas Grace (Jeroboam), Chapman Roberts (King Yusef).

AWARDS

Image Awards (1996) nominated: Outstanding Actress in a Television Movie, Miniseries, Halle Berry.

THE WEDDING (FOUR-HOUR MINISERIES, 1998)

CREDITS

Executive producers, Kate Forte, Oprah Winfrey; producer, Daniel Schneider; director, Charles Burnett; teleplay, Lisa Jones; novel, Dorothy West; cinematographer, Frederick Elmes; editor, Dorian Harris; music, Stephen James Taylor; art director, Geoffrey S Grimsman; set decorator, Jim Ferrell; costumes, Eduardo Castro; production manager, Daniel Schneider; aired in the US 22, 23 February 1998; ABC-TV.

CAST

Halle Berry (Shelby Coles), Eric Thal (Meade Howell), Lynn Whitfield (Corinne Coles), Carl Lumbly (Lute), Michael Warren (Clark Coles), Shirley Knight (Gram), Cynda Williams (Liz).

AWARDS

Golden Satellite Awards (1999) nominated: Best Performance by an Actress in a Supporting Role in a Miniseries or TV Movie, Shirley Knight. Image Awards (1999) nominated: Outstanding TV Movie or Miniseries; nominated: Outstanding Lead Actress in a TV Movie or Miniseries, Halle Berry.

INTRODUCING DOROTHY DANDRIDGE (TV MOVIE, 1999)

CREDITS

Executive producers, Halle Berry, Vince Cirrincione, Moctesuma Esparza, Robert Katz; producer, Larry Y Albucher; director, Martha Coolidge; teleplay, Shonda Rhimes and Scott Abbott;

book, Earl Mills; cinematographer, Robbie Greenberg; editor, Alan Heim; music, Elmer Bernstein; production designer, James Spencer; art director, A Leslie Thomas; set decorator, Robert Greenfield; costumes, Shelley Komarov; production managers, Robert Rothbard, Sally Young; debuted in the US 21 August 1999; HBO.

CAST
Halle Berry (Dorothy Dandridge), Brent Spiner (Earl Mills), Klaus Maria Brandauer (Otto Preminger), Obba Babatundé (Harold Nicholas), Loretta Devine (Ruby Dandridge), Cynda Williams (Vivian Dandridge), LaTanya Richardson (Auntie), Tamara Taylor (Geri Nicholas), DB Sweeney (Jack Denison), William Atherton (Darryl Zanuck), André Carthen (Harry Belafonte), Benjamin Brown (Sidney Poitier).

AWARDS
America Cinema Editors (2000) won: Best Edited Motion Picture, Alan Heim. American Society of Cinematographers (2000) won: Outstanding Achievement in Cinematography in TV Movies or Miniseries, Robbie Greenberg. Art Directors Guild (2000) nominated: Excellence in Production Design, TV Movie or Miniseries, James H Spencer. Casting Society of America (2000) nominated: Best Casting for TV Movie, Aleta Chappelle. Directors Guild of America (2000) nominated: Outstanding Directorial Achievement in TV Movies, Martha Coolidge. Emmy Awards (2000) won: Outstanding Lead Actress in a TV Movie or Miniseries, Halle Berry; won: Outstanding Hairstyling in a TV Movie, Miniseries or Special, Hazel Catmull, Katherine Gordon, Katherine Rees, Jennifer Bell, Virginia Kearns; won: Outstanding Cinematography for a TV Movie, Miniseries or Special, Shelley Komarov, Lucinda Campbell; won: Outstanding Art Direction for a TV Movie, miniseries or special, James H Spencer, A Leslie Thomas, Robert Greenfield; nominated: Outstanding Made-for-TV Movie; nominated, Outstanding Directing for a TV Movie, Miniseries or Special, Martha Coolidge; nominated: Outstanding Editing for a TV Movie, Miniseries or Special, Alan Heim; nominated: Outstanding Choreography, Kim Blank; nominated: Outstanding Supporting actor in a TV Movie, Miniseries or Special, Klaus Maria

Brandauer. Golden Globes (2000) won: Best Performance by an Actress in a TV Movie or Miniseries, Halle Berry; nominated: Best TV Movie or Miniseries; nominated: Best Performance by an Actor in a Supporting Role in a TV Series, TV Movie or Miniseries, Klaus Maria Brandauer. Golden Satellite Awards (2000) nominated: Best Motion Picture Made for Television; nominated: Best Performance by an Actress in a TV Movie or Miniseries, Halle Berry; nominated: Best Performance by an Actor in a TV Movie or Miniseries, Brent Spiner. Image Awards (2000) won: Outstanding TV Movie, Miniseries or Dramatic Special; won: Outstanding Actress in a TV Movie, Miniseries or Dramatic Special, Halle Berry; nominated: Outstanding Actor in a TV Movie, Miniseries or Dramatic Special, Obba Babatundé. Screen Actors Guild Awards (2000) won: Outstanding Performance by a Female actor in a TV Movie or Miniseries, Halle Berry.

PICTURE CREDITS

All pictures are reprinted by kind permission of Larry Edmunds, with the following exceptions:

Page 1 (top left): Halle Berry as a model – courtesy of Charles Knight/Rex Features

Page 8 (top): Halle Berry and David Justice – courtesy of StarTraks/Rex Features

Page 8 (bottom): Halle Berry with Judith Berry and Eric Benét – courtesy of R Hepler/Everett/Rex Features

ABOUT THE AUTHOR

A nationally known author and syndicated columnist, Frank Sanello has written seventeen critically acclaimed books on history and film, including *Steven Spielberg: The Man, The Movies, The Mythology*; *Reel v. Real: How Hollywood Turns Fact Into Fiction*; and *The Opium Wars: The Addiction of One Empire and the Corruption of Another*.

Sanello is currently writing *Faith and Finance in the Renaissance: The Rise and Ruin of the Fugger Empire*, a centuries-spanning epic about the influential family of bankers who were the German equivalent of their contemporaries, the Medicis.

A journalist for the past 25 years, Sanello has written articles for the *Washington Post*, the *Los Angeles Times*, the *Chicago Tribune*, the *Boston Globe* and the *New York Times Syndicate*. He was formerly the film critic for the *Los Angeles Daily News* and a business reporter for UPI.

The author graduated *cum laude* from the University of Chicago and earned a master's degree from UCLA's film school. He also holds a purple belt in tae kwon do and has volunteered as a martial-arts instructor at AIDS Project Los Angeles.

Sanello lives in Los Angeles with four stray cats, Cesare, Thisbe, Pellegrino and Catullus. He can be contacted at FSanello@AOL.com.

INDEX

Academy Awards 177–95
Access Hollywood 192, 201, 214
Addica, Milo 163, 168
Affleck, Ben 226
All That Jazz 79
Allen, Debbie 44
Allen, Tim 119
Allen, Woody 43
Anderson, John 89
Andress, Ursula 205, 207, 213
Anniston, Jennifer 119
Another 48 Hrs. 39
Archerd, Amy 221
Atherton, William 137, 248
Atkinson, Michael 175–6
Austin Chronicle, The 72

Bailey, Lee 193
Baltimore Sun 51
B.A.P.S 113–16, 236–7
Basinger, Kim 206
Bassett, Angela 129, 137, 178,
    184, 191–3
Beatty, Warren 119–20, 121, 147,
    164, 186, 237
beauty pageants 15–20, 24
Beck, Marilyn 78, 222
Bedford High School 11–16
Belafonte, Harry 131
Benét, Eric 125–8, 139, 143, 147,
    148, 155–6, 159–69, 172,
    183, 185, 197–205, 226
Berardinelli, James 58
Berry, Halle
    beauty pageants 15–20, 24
    car accident 143–8

divorce 96–108, 111
education 8–18
finance 20–1, 63–5, 87–8,
    100–101, 145–6, 174
health 26–8, 49–50, 76, 105,
    116, 143–5
marriage 55, 156
modelling 19–22, 24, 108–10
nudity 158–61, 167–8, 169,
    210–11
the Oscars 177–95
racism 8–11, 12–16, 61–2,
    218–19
relationships *see* Benét, Eric;
    Justice, David
suicide attempt 107–8, 138
therapy 8, 94, 100, 111–12,
    200, 201, 203
Berry, Heidi (sister) 3, 4–5, 127
Berry, Jerome Jessie (father) 2–8,
    99–100, 139, 184–5, 203
Berry, Judith (mother) 4–11, 15,
    20–21, 77–8, 87–8, 108,
    110, 155, 185
Beyer, Troy 115
Birnbaum, Roger 92, 236
Black, Shane 36, 230
Black Enterprise 44
Boggs, Eugene 163, 171
Bogle, Donald 129, 134
Boomerang 38–45, 63, 231
Box Office magazine 115
Boyle, Peter 187, 240
Brando, Marlon 163
Branton, Geri 132, 138, 140
Bratt, Benjamin 225

Brest, Martin 226
Brosnan, Pierce 201, 205, 206, 207, 209–11, 214, 218, 242
Brown-Eyed Girl 224
Brynner, Yul 83
Bulworth 119–22, 164, 237–8
Busey, Gary 37

Caan, James 232
Caine, Michael 222
Calhoun, Coronji 173–4, 240
Callaway, Libby 180
Campanella II, Roy 193
car accident 143–8
Carey, Mariah 160
Carmen Jones 128, 131, 133, 136–7
Carrey, Jim 115
Carroll, Diahann 131, 178, 184
CB4 57–58, 231–2
Celebrity Justice 1
Charlie's Angels 24
Chicago Sun-Times 32, 35–6, 58, 113
Chubbuck, Lyndon 225
Cinema Confidential magazine 161
Cirrincione, Vera 23, 30, 51–2, 108
Cirrincione, Vincent 23–5, 108, 129, 164, 165–6, 184, 224, 226, 247
Cleveland City Hospital 4, 133
Cleveland Plain Dealer 3, 52
Collins, Joan 24
Combs, Sean 'Puffy' 174–5, 240
Complete Directory to Prime Time Network and Cable TV Shows 25
Coolidge, Martha 132, 136, 224, 247
Cosmopolitan 158, 160

Cox, Brian 219, 243
Crawford, Cindy 21, 108, 189
Crowe, Russell 182–3, 184
Cruise, Tom 177
Cruz, Penelope 223
Crystal, Billy 147, 186
Cumming, Alan 216, 219, 243
Cuyahoga Community College 17–18

Daily Mail 43, 51, 198, 203
Daily Mirror 125
Daily Variety 40–41, 42, 139, 167, 174, 179, 213, 221, 223
Dalton, Timothy 218
Daly, Tim 47, 246
Dandridge, Dorothy 4, 90, 128–41, 178, 179, 181, 184
Daniels, Lee 164, 165–7, 169–70, 174, 178, 182, 186, 192, 240
Danson, Ted 61
Davidson, Tommy 34, 230
Davis, Bette 137
Davison, Bruce 150, 215, 239, 243
Days of Our Lives 24
De Niro, Robert 30, 163, 172
Dench, Dame Judi 177, 178, 242
Dennison, Jack 138
DeSanto, Tom 217–18, 238, 242
Deseret News 35
Desselle, Natalie 113
Devine, Loretta 133, 248
diabetes 26–8, 116
Die Another Day 205–14, 218, 241–2
Dinkins, David 61
divorce 96–108
domestic violence 5–7, 33, 101–3
Drew Carey Show, The 4
Drop Zone 37

drugs 31
    Whitney Houston and 1

Ebert, Roger 32, 35–6, 38, 58–9,
    113, 114, 115, 123, 137,
    166, 170, 175
Ebony magazine 100–101, 104,
    107, 126, 133, 204
Edelstein, David 121
education 8–18
Elliott, Alison 25, 28, 245
English, Kimberly 218
Entertainment Tonight 201
Entertainment Weekly 223, 224,
    225
Epps, Omar 59, 232–3
Erman, John 49
Essence magazine 100, 159–69,
    198, 200, 201, 202
Evans, Linda 24
Executive Decision 87, 88–9, 234–5

Farber, Stephen 72
Farley, Christopher John 134,
    178, 192, 194–5
Father Hood 58–9, 232
FHM 207
Fichtner, Christy 17
Field, Sally 183
filmography 229–43
finance 20–21, 63–5, 87–8,
    100–101, 145–6, 174
Fitzwater, Terrie 15
Flintstones, The 67–73, 233
Forster, Marc 164, 165, 167, 169,
    170, 172, 175, 185, 240
48 Hours 37
Fosse, Bob 79
Fossett, David E 193
Foster, Nicole 103
Fox, Vivica A 123, 184, 192, 238

Foxy Brown 224–5
Frances 79
Freedman, Syd 19–20
Fried, Jonathan 114

Gandolfini, James 225
Gartner, Alex 225
Gibson, Mel 37
Gigli 226
Gilbert, Lewis 222
Girl 6 90–91, 235–6
Givens, Robin 39, 43, 231
Glitter 160
Globe 5, 200
Glover, Danny 37, 50
Godsick, Jeffrey 220
Goldberg, Whoopi 61–2, 178,
    180
Gooding Jr, Cuba 39, 234
Goodman, John 18, 67, 233
Gossett Jr, Louis 191
Gothika 223
Graves, Renée Berry (half-sister) 3
Grazer, Brian 42, 231–2
Greene, Peter 92, 104–5, 236
Guide, The 223–4
Guthmann, Edward 81
Guy, Jasmine 129
Gyllenhaal, Stephen 76, 79, 92,
    233

Hagman, Larry 222
Haley, Alex 10, 47–8, 246
Hallenbeck, Joe 37
Harris, Danielle 37
Hawkins, Judith *see* Berry, Judith
    (mother)
health 105
    car accident 143–5
    diabetes 26–8, 116
    horse riding accident 49–50

scratched cornea 76
Heatwave 33–4
Hepburn, Katharine 137
Heskett Middle School 11
Hichens, Kelli 15
Hicks, Chris 35
Hicks, Greg 230
Hollywood Reporter 87, 88, 139, 217, 223
Hooks, Kevin 33–5
Hope, Bob 17
Horne, Lena 184, 193
Houston, Cissy 1, 2
Houston, John 1–2
Houston, Whitney 1–2, 129
Howe, Desson 32, 38, 175
Hudlin, Reginald 43, 231
Hudlin, Warrington 39–40, 42, 44, 231
Huvane, Kevin 186

I Dream of Jeannie 222
Ice Cube 57, 232
In Style magazine 107, 144–5
Indecent Proposal 92
Interview magazine 160, 171, 205
Introducing Dorothy Dandridge 129–41, 155, 226, 247–8
Introducing Halle Berry 134

Jackman, Hugh 152, 156, 157, 215, 239, 240, 243
Jackson, Janet 129
Jackson, Samuel L 30–31, 39, 76, 80, 161, 171, 191, 205, 229, 234
Janssen, Famke 216, 239, 243
Jet magazine 63, 100, 165
John, Elton 189, 191
Jolie, Angelina 201
Jones, Amy Holden 92, 104–6, 236

Jones, Tommy Lee 163
Jungle Fever 29–33, 35, 80, 109, 229
Justice, David 51–7, 60, 65, 87, 94–108, 111, 125, 159
Justice, Nettie 54
Juvenile Diabetes Foundation 28

Kelly, Grace 178
Kempley, Rita 81
Kidman, Nicole 177, 180, 191
Kim, Rob 188
King, Rodney 41, 44, 96
King Kong 79
King Solomon's Mines 41
Knight, Shirley 118
Knots Landing 33, 245

Lackawanna Blues 227
Lange, Jessica 75, 78–80, 81, 234
LaSalle, Mick 88
Last Boy Scout, The 33, 36–8, 43, 158, 230
Lazenby, George 218
Learned, Michael 25, 245
Ledger, Heath 170, 240
Lee, Spike 29–30, 32, 62, 104, 186, 188–9, 229, 235
Lethal Weapon 37
Levant, Brian 67–9, 71, 233
Lieberman, Josh 186
Living Dolls 25–6, 28, 245
Lollobrigida, Gina 83
Lopez, Jennifer 180, 223, 226
Los Angeles Daily News 55, 99, 120
Los Angeles Times 6, 26, 40, 43, 44, 89, 90–91, 93, 113, 121, 158, 168, 188, 192, 193, 213
Losing Isaiah 70, 75–81, 109, 233–4
Lumbly, Carl 118

Lumet, Sidney 225
Lymon, Frankie 122–3

MacLachlan, Kyle 69, 233
Make-A-Wish Foundation 218
Maltin, Leonard 79
Mandela, Nelson 189
Mandoki, Luis 223
Maple, Marla 88
Margolis, Edward 64
marriage
    David Justice 55
    Eric Benét 156
Marsden, James 239, 243
Maslin, Janet 88, 115, 122
Mazursky, Paul 122
McDaniel, Hattie 135, 178
McDonald, Christopher 92
McKellen, Sir Ian 150, 152, 215,
    239, 243
Menace II Society 45, 60
Meola, Marisa 144
Meyer, Neil 186
Mills, Earl 129, 132, 248
Mitchell, Elvis 152
Mitchell, Kay 19
modelling 19–22, 24, 108–10
Mohberg, Laura 190
Monster's Ball 163–76, 191–2,
    201, 206, 207, 223, 240–1
    see also Oscars
Moore, Dawn 180
Moore, Demi 50, 92
Moore, Roger 212, 218
Morris, Wesley 152
Mortal Thoughts 50
Moscow, David 25, 245
Movieline magazine 72
mugging 109–10
Murphy, Eddie 37, 38–45, 98,
    104, 231

Musto, Michael 109
Mystic Pizza 92

NAACP (National Association for
    the Advancement of Colored
    People) 121, 139
Nappily Ever After 225–6
National Enquirer 99
Need 223
New York Daily News 2
New York Observer 61
New York Post 113, 180, 189–90,
    197
New York Times 88, 99, 103, 115,
    122, 123, 152, 159, 212, 213
Newsweek magazine 139, 153,
    191–2, 218
Nicholas, Harold 132, 137–8
Nolte, Nick 37
nudity 158–61, 167–8, 169,
    208–9

October Squall 225
O'Neal, Shaquille 57
Orange County Register 26
Ortenberg, Tom 185, 192, 193–4
Oscars see Academy Awards
Owen, Clive 92

Pageantry magazine 18
Paquin, Anna 150, 239, 243
Park, Ray 151
Paseornek, Mike 185
Penn, Sean 163
People magazine 32, 53, 84, 89, 95,
    96, 98, 144, 155, 167, 173,
    207
Perelman, Ron 189–90
Phillippe, Ryan 201
Phillips, Joseph C 34, 35, 230
Pinkett, Jada 129, 184

Pitt, Brad 18
Playboy magazine 38
Poitier, Sidney 131, 181–2, 189, 193
Posey, Demonte 155
pre-nuptial agreements 201
prejudice *see* racism
Premiere magazine 205, 207
Preminger, Otto 136–7, 179
product placement 219–20
Program, The 59–61, 232–3
prom queen 13–14
psychologists 8, 94, 100, 111–12, 200, 201, 203
Purvis, Neal 212

Queen 10, 47–51, 55, 70, 94, 245–6

Race the Sun 89–90, 234
racism 8–11, 12–16, 61–2, 77–8, 218–19
Randle, Theresa 90–91, 235
Raythata, Heta 143–7
Relate magazine 200
Remini, Leah 25, 28, 245
Revlon cosmetics 108–10, 189–90
Rich Man's Wife, The 91–3, 104–6, 236
Richardson, LaTanya 133, 248
Richmond, Ray 26
Riley, Julia 197–8, 200, 201, 203, 204
Roberts, Julia 83, 92, 182
Rochon, Lela 123
Rock, Chris 57, 232
Rodong Sinmun 211–12
Rokos, Will 163
Rolling Stone 44–5, 90, 91, 152
Romijn-Stamos, Rebecca 215, 239, 243

Ronan, Dr John 63–5
Rose, Rista 156
Rosenberg, Howard 26
Rosenblum, Bobby 198
Ross, Diana 178
Roth, Joe 92
Roush, Matt 51, 118–19
Russell, Kurt 88–9, 234
Ryder, Winona 147

Saab, Elie 179–80
Samfilippo, Karen 189, 195, 202
San Francisco Chronicle 81, 88, 89–90, 123, 158, 214
San Francisco Examiner 93, 152
Santiago-Hudson, Ruben 227
Sciorra, Annabella 31, 229
Scorsese, Martin 222
Scott, George C 18
Scott, Tony 36, 230
Seagal, Steven 88, 234
Seinfeld, Jerry 56
Seltzer, Nancy 2
Set-Up, The 225
Sheffer, Craig 60, 233
Shulgasser, Barbara 93
Silver, Joel 88, 156, 161, 169, 186, 223, 230, 234, 239
Sims, Yvonne Nichols 11–13, 144
Singer, Bryan 150, 151–2, 216–18, 238, 242
Slate internet magazine 121
Smith, Liz 189–90
Smith, Will 39, 181, 222
Smits, Jimmy 83, 247
Snipes, Wesley 31, 32, 37, 98, 103–4, 229
Solomon & Sheba 83–5, 246–7
Spacek, Sissy 177, 182
Spelling, Aaron 24

Spielberg, Steven 58, 67, 69, 71, 219
Sports Illustrated 53, 54
Stack, Peter 89–90
Stallone, Sylvester 221–2
Star, The 3, 64, 99, 110–11, 197
Stauff, Tami 127
Stevens, David 48
Stewart, Patrick 150, 152, 215, 219, 239, 243
Stone, Oliver 163
Stone, Sharon 41, 56, 67–8, 176
Streep, Meryl 30, 172, 192
Strictly Business 32, 33–6, 229–30
suicide attempt 107–8, 138
Sunday Times 168, 170, 183, 187, 188–9, 203, 205, 206, 224
Swayze, Patrick 58, 232
Sweeney, DB 138, 248
Swordfish 88, 156–8, 169, 208–9, 239–40

Tamahori, Lee 208–9, 213, 223, 241
Tarantino, Quentin 90, 235
Tate, Larenz 122
Taylor, Elizabeth 70, 233
television appearances 245–9
Thal, Eric 118, 247
Their Eyes Were Watching God 227
therapy 8, 94, 100, 111–12, 200, 201, 203
Thomas, Trisha 225
Thornton, Billy Bob 168–70, 171, 187, 201, 240
Time magazine 194
Times, The 30, 62, 111, 176, 197, 200, 206, 219
Tomei, Marisa 223
Townsend, Robert 115, 236
Travers, Peter 44–5, 152

Travolta, John 156–7, 240
Tucker, Deborah 25, 28, 245
Turan, Kenneth 43, 90–91, 93
TV Guide 138, 197, 202
Tyson, Cicely 178

US Weekly 96, 100, 145, 183, 186, 190, 201
USA Today 51, 96, 118–19
USA Weekend 31, 199

Vanity Fair magazine 186
Variety 224
Venice magazine 164, 173–4, 217, 222–3
Village Voice 109, 175–6, 214
violence 5–7, 33, 101–3
Vogue magazine 202–3, 206

Wade, Robert 212
Walters, Barbara 107–8
Walters, Julie 222
Ward, David S 59, 232
Washington, Denzel 178–9, 181, 188, 193, 194, 222
Washington Post 32, 38, 81, 146–7, 163, 175
Wayans, Damon 37, 230
Webb, Veronica 29
websites
  codependency 7
  CTVNEWS.com 178
  Halle Berry's 10–11, 14, 190–91, 199–200
  The Last Boy Scout 36
  Movie Times 39
Wedding, The 117–19, 247
Why Do Fools Fall in Love (film) 122–3, 238
'Why Do Fools Fall in Love?' (song) 122

Williams, Christopher 104
Williams, Cynda 134
Williams, Gary 224
Williams, Vanessa 129
Willingham, Noble 37, 230
Willis, Bruce 36, 37–8, 43, 50, 230
Wilson, Michael 213, 241
Winfrey, Oprah 44, 116, 117–18, 186, 187, 191, 227, 247
Witherspoon, Reece 201
Wojda, Hank 11–12
Wolper, David 48–9

Woman's Day 197, 201

X-Men 149–53, 158, 206, 238–9
X-Men 2 215–20, 242–3

Yeoh, Michelle 208–9
Yun Lee, Will 211, 242
Yune, Rick 211

Zacharek, Stephanie 158
Zellweger, Renée 177, 178
Zurawik, David 51